BY THE SAME AUTHOR

Our Knowledge of Other Selves
The Existentialist Outlook
The Language of Philosophy
Gandhi's Religious Thought
The Religious Spectrum
Concept of Spirituality

PHILOSOPHICAL ENQUIRIES

MARGARET CHATTERJEE

MOTILAL BANARSIDASS
Delhi Varanasi Patna
Bangalore Madras

First Published: Calcutta, 1968
Second Edition: Delhi, 1988

MOTILAL BANARSIDASS
Bungalow Road, Jawahar Nagar, Delhi 110 007

Branches
Chowk, Varanasi 221 001
Ashok Rajpath, Patna 800 004
24 Race Course Road, Bangalore 560 001
120 Royapettah High Road, Mylapore, Madras 600 004

ISBN: 81-208-0316-7 (Cloth)
ISBN: 81-208-0317-5 (Paper)

PRINTED IN INDIA
BY JAINENDRA PRAKASH JAIN AT SHRI JAINENDRA PRESS, A-45 NARAINA INDUSTRIAL AREA, PHASE I, NEW DELHI 110 028 AND PUBLISHED BY NARENDRA PRAKASH JAIN FOR MOTILAL BANARSIDASS, DELHI 110 007

FOR EDITH

Contents

Preface to the Second Edition ix
Preface to the First Edition ix

PART ONE

GENERAL

I PHILOSOPHY AND SCIENCE 1
II PHILOSOPHY AND RELIGION 16
III PHILOSOPHY, LANGUAGE AND LIFE 29
IV THE POSSIBILITY OF METAPHYSICS 47

PART TWO

THE NATURE OF KNOWLEDGE

V THEORIES OF KNOWLEDGE 64
VI A PRIORI KNOWLEDGE 102
VII THEORIES OF TRUTH 114

PART THREE

MAN AND NATURE

VIII MATTER 133
IX SPACE AND TIME 144
X CAUSATION 159

PART FOUR

GOD, MAN AND VALUE

XI MIND AND BODY 171
XII EVOLUTION 185

XIII SELF 200
XIV FREEDOM AND NECESSITY 215
XV THE PROOFS OF THE EXISTENCE OF GOD 229
XVI THE PROBLEM OF EVIL 253
XVII THE NATURE OF VALUE 263

Epilogue 279
Selected Bibliography 284
Index 291

Preface to the Second Edition

The first edition of this work was published by New Age Publishers Private Ltd., Calcutta in 1968.

As it has been out of print for several years and yet there is still a demand for it, I am grateful that Motilal Banarsidass thought of bringing out a new edition.

Indian Institute of Advanced Study M.C.
Shimla

Preface to the First Edition

In the succeeding pages an attempt has been made to discuss some of the central enquiries which may be described as philosophical. It is easier, most students of philosophy would agree, to pinpoint a philosophical problem than to say what philosophy itself is. In avoiding the task of defining philosophy at the outset, I am, admittedly, open to criticism. I felt, however, that it was better to plunge in *medias res* by trying to show what philosophical enquiries were like, or, to put it another way, what philosophical problems are, than to tie oneself down by a straight-laced definition right from the start. In the epilogue it is suggested that, whereas it may not be possible to say what exactly philosophy is, we can perhaps more easily find out what the activity of 'philosophising' may be like. Philosophising, in turn, is not to be defined but rather to be 'shown'.

Even then some further apology might be needed for the presumption of adding to the already voluminous list of introductory books on philosophy. Here I may say that, in large part, I had the needs of my own students in mind, and that this consideration lies behind my historical method of procedure and the attempt to indicate (alas most briefly) the nature of the contemporary treatments of the problems chosen. The philosophy of the west, especially, cannot be properly understood without some knowledge of the background out of which that philosophy grew. I believe, for example, in studying Locke's stand in the controversy concerning innate ideas it is helpful to bear in mind that Locke was a staunch advocate of freedom in non-philosophical fields as well, and that he was an opponent of the Divine Right of Kings. The historical material introduced, therefore, is intended to provide a certain amount of background, which, in my view, serves to assist in making particular philosophical enquiries intelligible. In philosophy there can be no substitute for the actual study of philosophical texts. Too often the student is introduced to a number of problems particularly in courses of 'general philosophy' or 'metaphysics' and is expected to treat them for the most part in abstraction from the history of philosophy. It is in reaction to this approach that this book has been written. I am very aware, however, that the treatment I have given is far from complete. But if, in reading it, the student or general reader feels encouraged to look at the classical philosophical texts for himself its purpose will have been amply fulfilled.

In writing a work of this kind an author is indebted beyond measure to what he has been taught, what he has read and what he has unconsciously assimilated. Finally I would like to acknowledge with grateful thanks the help given me by Dr N.V. Banerjee, formerly Professor and Head of the Department of Philosophy and Psychology in the University of Delhi, especially by way of searching criticism, and, as ever, by way of encouragement.

PART ONE: GENERAL

1 Philosophy and Science

Science and its characteristic method

It is fitting that the first of our philosophical enquiries should concern the relation of philosophy and science for there are some who think that philosophy itself is a kind of science in the sense of 'branch of knowledge' and there was a time when science called itself 'natural philosophy'. When we look closer we find that over the centuries science has come to have a special meaning and that central to this meaning is the notion of 'scientific method'. It is, therefore, with an enquiry into the meaning of scientific method that we must begin. The main methodological procedures of modern science were laid down in the seventeenth century. Not that the preceding centuries had been non-scientific. For example, the science of astronomy, engineering and medicine, to mention just a few, had a long history dating from ancient Egyptian and Greek times. Medicine most certainly had been conducted in an experimental way. But a number of factors combined to make the seventeenth century a particularly fertile one in the history of science. Among these factors may be mentioned progress in the making of precision instruments, growth of mathematical techniques, capital available for investment in new industries demanding scientific knowledge and the presence of a galaxy of men possessing the scientific spirit in a high degree. Men like Copernicus, Bacon, Kepler and Galileo began the work which was to be perfected by Sir Isaac Newton some years later.

The characteristic stages of scientific investigation are as follows : the choice of a problem, the collection of facts which are apparently relevant to its solution, the search for a hypothesis which can illuminate the chosen field, the organisation of an experiment to verify the hypothesis and the summarising of the results in the shape of a formula. As to the first of these stages, the choice of a problem, there can obviously be no recipe for this. Problems strike the working scientist while he is in the midst of his work. 'Why?' is most probably one of the ultimate categories of human thinking. The second stage amounts to what is commonly called observation. But on reflection it will be found that it is not possible *just* to observe or *just* to think (as critics of Descartes were quick to point out). Karl Popper recounts* his experience of asking a class of physics students to 'Take pencil and paper, carefully observe, and write down what you have observed'. Naturally the first thing they asked was 'What shall we observe?'. It is necessary to have a problem and to make a hypothesis about your problem before you are in a position to say what observations are relevant to its solution. What exactly is meant by 'relevant' in this context is not easy to pin down. To assume that some things are not relevant to a particular investigation presupposes the principle of the isolation of systems. If, for example, you are engaged in medical research and are trying to find out the causes of cancer it will not be relevant to your task for you to bring in calculations about the movements of the heavenly bodies. This, of course, is an extreme example. But the determining of what exactly is relevant may be very difficult. In our example, say, can we rule out the working of the glands, the amount of haemoglobin in the blood and so on? Controversies about the effects of smoking show quite well how difficult it is in practice to pin down what is relevant to what. Only by successive experiments under carefully controlled laboratory conditions, and this brings us to the next stage, do the causal lines in nature reveal themselves.

At the stage of experiment the various hypotheses regarding the chosen problem are eliminated one by one until the hypothesis which 'works' is isolated. What we have found out by means of our experiments amounts to this, that under a given set of conditions a certain result can, other things being equal, be predicted. The factors which are grouped under 'other things being equal' are enormously important. In medicine this is particularly evident. The operation may be pronounced successful and yet the patient may die on the operating table thanks to factors which may seem infinitesimal but which turn the balance between life and death. It is in fact through the

* *Conjectures and Refutations*, p. 46.

investigation of infinitesimal factors that science advances. No scientific law is absolute. Scientific laws give us probable knowledge (if such a phrase be for the moment epistemologically permissible). Scientific laws are expressed not in ordinary language, but, for the sake of precision and accuracy, in notational language or formulae, a conventional short-hand which summarises whatever has been discovered in a convenient form. A scientific law does not in any way prescribe to nature (the word 'law' should not mislead us) but is really a condensed description of the way in which nature has been found to behave.

The real world for the scientist is the measurable world. Not that the scientist denies that the world of so-called secondary qualities exists, but many of the secondary qualities may be irrelevant to the task he has in hand. If he is a botanist working in a field in which the chlorophyll content of leaves has to be taken into account then for him colour will be relevant. If he is a nuclear physicist then colours will be irrelevant. But the scientist, whatever his specific field, is always concerned with quantities. In this respect his concern is quite different from the artist's concern with the qualitative world. This serves to bring out the highly selective character of the sciences. The advances made in general theory by a Copernicus, a Newton or an Einstein, come but rarely. The bulk of scientific advances come about through intensive specialization. It is for this reason that science strikes the layman as dealing only in abstractions. Now the word 'abstraction' can be misleading. The formula H_2O is an abstraction in the sense that it gives us the composition of water in 'abstraction' from its admixture with salt or sugar or bicarbonate of soda. Indeed as a formula it does not claim to tell us more than this. It expresses in a quantitative form what happens when certain parts of hydrogen are combined with certain parts of oxygen. Not only this. The formula H_2O is a telling example of the relational character of the information which science gives us. There can be no essentialist answer to the question 'What is water?' Water, one might say, is what happens when hydrogen and oxygen are related in certain proportions. Science substitutes relational properties for essences and qualities.

Nothing can mark more clearly the scientist's abandonment of the quest for inner natures than Newton's pronouncement 'All the difficulty of philosophy* seems to consist in this—from the phenomena of motions to investigate the forces of nature and from these forces to demonstrate the other phenomena'. This quotation shows also that the notion of demonstration, of system, is something that has always been in the forefront of the scientist's programme. Now the helter-skelter world of perceptual data hardly forms a system. Only by moving away from the concrete world of bewildering variety is it possible to lay bare the skeletal system which underlies it. System is achieved at a cost. But there are rewards too. If we discover the separate causal lines which underlie phenomena this enables us to predict and, ultimately, to control phenomena. The growth of science is intimately connected with the spread of the industrial revolution and, in our own day, with technology. The connection of the notion of system with that of demonstration is derived from the immense influence which the pure science of mathematics had and still has, on the natural sciences. Today we speak of 'system' with a far greater variety of connotations. We speak of the capitalist system, the respiratory system, the solar system and the like. The simplicity and analytical coherence of mathematical systems, however, is an ideal which has, since the time of Pythagoras down to the present day, been tantalisingly attractive to the natural scientist and particularly to the physicist. Mathematics has been the language of discovery. Mathematics on the one hand and observation on the other are the twin tools of scientific advance. In themselves these tools strike one as being extremely diverse until it is remembered that in experiment both unite in a rare combination. Experiment means controlled observation, control made possible through the precision of measurement, that is, through the use of numerical notation. Within science itself the respective roles of theory and observation were thrashed out in the controversy between Poincaré and Mach. In philosophy the controversy appears in the guise of the long debate between demonstration

* He is referring to natural science.

and sensation as sources of knowledge, or, more simply, the contest between reason and experience. It was not until the time of Kant that philosophy caught up with the synthesis of reason and experience, hypothesis verified by observation, that, for many decades before his day, had been the daily bread of the scientist working in his laboratory.

Philosophy compared with Science

The most striking contrast we come across when beginning to compare the two disciplines is the absence of any single characteristic method in the case of philosophy. There is nothing in the history of philosophy comparable to the growth of the experimental method which we found to be the dominant theme in the history of science. Indeed critics of philosophy in general have usually based their criticism on the alleged a priorism of metaphysicians, and a priorism, in the view of such critics, is tantamount to absence of method at least in the scientific sense. This criticism is not altogether just. There have been philosophers (like Hume) who have done their best to introduce the 'experimental method of reasoning' into philosophy. A priorism itself encompasses many possible approaches, as can be found, say, on comparing Descartes and Hegel. The desire to find a method which should be as fertile for philosophy as experiment is in the case of science has been the dominating motive in philosophers as varied in outlook as Descartes, Bacon and Kant.

It is not surprising that philosophy should search for a method of its own. We have seen that the scientist's results really amount to a kind of description, although, of course, a highly technical kind of description. In order to describe, scientists have evolved their own kind of methodology. Not many philosophers, however, in the history of philosophy, have thought that what they were doing was describing. Much of Aristotle's work springs from a classificatory temper that is typical of the biologist, and yet the vocabulary Aristotle uses, a vocabulary of words like 'substance', 'essence' and 'accidents', is far from the language of mere description. Some contemporary philosophers, deriving from Wittgenstein, think that the philosopher's business *should be* with description and what they usually mean by this is that philosophers should describe or analyse the various uses of language. Strawson develops this thesis in his distinction between 'descriptive' and 'revisionary' metaphysics in his book *Individuals*. The attempt to impose one single method on philosophers is something in which philosophers themselves have always taken an interest. Anything else, it was felt, would lead philosophy into the bog of mere speculation, into a groping among mere concepts. It is plain from all this that philosophers are as preoccupied as ever with the general question of methodology even today, whereas when the scientist is concerned with method it is a question of what particular procedure to adopt within a general framework of ultimate appeal to the verdict of controlled observation, an appeal the propriety of which he takes for granted.

The main trouble is that the speculative instruments used by the philosopher are not such that any particular experience is relevant to their verification. If (as a pupil chemist) I hazard the hypothesis that, if I burn sugar carbon dioxide will be given off, this is something that I can test for myself by going into the laboratory. If, however, a philosopher hazards the hypothesis that the Absolute is real or that reality is made up of monads or that the perceptual world is a world of appearances there is no possible experience which could tell him whether he is right or wrong. If the philosopher defends himself by maintaining that the sorts of things he says are of a special order and that of course they cannot be verified then the onus of proof rests on him and it is incumbent on him to tell us exactly what he *does mean*. If we compare the philosopher's procedure with that of the scientist in respect of the series of stages of investigation we can now see precisely where there is a parting of the ways. Like the scientist the philosopher begins with a problem, finds material which is apparently relevant to its solution and makes a hypothesis about it. Here we must, in fairness to both, make a qualification. The problem with which the philosopher begins is likely to be of a highly general sort, like, say, 'Are space and time relative?' or 'Is an effect entailed in its cause?' This means that the philosopher's problem, unlike the scientist's problem, is not suggested by any specific set of data (we noted above that the scientist too, at times, comes up against questions concerning general theory). But the real point of our comparison is this. Whereas the scientist uses his hypothesis for the actual exploration of nature, the philosopher stops short here and has to remain content with a mere hypothesis. This distinction between the two disciplines is perhaps the most fundamental of all.

Is there no way out for the philosopher? One alternative is for him to give up the project of making overall theories and to turn to piecemeal investigations. In this way his procedure will more resemble that of the scientist. The greatest advocate of this alternative in our own day is Bertrand Russell. Even in so doing, however, the philosopher will usually be making some overall assumption or other which may not be strictly "scientific". For example Russell, at one stage in his career, took for granted that reality was atomic in structure, and the contemporary analysts (diverse though they be) take it for granted that the only concern of philosophy is with language. Even piecemeal philosophizing, therefore, is not as "scientific" as it seems.

One thing we discovered about science was its intimate connection with mathematics. Now the rationalist philosophers have all shared the conviction that the method of demonstration, which belongs peculiarly to geometry, is something which would be fruitful for the philosopher too and that its utilisation would make philosophy "scientific". But on the other hand there are branches of philosophy like ethics, aesthetics, epistemology, and philosophy of religion, which have no relation to mathematics at all, and if to be scientific means to be connected with the possibility of measurement then all these disciplines are very far indeed from science. It is mathematics that has given science its precision of language. But philosophical language cannot have such precision. If ordinary language has an 'open texture' philosophical language has this characteristic even more. Think of, say, the philosopher's use of the word 'real'. This is a word which is capable of bearing a myriad connotations.

We said that science gives us a relational view of things. The importing into philosophy of this approach was largely the work of David Hume. Hume found that the temporal nature of our experience was a matter which traditional philosophers had completely ignored. The relation with which he was concerned, then, was the temporal relation. The ontological view of reality (to be found in scholastic and in rationalist philosophy) tried to give an account of things as *they* are, that is to say, out of relation to other things. The Aristotelian metaphysic of substance which was the ancestor of this kind of philosophizing, accounted for things according to their natures, that is, in terms of essence and accidents. The view that substantiality (one might call it simply 'being something') was bound up with 'independence' died hard, and it was strictly an 'unscientific' view in the sense that it is the business of science to tell us about the transactions between things, or even more strictly, to show us that things themselves are nothing other than such transactions. (To the traditional substantialist change and motion could only be accounted for by bringing in some extraneous principle or *Deus ex machina.*) The scientist, one could say, was responsible for splitting up the ontologist's one big question 'What is Being?' into a number of smaller questions like what is salt, what is living matter, and the like, and to these smaller questions he gave relational answers. Instead of asking what things *are* we were told to ask what things *do*. Substance was replaced by function.

However, many philosophers feel that, in spite of the success of science in investigating the realm of the relational, there is no occasion for philosophy to abandon the search for the 'natures' of things. Many of our concepts can perhaps be analysed in terms of their functions in experience, and it was precisely in this way that Kant attempted to bring back philosophy into her own as queen of the sciences. But ontological questions are still posed in the works of Whitehead and, differently, by many existentialists. If the scientist must be given pride of place where investigating physical nature is concerned—and there are perhaps no philosophers today who would wish to resurrect for philosophy her one-time task of speculating about the cosmos—there are problems to do with man himself and his nature about which science has no *prima facie* authority to pronounce judgement. 'What is man?' This is still a question about which neither science nor philosophy has been able to say the last word.

The laws which science discovers are abstractions from the concrete world of perceptible objects. The idealist philosophers referred to these laws most critically as 'abstract universals' in distinction from what they called 'concrete universals' or 'individuals'. The philosopher also, it may seem to the student, deals in abstractions. Words like 'substance', 'cause', 'free', 'determined' etc. certainly do not refer to anything tangible. They are concepts of high generality. Words like 'meson', 'neutron' and 'proton' are abstract in a different sense. They are shorthand terms for complicated operations in nature, theoretical constructs or 'lenses' (to use a metaphor) through which the processes of nature become capable of explanation. The concepts with which philosophy deals are in a sense more basic than these. They are, as Collingwood puts it, 'absolute presuppositions'. Some of them, moreover, do not concern physical nature but man. When we try to analyse the meaning of 'good', 'time', or the concept of God, we are doing something different from the scientist's procedure of isolating the uniformities in nature. Furthermore the philosopher's abstract analyses are constantly referred back to the data of concrete experience. This is quite easy to understand in the case of ethics. The moral philosopher does not generalise about the meaning of right and wrong without illustrating what he has to say from actual ethical situations. The cry of 'back to experience' is always one that appeals to the philosopher no matter how 'schematic' his work may appear to be.

If, in order to delimit the sphere of relevance, the scientist assumes the isolation of systems, the philosopher is for the most part loath to abandon his search for a single system. Kant cannily detected this search for a total system as being most characteristic of the philosopher's activity, although he took pains to point out that the unity which the philosopher seeks is only a projected unity, a heuristic concept which guides and stimulates him but which must not be taken to exist in fact. This warning given by Kant was not heeded by many who succeeded him and those who later talked of the Absolute were in fact refusing to accept the limits which, as Kant had so carefully shown, attend the projects of pure reason. Philosophers who felt convinced of the pluralistic nature of the universe reacted against the systematisers, thinking that the absolutists, as Russell somewhere vividly puts it, had made of the universe one big blancmange. And so the controversy between the tender-minded and the tough-minded may still be said to continue, with the systematisers in the former camp. All of which only shows how dangerous it is to generalise about what philosophers do.

The impact of Science on Philosophy

The impact of science on philosophy is a fascinating subject of inquiry for the historian, but it is no less important for anyone who wishes to find out the inside story of the issues which form the skeletal framework of the history of western philosophy. The science of astronomy gradually made redundant the cosmological speculations of the ancients and turned men like Socrates to a field where the evidence was closer to hand, namely to man himself. The scientific and philosophic tempers were, as has been hinted, closely fused in Aristotle. His theory of natural kinds is dogmatic and metaphysical, and yet, at the same time, it bears the empiricist stamp of a clear realisation of the *de facto* differences between things. It was, however, the 'philosophical' part of what Aristotle had to say that proved most influential in succeeding centuries and which was in the last analysis responsible for 'scholasticism', a movement against which those interested in making philosophy scientific reacted most forcefully. That philosophers in the seventeenth century should at all have had the idea of making philosophy 'scientific' was itself a sign of the times. Instead of nature being teleologically subordinate to man, and man to God, nature appeared to be a mechanical system. Things were to be explained not in relation to man but in relation to each other. The astronomical discoveries of Copernicus confirmed thinkers in stressing the fertility of the geometric method and the distinction which Descartes and his successors made between primary and secondary qualities was a distinction which had already been made by Kepler and Galileo. The processes of nature could only be investigated if motion were done justice to and motion was to be regarded as a dynamic concept. Small wonder that all philosophers from Descartes to Hume, no matter what school of thought they belonged to, referred to Sir Isaac Newton as the greatest man of the times. To substitute the Aristotelian world of final causes by a world of efficient causes was in fact the achievement of the scientists. This meant, at one blow, to make the philosopher's traditional concern with the static and the eternal obsolete. Thus, although Hume knew far less of science than Descartes or Locke, it was only he who brought into philosophy the most significant discovery of philosophical import that had been contributed by science — the discovery of time.

If, however, the universe was a mechanical one whose motions were capable of investigation by man, the status of God in the scheme of things became problematic indeed. Was His existence "necessary"? This question took on a new poignancy and a new connotation. The implicit threat to traditional theology did not emerge at once for Newton was a deeply religious man, and an ingenious piece of mythologising, the idea of the universe being God's *sensorium*, kept at bay a virtual rift between the mechanical and teleological ways of regarding phenomena which taxed the wits of men like Leibniz exceedingly. Was the existence of God an unnecessary hypothesis? Without the advent of science so shocking a question could not have been asked. The comfortable Deism of the eighteenth century shelved the question, but it is significant that all the philosophers of those times devoted a considerable amount of space in their writings to dealing with proofs of the existence of God. Not only this, but, as E. A. Burtt has shown most ably and convincingly in his book *The Metaphysical Foundations of Modern Science*, the intelligibility of the universe had traditionally been guaranteed by the presence of rationality in three places, in God, in man, and in the universe, a rationality which in the last two cases derived from the creativity of God as a rational Being *par excellence*. If the existence of God were problematic then problems of epistemology would prove difficult indeed. This is in fact exactly what we find if we examine the history of philosophy from the seventeenth century to the present day. The philosophical scene has been hag-ridden by problems of epistemology.

Newton's attack on unverifiable hypotheses is a theme which is still being developed by the logical positivists of this century. The immediate effect of his work for our purpose, however, is the inspiration that Newton undoubtedly provided to the empiricist movement. If the mathematical character of scientific procedure was grist to the mill of rationalism and led up the path of dogmatism, there can be no doubt that the scientific stress on observation was something which men like John Locke learnt from friends like Boyle. That the role of the spectator is something without which observation is blind could have been discerned from a close study of the writings of Copernicus, but this blind spot in empiricism was not to be corrected until the advent of the work of Kant and, in our own day, the work of Heisenberg and Bohr. This particular aspect of the impact of science brought many new issues into philosophy among which may be mentioned for the first time a critical examination of the concepts of substance, causality and God—all which had previously been sacrosanct—and a new awareness of the importance of the relational, especially the relation between the knowing subject and the object known. Science was, however, indirectly responsible for an over-simplified view of the nature of mind, an influence which probably we have yet to grow out of. Observation was identified with simple sensation and this was, after all, a gross trivialising of the highly skilled techniques of observation exemplified in the laboratory. The necessarily reductionist procedures of the chemist were taken over in the composition theory of the mind which initiated an atomic picture of the mind and its contents which survived as far as the works of Bertrand Russell, and the notion of scientific law inspired a parallel notion of laws of association in the mind which even Kant and the Gestalt psychologists between them have not completely succeeded in quashing.

The biological sciences brought with them an entirely new set of categories, the most important of which was that of evolution. Instead of the notions of mere change and process biology made use of the concepts of growth and development, concepts which had a peculiar relevance to the world of living things. Idealists were quick to note that these were characteristics which were peculiar to mind in general. Thought cannot be analysed into a series of items or discrete particulars. It possesses a unity, a life of its own. Strangely enough this was an aperçu which was to lead the philosopher away from the inspiration of science, away from nature, to the very different field of history, to society and its laws. If to Hegel the main inspiration is history, to Bergson once more it was the science of biology—although perhaps interpreted in a somewhat unscientific way—which provided the philosopher with some of his leading concepts.

The progress of science in general may be said to have been behind the naturalistic temper of the greater part of nineteenth philosophical thought. Positivism and Marxism were avowed attempts to make philosophy scientific. Many of the leading positivists were themselves scientists, and Marxism took from science not only the view that just as there are laws of nature there are also laws of society, but, perhaps even more significant metaphysically, the view that reality is not something given but something that can be controlled, something that can be changed. The infant science of psychology has made its impact too. Behaviourism has left its mark on the concept of mind, and Freud and Jung's work on the unconscious has made Leibniz seem nearer the mark than ever Descartes was. Relativity physics had its influence on Whitehead and Russell, one small example being Russell's shift from the vocabulary of events to that of fields at one stage in his career. Scientific discussions of indeterminism are seen to be not irrelevant to the problem of freewill and Heisenberg's work seems in some quarters to offer encouragement to the general trend towards relativism which straddles contemporary discussions whether of perspectivist theories of perception or of ethical language.

A glance at contemporary philosophy reinforces the sense of how great the impact of science has been on philosophy. The philosophy of linguistic analysis is really naturalism in another form. Instead of describing the world (with the scientists) we describe our ways of describing the world*. In this way language becomes one natural object among others. Activist philosophies of the pragmatist type continue to have a certain vogue and are in sharp contrast to the contemplative mould of traditional philosophy. Whether philosophy should try to be scientific at all is a highly debatable question. There are three other alternatives that are sometimes put forward by philosophers themselves. According to the first of these the philosopher's business is to analyse the presuppositions of the sciences. A good example of this method is to be found in Collingwood's *Metaphysics*. Such a procedure is bound to be historical and it has something to recommend it. The concepts of substance and cause which, *inter alia*, Kant subjected to critical examination, were certainly concepts operative in Newtonian science. Kant was, however, surely doing more than to lay bare the basic concepts of the science of his day. The traditional scope of metaphysics, moreover, has always included matters which do not fall within the field of science at all. The second alternative is to look upon the task of philosophy as essentially that of supplementing the sciences by dealing with what is left over after the various sciences have delimited their own specialist fields. The trouble with this view is that it makes it necessary for the philosopher to delimit his own special field, to give his own discipline a special subject matter of its own and this is a programme which perhaps no philosopher has been able satisfactorily to carry out. The attempt to define philosophy by reference to a specific sort of subject matter lays it open to all the charges of the verificationists, for since, *ipso facto*, the alleged subject matter must fall outside the purview of the sciences it can be 'located' only in the realm of the supersensible. The third alternative is to maintain that there often arise clashes between the various sciences themselves and that it is the business of philosophy to adjudicate between these. For example a clash between physiology and psychology gives rise to the mind/body problem, and a clash between theology and geology gives rise to a metaphysical problem concerning the creation of the world. Here again the question might be raised whether such

* There is of course more to linguistic analysis than this.

seeming clashes do not properly concern the actual disciplines themselves, and whether there is any occasion for a putative super-science to arbitrate between them.

There can be no doubt, however, that historically the relation between philosophy and science has been close indeed and that the traffic has not been altogether one-way. The physicists of this century owe perhaps as much to Kant as to Einstein. Newton, Kant and Einstein are leading figures in the history of both science and philosophy. It would be a mistake to imagine that philosophy can, in any way, ever be a rival to science. There is probably no longer any room for speculative cosmology in philosophy. The days are gone when it was possible for the philosopher to speculate about 'nature'. Many problems still remain, most important of all, the puzzle concerning the status of man in the scheme of things. It may be that to reflect on problems like this constitutes a special kind of activity—the activity of philosophizing, and that instead of asking in a old-fashioned essentialist way "What is philosophy" we should ask a different question—"What is it to philosophize?".

II Philosophy and Religion

The nature of Religion

WHEREAS philosophizing is a sophisticated and highly critical activity, being religious seems to be natural and spontaneous. Even though many may disclaim any familiarity with religious experience it is usually found that they do have some substitute which in certain ways resembles it. To characterise religion, however, is a task fraught with difficulties and indeed dangers, for he would be rash indeed who would hazard a definition covering the immense variety of religious forms of life, from animism and totemism, to Buddhism, Confucianism and the diverse types of monotheism. Whatever we say will be constantly open to modification in the course of detailed examination of any one particular religion.

To begin with, religious beliefs are matters of intimate concern. They encompass life in its totality. Religion does not concern man in his cognitive moments only, but enlists his feelings, inspires certain patterns of overt activity and has an impact on his social and cultural life too. Each of these aspects may be considered in turn. The cognitive element in man's religious experience is difficult to pin down. The object of religious knowledge is not a sensible object at all, although sensible objects may, in their symbolic functions, form an important part of worship. Thus an 'eidolon' or idol is not taken literally by the worshipper but is regarded for what it symbolises. If this were not so idols would not be submerged in rivers when the religious rituals involving them are over. The role of the sensible object is therefore an oblique one. Wherein lies the cognitive element in religion if it cannot strictly be said to lie in sensible experience? Those who take a strict empiricist or realist view of cognition will ask this question in a rhetorical way. The religious man, though, will claim that the cognitive element in religion is provided by faith. To this we shall return later.

The second element in religious experience is the emotional. The feelings involved in religion range from the fear and awe felt by primitive man in the face of the tremendous powers of nature, to the feelings of love and devotion felt by the followers of a personal God. Schleiermacher considers that the 'feeling of absolute dependence' is the most basic of all these feelings, and that this is the most characteristically religious feeling. But, as Cook Wilson has pointed out, a feeling can only be felt in relation to an object, and it presupposes at least some conception of a spiritual being. The epistemological problem, which we noticed earlier, cannot be short-circuited by an appeal to feelings, however important these may be as elements in religious experience, and even perhaps as forming part of the subjective conditions requisite for religious knowledge.

The third element in religious experience concerns man's actions. Religion is a practical and not merely a theoretical activity. Religions lay down certain things to be done, times of the day and year for prayers and festivals, areas in space to be set apart as holy in the form of places of pilgrimage and shrines for regular worship. Sacrifices are to be offered on special occasions. Ritualistic acts laid down in connection with the preparation of food, and religious ceremonial bound up with marriage and burial rites show how closely related religion is to the cultural and the social life of man. In all these various ways, then, religion is a matter of intimate concern, something that cannot be cordoned off into any one department of man's life.

Furthermore religion has been described as a matter of *ultimate* concern. Religion deals with the ultimate matters of life and death, whence we came and what we may hope for—the ultimate meaning of existence. Surely, the question may now be raised, the most ultimate question of all concerns man's relation to God? If it were possible to define religion by reference to belief in God then our task would be made easier. This is not possible however for our definition has to cover religions where the concept of God is lacking and such religions like animism and totemism, 'philosophical' religions like Buddhism and Confucianism, 'manufactured' religions like Comte's worship of Humanity, and secular religions (if this is not self-contradictory) like Freudianism, Nationalism, Fascism and a host of other substitutes to which this century in particular is partial.

Religion, in the usual sense of the term, constitutes a response on the part of man to the supernatural. This has been described best by Rudolf Otto as man's response to something he regards as 'numinous' or 'holy'. This sense of the numinous is like a sense of the uncanny, the eerie, and yet carries with it a recognition of something of value, a response to something given which calls forth and demands a reaction on the part of the worshipper. Otto's category of the numinous probably constitutes the most significant of the attempts to isolate exactly what the differentia of the religious is, and it seems capable of embracing the experiences of 'fascinosum' and 'tremendum' described by Joachim Wach as well as the variety of religious experiences dealt with by William James.

One characteristic of religion which is closely related to the preceding one is its intensely subjective nature. It was not for nothing that Kierkegaard pronounced in his *Concluding Unscientific Postcript* that 'religious truth is subjectivity'. The unbeliever has no awareness of the burning bush, no awareness of the numinous. Ecstatic experiences are private and incommunicable. Religious truths are distorted by being put into propositional form. The truths of religion are to be realised vividly in personal experience or not at all. This is so because religion is bound up with the paradoxical. It is paradoxical to say that an incarnated being is both God and man. It is paradoxical to claim that in prayer it is possible to communicate with a transcendent being. It is paradoxical to claim that a mere mortal can have eternal life. Such paradoxes are 'beyond reason'. Reason has to be supplemented by faith, indeed to make room for faith, if religious truths are to be acceptable.

The subjectivity of religion stems, moreover, from the fact that religion is deeply founded in certain basic human needs. Schleiermacher is partly right in speaking of the need for dependence on a spiritual power. There is a need to believe also that the power believed in is in some way responsive to man. There would be no point in prayers and sacrifices if this were not so. Anthropologists have much to say about the relation between religion and magic, and, without making the mistake of committing the genetic fallacy, man in his relation to the object of his worship seems to believe not only in the causal efficacy of the adored object but also to have some faith in the efficacy of his own activities towards that object. Man feels the need of a supernatural ally. Primitive man is constantly made aware of the powers of the invisible—the sudden disease which strikes in the night, the mysteries of sky and earth. The supernatural ally whose help he seeks is a usually a being who has the power to bring about disasters as well as to bestow benefits. From lowly origins such as these evolves the notion of a being who can bless and of ways in which this blessing can be evoked. Finally the claim is made by the devotee that he can enter into personal fellowship with the god he worships. At this stage of religion the divine object is regarded as the ultimate power in the universe and endowed with qualities like goodness, justice and loving-kindness.

The most characteristic need which is to be found mirrored in the so-called higher religions is the need for salvation or liberation. These are by no means the same, but they do possess a common nucleus of meaning in the sense of the possibility of living a life of very different quality from the one that we normally lead. The different religions lay down 'ways' in which this 'higher' sort of life can be entered upon. A striking feature of some theistic religions is the view that God Himself is interested in His followers attaining salvation and takes an active part in bringing about a closer relation between Himself and His worshippers. Some religions, that is to say, carry with them conceptions of divine grace and various media of revelation.

Together with all the aspects so far mentioned goes an element of authority which is one of religion's most typical features. The potency of the totem cannot be questioned, the scriptures are to be accepted either as they are or as interpreted by the priest. The ecstatic experience of the seer is taken to be evidence of fresh authoritative revelation. The dogmas of the church are not to be tampered with. The authoritative element in religion is bound up with faith. Faith is the subjective condition of the reception of revelation. The sceptic or the extreme rationalist (and your extreme sceptic is often a rationalist manque) is in no state of mind for accepting the authority of revelation. Not that the dictates of doctrine and dogma (and these must not be confused) are always counter to reason. The Catholics, for example, have worked out their teachings on a most coherently argued basis. But, to put the matter in more philosophical language, the truths of religion are expressed in a categorical form. Anything less than this is tantamount to doubt, or even unbelief.

Philosophy compared with Religion

The critical discipline of philosophy is directed towards a cognitive goal, the goal of understanding. Even in a philosophy like Plato's where the crowning conception, that of the Form of the Good, is regarded as the goal of both theoretic and ethical endeavour, the vehicle for attaining this summit is *noesis*, i.e. a form of knowledge. The goal of the religious life is salvation or liberation, and the way of attaining it, the life of worship. There are branches of philosophy which are concerned with highly specialised studies—for example logic is concerned with 'form' (whether of thought or of sentence-frames need not occupy us here). Metaphysics is the branch of philosophy which is the most all-embracing in its scope, but the main aim of the metaphysician remains knowledge, even though sometimes he may lay claim to the possibility of a form of cognition which is other than the ordinary. The philosopher is supposed to keep his feelings out of his philosophizing. Bertrand Russell in his book *Our Knowledge of the External World* includes a very critical passage about Bergsonianism in which he criticises Bergson on the ground that much of what he says is mere wishful thinking. This does not mean, however, that a philosopher need not write with a deep sense of the urgency of what he is saying, with a sense that he is making 'judgements of importance'. No one can read Spinoza without being aware that the philosopher was writing about a way of life to which he himself was fully committed. Since the time of the German Romantics, moreover, there has been a style of writing in philosophy which considers it to be the philosopher's business to deal with "Life", and the contemporary existentialists are examples of philosophers of this tradition. There are activist philosophies too of varied brands—

those of Nietzsche, Marx, Blondel, pragmatism and existentialism—which take the scope of philosophy outside the realm of the purely cognitive. Even so there is no great need substantially to modify the generalisation that philosophy has for the most part been intellectualist and contemplative in mould. Philosophy concerns *theoria* rather than *praxis*.

Although defining religion with reference to the concept of God would have simplified our task, this was an alternative that we had to eschew. In most of the religions, however, it is possible to trace a notion of the divine, however, embryonic the notion may be. What stand does philosophy take in relation to the concept of God? It is far too facile to say that religion begins with God and philosophy ends with God. Many religions neither begin nor end with God, and many philosophers do not entertain the concept of God at all. Many philosophers have found it necessary for metaphysical or epistemological reasons to attempt to prove the existence of God. But, as Hume showed, matters of existence cannot be proved anyway, whether it be a question of proving the existence of the external world, the existence of the self or the existence of God—the three existences which have attracted the attention of philosophers. But if this result should appear disappointing, it is worth pointing out that the philosopher cannot *disprove* God's existence either.

Does philosophy have anything to say about the 'numinous' in general? If it be true to say that the philosopher's sole tool is pure reason then he will have nothing to say about matters which are not accessible to reason. If, however, the philosopher takes his stand on a kind of extended empiricist programme, including within the fold of 'experience' things which are not strictly within the range of 'sense' experience at all, then the numinous may be something of which such a philosopher will take account. One sort of question which a philosopher might raise (and which, I believe, is one that interests Professor H. H. Price) is what relation mystical experiences have to 'psi' experiences in general, and this is a very crucial question if we are going to admit that there are experiences other than sense experiences, and, after all, outside the ranks of the philosophers everyone does use the word 'experience' in this wider extension.

There are philosophies, especially in the East, where the question of the nature of reality is not kept separate from the question of leading a specially transformed sort of life. To dub all such philosophies as mystical is perhaps to do an injustice to their variety. It is not unreasonable to suppose either that only leading a certain kind of life will enable one to attain a certain sort of knowledge (indeed Plato maintained this too) or that only those who have attained a special level of illumination are able to live in a certain way. The main tradition of western philosophy, however, insists that, where knowledge is in question, the object of knowledge must, *ipso facto*, be distinct from the subject of knowledge. Where there is a claim to fusion of the two then we must speak of being and not of knowing. Time was, in the Middle Ages, when philosophy and theology (rather than religion) were more or less identified. But it was never thought to be the role of the professional philosopher to point the way to a higher form of existence. Such a view of the role of the philosopher is furthest of all from the practice of the contemporary philosopher.

The reason which impels philosophic thought cannot but be hostile to the shackles of the authoritarian spirit. As long as he is philosophizing, faith, belief and authority have to be kept in their proper place by the philosopher. How the philosophic temper revolts against anything that would bind thought can be seen in the writings of the seventeenth century pioneers in methodology. Locke speaks of how the dogma of innate ideas in the field of 'practical principles' cripples intelligent thinking in ethics, and no less scathing criticism of traditional shibboleths is to be found in Mill's criticisms of Paley's *Natural Theology*. The dogma of the existence of the soul acted as a barrier in the path of the growth of empirical psychology down the centuries. Sometimes philosophic methods too had the force of dogmas, such as the stranglehold which syllogistic ways of thinking had in the history of metaphysics until quite recent times. The philosopher, then, does not take to authority kindly. The pioneers in philosophy have tended to start from scratch, taking nothing for granted, beginning with studies that try to be as foundational as possible.

The philosopher has objectivity as his goal and in the search for objectivity it is his business to dissolve the paradoxical. Kant showed that many of the projects of pure reason lead to antinomies or alternative points of view between which, on purely rational grounds, it is impossible to decide. There are, for example, as many arguments to show that man is free as there are arguments to show that he is determined. On some other ground, say, the moral one, we may come to the conclusion that if he were not free then it would be impossible to make sense of the moral life. Hegel maintained that it was possible for the movement of thought to embrace opposing points of view in a third point of view which included both the opposites. In this way, he said, thesis and antithesis can be 'sublated', that is to say, taken up and transformed into what he called 'synthesis'. But apart from the Hegelians philosophers have been ruled for the most part by the Law of Contradiction and the Law of Excluded Middle, both of which make sense if one is an ontologist, for of what *is* it is meaningless to raise the question whether perhaps it is not. Substances are and there is no room for their becoming what they are not, although Aristotle did conceive of his substances as moving from potentiality to actuality, but this was really an unrolling of what they already had it in them to be. What we are here concerned to stress, however, is that paradoxes are properly foreign to philosophy. Kierkegaard is a religious thinker rather than a philosopher.

So far nothing has been said about that vexed phrase 'ultimate reality'. Some people maintain that there is considerable resemblance between philosophy and religion because both are attempts to say something about 'ultimate reality'. The word 'real' is one that is much abused by philosophers. We know what a real dog is in contrast with a toy one, what a real oasis is in contrast with a mirage, what being really sorry is compared with merely pretending. What does 'ultimate reality' mean? One common meaning of our various uses of 'real' seems to suggest 'something other than this', 'something in contrast with which what we have before us is a mere show'. Evidently some philosophers have taken this stand towards the world in general. There must be something else in contrast with which this world is a mere appearance. It is only fair to point out that there are many philosophers who do not share such hankerings. There are technical branches of philosophy like logic and epistemology where it is possible to get along (indeed, in the case of logic, positively necessary to get along) without so much as mentioning 'ultimate reality'. In metaphysics and ethics, however, the philosopher often finds it tempting to appeal to the transcendent, that is, to an order of being which lies beyond experience, and this order he may regard as ultimately real. The phrase itself suggests that reality is capable of degrees, a viewpoint which many philosophers would find repugnant. Empiricists and realists, moreover, would think it improper for the philosopher to say anything about what lies beyond experience. Whereof one cannot speak one should be silent. So philosophers by no means all take it upon themselves to pronounce about the nature of ultimate reality. Some would even deny that the phrase had any meaning. In any case those speculatively inclined philosophers who do say something about it do so in a purely theoretical way. One of the biggest issues in the whole history of philosophy is the question whether unaided reason can in fact establish any sort of theoretic relation to the transcendent at all. Here religion has an advantage, for religion maintains that reason needs to be supplemented on the one hand by faith, and, on the other hand, by supernatural aid or revelation. The relationship which religion seeks to establish is, therefore, seen to be a practical one and not a merely theoretical one. The relationship, moreover, is for religion a highly personal one. So any comparison we may make between philosophy and religion on the ground of their both being concerned with 'ultimate reality' should be made advisedly.

Philosophy of Religion

In view of the many contrasts discovered above it is not surprising to find that many thinkers find the phrase 'philosophy of religion' an objectionable one. On the side of the philosophers, the verificationists, that is, those who confine the meaningful use of language to matters which we can verify in experience, naturally deny that sentences about religious experience have more than emotive value. Such rentences will be emotive in a two-edged sense, expressing certain feelings in the person who utters them, and arousing certain feelings in those who hear them. A more generalised philosophical objection is that, as human knowledge is relative and finite, *ipso facto*, nothing can be known in the strict sense about the field which purports to be dealt within religion. Various conclusions can be drawn from such a position. The most convincing is that of Kant who said that in the field of religion reason must make room for faith. The least convincing was that of Herbert Spencer who said that religion was concerned with the Unknowable.

Objections to the idea of a 'philosophy of religion' from the side of religion come mainly from two sources, from neo-Calvinism and from neo-Thomism. To take the first, if we believe that revelation is the main source of religious knowledge it will be out of place for man with his puny understanding to speculate about religion. There will be little scope for the exercise of that critical faculty which we associate with the philosophical approach. The most authoritative exponent of this way of thinking today is Karl Barth. To the neo-Thomist on the other hand, thinking about religion is synonymous with theology and Thomist theology at that. Now the theologian's approach is essentially that of apologetics. There are various theologies, and each expounds the doctrines of a particular historic religion. Theologies are elaborate systems of teaching which grew up thanks to the historic demands for defining the doctrines of a particular religion in contrast to other religions, the need for training a priesthood in those doctrines, and the need for redefining doctrines in the face of new challenges from science and elsewhere. On the Catholic view, that is, there may be room for the study of comparative theology, but not for anything called 'philosophy of religion'.

And yet the subject does exist. The neo-Platonists were interested in many topics which nowadays we should classify under this heading. Leibniz and the Deists in general tried to show that religious and philosophic motives harmonise, but, in emphasising only the rational side of religion, their view was rather one-sided. Hume's writings on religion, like his other writings, had a strong psychological bias, but his *Dialogues*

Concerning Natural Religion remain a masterpiece in this genre. Kant's attacks on rational theology confirmed succeeding generations of German theologians in their belief that religion was to do with faith rather than reason. It is interesting to note that Kant's contemporary in Koenigsberg, Hamann, said much the same as Kant as far as the limits of reason were concerned, and that Hamann, through Kierkegaard, exercised a great influence on Protestant thinking. The place of feeling in religion was stressed by Schleiermacher, while Ritschl and Hoffding focussed on value and the impulse to conserve value as the central thing in religion. Historically though, it was a rationalist in the grand manner who was to give philosophy of religion the most elevated status of all. Hegel's *Philosophy of Religion* remains one of his most readable books, although the anthropological material in it may give us pause today. The most important thing that Hegel emphasised was that philosophy of religion must be historical. Religion has a history, it has evolved and must be studied accordingly and apart from the traditional approach of natural theology. There was little comparative data available in Hegel's day, but he was the first to make reference (however wide of the mark sometimes) to religions other than the Christian. His was a speculative method no doubt, a method elaborated by Caird, and he went as far as to give to philosophy a position beyond religion and this was only to be expected in view of his treatment of philosophy as a sort of super-science.

From the standpoint of this century, and bearing in mind the considerable amount of comparative data available to us about various religions, are there any characteristically philosophic issues to be extracted from religion? To begin with, if we admit (as we must, in view of the amount of material at hand from empirical theology, the descriptive accounts given in books like William James' *Varieties of Religious Experience* and the records of mystical experience from other sources) that religious experience is an important part of experience, then, as such, it calls for philosophical interpretation. This, after all, is good empiricist procedure. Is the claim to knowledge of a transcendent being justified? As long as the religious man makes use of the word "know" this usage falls within the legitimate scrutiny of epistemology. The family of uses of 'know' is constantly expanding. Now we have 'knowing how' as well as 'knowing that'. We also speak of 'knowing' other people. In what sense God can be 'known' is certainly something which it is the business of the philosopher to scrutinise. If the question of the proofs seems to have been finally put in its place by Hume and Kant there still remains the vexing question of the nature of religious truth. Just as the nature of perception is still a live issue in philosophy so also might be the question of the distinction between the illusory and the veridical in religious experience, although this is a matter which the philosopher has scarcely touched as yet.

The traditional problems of philosophy of religion may not all strike us today as being live issues. One such problem is that of determining the relation between God and the Absolute. For those philosophers who regard the Absolute as being a mere concept there will of course be no such problem. What can be meant by speaking of God as a divine person, however, is still a question worthy of consideration. The proofs for the existence of God may seem to have only historical interest, but even in this field, in recent years, some of these proofs have come in for rethinking. The nature of religious experience remains a matter of tremendous variety and whose diverse patterns have yet to be adequately plotted. Much contemporary work in philosophy of religion must needs concern clarification. The question of proof has largely given way to that of understanding. Philosophy of religion today needs to be analytic, comparative and critical, but yet, at the same time, sympathetic. That philosophy of religion is capable of wearing a new look is well-illustrated in the various works on 'philosophical theology' which have appeared in recent years. Many one-time strictly theological controversies are now being treated within the framework of a more or less linguistic approach to philosophy. Instead of, say, asking 'Did God create the world?' the question can be asked what creation might possibly mean outside the context of sense experience. Interestingly enough one can discern in such writings a strong analogical slant, but instead of the analogical thinking being geared to ontology, as it certainly was in classical theology, the analogies are laid bare within language itself. In conclusion, one might hazard the conclusion that, in spite of the attacks of the latest form of positivism, philosophy of religion seems to have taken on a new lease of life in recent decades.

III Philosophy, Language and Life

Philosophy and Language

IT was the mark of traditional philosophies, i.e. metaphysical systems, that they provided accounts about the nature of things, and this approach to philosophy is what is known as 'ontology'. The epistemological approach, by contrast, centres not on the nature of things but on our manner of knowing things. Such was the philosophy of Locke and Kant. Many contemporary philosophers have adopted yet another approach—philosophy is concerned not with things but with the way we talk about things, that is, with language. Now in so far as philosophers have always been engaged in argument they have, in one way or another, always been concerned with language too, although language was not, until this century, regarded as the philosopher's main concern. When Plato wishes to mark the difference between perception and the highest form of knowledge he uses a special word *noesis*, to refer to the latter. The nominalist philosophers of the Middle Ages believed that the controversy about universals was entirely one about language and that a universal was in fact a word instead of a concept (as the conceptualists thought), or an entity (as the Platonists thought).

Since those times empiricist philosophers have showed the most evidence of being interested in linguistic matters and in what they call 'analysis'. The third book of Locke's *Essay concerning Human Understanding* contains much material which is of interest to the contemporary linguistic philosopher. Berkeley's criticism of 'abstract ideas' forces us to look at words like 'force' and 'motion' anew. His criticism of the concept of material substance amounts in its positive aspect to an analysis of the meaning of material object sentences. When I say that the table I write on exists I *mean* that 'I see and feel it, and if I were out of my study I should say it existed' etc. Berkeley's use of the words 'notion' and 'idea' reflects his conviction that it would be inappropriate to use the same language for treating of selves and objects. Throughout, Berkeley insists that language can be misleading and can easily lead us to confusion. Hume likewise can be understood as providing an analysis of the meaning of 'cause' and 'self'. It is necessary, however, to distinguish between such 'analysis' and the contemporary type of linguistic analysis. Modern protagonists of linguistic philosophy go much further than any of the philosophers so far mentioned in insisting that the only function philosophy can have is that of analysing the way we talk. The influences which contributed to the formulation of this extreme view are worth looking into.

To begin with, the idealist speculations of Bradley and McTaggart stimulated a rebound movement, a return to commonsense. To some the contrast of the judgements formulated by idealist philosophy with the propositions of science was the most striking. To others the departure of a standpoint which could profess that time was unreal from what we ordinarily believe in our everyday conduct of affairs was the more remarkable. At all events the commonsense point of view for the first time (barring the important exception of pragmatism) became the favoured oracle and pure reason fell into disfavour on the ground that its findings landed us in propositions which were manifestly untrue. The classroom technique of G. E. Moore became a model for all who wished to counter the excesses which speculation had been instrumental in producing. If it be true that I have had my breakfast and that I shall (God willing) have my lunch in due course what meaning can there be in saying that time is unreal? When I lift up my hand in front of me I am perceiving a hand and only a hand and to say that I am perceiving an idea is not so much untrue as plain silly. It is not so easy, however, to say exactly what the commonsense point of view consists in, for, above all, this is a point of view which is unformulated. We may describe it, following Professor Price, as an attitude of taking for granted, as a feeling of familiarity.

One way of specifying what commonsense dictates is by appealing to ordinary language and Moore's technique did in fact include an appeal to our ordinary use of language. Ordinary language can be initially defined as language which is devoid of technicalities, especially the technicalities of scientific formulae and numerical symbolism. Thus, at a time when Continental philosophers were intent on building complicated symbolic systems, Moore himself used the language of the man in the street. The analysis of ordinary language, it was thought, could provide a fruitful approach both to the understanding of ethical concepts as well as to the analysis of material object sentences in the study of which British empiricists were already engaged. Moore's kind of philosophizing was certainly piecemeal but it can be distinguished from that of Russell, *inter alia*, by its comparative lack of reliance on the findings of modern logic. The linguistic method proper appeals to actual use, whereas Moore's method, one could say, veers between appeal to the actual use of language and appeal to 'the facts'. But the appeal to unverbalised experience i.e. ostensive definition, obviously has its dangers and subsequent analysts have been wary of it. The commonsense appeal to the facts has a certain fascination in that it short-circuits all the problems connected with the epistemology of perception, problems with which it is the philosopher's business to deal. Moore's position with regard to the whole linguistic movement is important although he would not have wished at all to be remembered among those who think that philosophy deals only with language. He believed that the answer to the question "What do you mean by . . .?" could not be extracted out of a mere analysis of the words we use. In a sense, then, "analysis" for Moore was something far closer to the work of Locke and Hume than to that of the linguistic analysts proper. The final appeal for him is always to something extra-linguistic.

Russell's "theory of descriptions" played a big part in turning the attention of philosophers towards the analysis of language. His theory in effect was a theory about the way in which phrases of the form 'the so-and-so' are to be defined. In sentences which contain expressions of this form we can, Russell said, substitute the expression by a descriptive phrase, the advantage of this procedure being that we thereby make the meaning of the sentences much clearer than it was before. For example, by translating the sentence 'The round square cannot exist' into 'No one thing can be both square and round' we guard against the suggestion that the subject of a negative existential sentence nonetheless possesses a certain quiddity. Moreover, reduction of nounal sentences to descriptive sentences protects us against the general tendency to look upon nouns as standing for entities, a generalised procedure which is to be found in a paradigmatic form in the metaphysics of Aristotle. Russell's contribution in this field was of importance not only in logic but also bore specific linguistic fruit in the development of phenomenalism, for what was the phenomenalist thesis but the assertion that all material object words functioning in sentences could be substituted without loss of meaning by a series of sentences containing no material object words but only references to sense contents.

Interest in language was further stimulated in Cambridge by the publication of Ogden and Richards' book *The Meaning of Meaning*. Among other things the writers showed how language had moved far from the stage when most words could be regarded as merely 'naming' things. In addition to the referent use of language there was also an 'emotive' use of language, a use which was exploited by some philosophers working in the fields of ethics and aesthetics. That language could not be exhaustively classified into these two categories and that there could be mixed types, was a discovery yet to come. The development of non-Euclidean geometries also left its mark on the linguistic movement. Just as in geometry it had been found that there was no one system which was especially geared to the physical world but that the initial set of axioms on which a particular geometry was based was a matter of decision or convention, so it could be pointed out that, after all, every symbolic system was based on convention. The parallel between a geometric system and a linguistic system was of course closer in the case of an artificial syntactical system than in the case of a natural language. The acid test of the 'powers' of a natural language must inevitably remain grounded in usage, whereas some geometric systems may have significance in the realm of pure mathematics alone and not at all (or at least with our present state of knowledge) in the applied sphere.

Apart from the influences that have been mentioned, there can be no doubt that the biggest single fillip to the linguistic movement was provided by logical positivism, however proper it be, nonetheless, to distinguish the two movements from each other. Analytic work had already been done by the positivists themselves in their sharpening of the distinction between tautologies and synthetic propositions. Since any third type i.e. metaphysical sentences, was *ipso facto* ruled out, it remained to be shown what exactly the positive task of philosophy was. A programme for the philosopher was set out clearly by Ayer in his book *Language, Truth and Logic*. The critical function of philosophy was in no way intended to provide a super-criticism of science for this would be to intrude on the role of the scientist himself. Rather the philosopher should confine himself to clarification and analysis, the sort of thing that the founding fathers of empiricism, Locke, Berkeley and Hume among others, had done. The philosopher is 'concerned only with the way in which we speak about' things. Philosophy is a department of logic. The philosopher has always been in search of definitions. But the definitions of which the linguistic analyst speaks are of a very different order from the definitions employed by the classical rationalists and from which the latter had thought deductions could be made. Philosophical definitions are definitions in use and they help us to dispel confusion about the different types of sentence in our language. Such an understanding of the word 'definition' stems directly from the work of Wittgenstein whose whole contribution to contemporary philosophy is regarded by analysts as an object lesson in what linguistic analysis can be.

The influence of Ludwig Wittgenstein made itself felt in Cambridge and beyond and dated from as early as the days when Russell was working on his book *Our Knowledge of the External World*. Wittgenstein's early views on language were contained in the *Tractatus* where he agreed with Russell in thinking that the main business of language was to mirror the facts. Atomic sentences were to reflect atomic facts. This simple copy theory of language was later given up by Wittgenstein. There could be no simple correspondence between language and fact for the reason that language enters into the very constitution of fact. The facts cannot be cut off from interpretation, from talk, and talk is a part of life. Linguistic activity is one activity among other activities. There are different language games and the rules of any particular language-game are determined by usage. 'Do not look for the meaning. Look for the use'. This was, in a nutshell, the message that Wittgenstein bequeathed to his successors. The aim of philosophy is 'To show the fly the way out of the fly-bottle', that is to say, the way out of the tyranny of misleading expressions which lead to puzzlement and confusion. Instead of the battle-ground of metaphysics, the nature of which Kant had described in very different terms, we have 'a battle against the bewitchment of our intelligence by means of language.' It is Wittgenstein who was responsible for turning the attention of analysts from the study of artificial language systems and stressing the immense unexplored fertility of natural language. The teaching no doubt fell on ground that had already been partly prepared by the work of G. E. Moore.

Linguistic philosophy has subsequently developed in two directions. The syntactical approach was pioneered by Carnap and is being continued by Tarski. Linguistic analysis in this approach amounts to intensive study of the logic of science. But this is not a path that can be followed by any but mathematical logicians. The alternative informal type of analysis has centred round the concept of linguistic 'therapy'. The radical therapy recommended by the early positivists may be likened to a successful operation which unfortunately kills the patient. Later practitioners of analysis have prescribed less drastic remedies. One example of such therapy is to be found in Ryle's article on 'Systematically Misleading Expressions' which appeared in 1931. His subsequent work is intended to continue the treatment. As to what was to follow the therapeutic programme of clarification, what was to happen to the patient when he was cured, the analysts are conspicuously silent. (The problem is analogous to that posed by Jung at the end of his book *Modern Man in Search of a Soul*—what is to happen to the patient after his course of psycho-analysis is presumable successfully completed).

Contemporary linguistic analysis certainly accommodates a considerable variety of exponents within its folds. Ayer in his Inaugural lecture at Oxford in 1960 upholds his former position that philosophy is a "second-order" subject, concerned with 'talk about talk', but he thinks that in so doing it is important also to 'examine the architectonic features of our conceptual system'. That this programme need not be embarked on in a Kantian manner he shows by mentioning as examples the work of Strawson and Hampshire. The analyst has to be prepared for the often bewildering variety of language structures extant in the world. Work on ideographic languages in Cambridge is trying to correct the almost exclusive emphasis on the structure of Indo-Aryan languages which has for the most part attracted notice to date. The last few decades have seen a progressive increase in the admitted categories of legitimate sentence. Ethical writers drew attention to the importance of prescriptive language in ethical discourse and stressed that the distinction of truth and falsity was absolutely inappropriate to such language.

Austin's discovery, for such it was, of the 'performative sentence' (e.g. 'I promise', 'I believe') indicated another type of sentence which could be neither true nor false. Moreover such sentences were not merely a sort of saying but a sort of doing. Here indeed was a vindication of the Wittgensteinian insistence that language was a part of life. That one could 'do things with words' had already been shown by Stevenson in his book on ethics and language. A 'persuasive definition' indicated language intended to get someone to do something. Austin had much more to say on this subject in the book published posthumously *How to do things with words.* Reference to the various meanings that a single word could have amounted at once to an illustration of meaning in use more detailed than anything that Wittgenstein had himself provided, and an elaboration of the theme of 'open texture' which F. H. Waismann had spoken of years before. That the linguistic analyst is concerned with mere lexicography is belied by Austin's most stimulating book. That there are often insincerities, infelicities, misleading statements and rough statements shows that the traditional dichotomy of sentences into true and false is all too simple-minded. That speech acts occur in a total speech situation is something that needed saying. There can be no doubt that, if one of the defects of traditional philosophy be its excessive adoption of the contemplative standpoint and excessive absorption with the problem of cognition, the alternative of seeing language as one activity among the other human activities bears the promise of correcting this. It is from Austin too that we have the admission and the warning that if ordinary language is not the last word 'only remember it is the first word.'

One further category of sentence remains to be mentioned, that of emotive sentences. Schlick, Ayer and Stevenson between them have made much of this particular category in their analysis of ethical language. The recognition that even a simple type of sentence can have an inner complexity emerged in Ayer's point that the emotiveness of a sentence consisted not only in its expressing of the emotions of the speaker but in its capacity to arouse feelings in the listener. Since then the 'mixed' nature of certain classes of sentences, especially in ethical discourse, has come in for analysis, by Hare and Nowell-Smith most notably. That language cannot be tortured on a Procrustean bed would be generally recognised by analysts today.

That there can be no radical rift between thought and action has been stressed by thinkers as different from each other as the pragmatists, John Macmurray and Stuart Hampshire. One way of doing justice to the interrelation between thought and action is by bringing language into the forefront of philosophic consideration, for if thinking be a kind of doing and doing a kind of thinking (performing well, for example), language is surely both. But to say that the entire scope of philosophy can be exhausted in the analysis of language is thought by many to be going too far. To say that philosophy consists in linguistic analysis is to confine philosophy to description, albeit a special kind of description, and this, as Gellner has pointed out,* is to reinstate naturalism. The alternative, Strawson has said, is some form of 'revisionary' metaphysics, revisionary in the sense that we revise language, we decide to use language in a different way. But recent work has surely thrown up the fact that 'ordinary' language itself is extraordinarily rich. If the meanings of words are to be defined in use, then we have to admit that this use is in constant process

* Vide *Words and Things.*

of revision. Even in ordinary usage we can decide to give a new meaning to a word. What the metaphysician does is to use words in such a way as to draw attention to a new range of facts, or a new angle on the facts. Language is *about* something and this is lost sight of if we confine ourselves to merely 'talk about talk'. The way in which linguistic analysis can lose sight of the original field from which it took flight is exemplified in the branch of contemporary philosophy known as meta-ethics. This consists of talk about ethical talk, which is all right as long as the original problems of the nature of moral experience, choice and allied matters are not lost sight of, as they usually tend to be. Many philosophic problems, it could be urged, are not based on linguistic confusion at all, problems like that of evil and the existence of God which are grounded in something positive in human experience. 'Clarity is not enough' has become the watchword of a group of philosophers as divergent in opinion as Price, Ewing and Findlay. Can philosophy so easily give up the synoptic task which seems given to it as it is given to no other discipline? To say that philosophy is properly only concerned with the analysis of language is to adopt the standpoint of dogmatism, something which, in their original programme at least, the analysts were pledged to eschew.

Philosophy and Life

THE contemporary crisis in philosophy has been marked on the one hand by a determination on the part of some philosophers to eliminate metaphysics and an insistence that philosophy should concern itself with linguistic analysis, and an equal determination on the part of others to find a fresh terrain for metaphysical thinking by a return to the promised land of experience, a return to the concrete life of man as a being who not only thinks, but feels and acts and suffers. The second of these two outlooks runs directly counter to Schlick's dictum that 'the philosopher as such is not interested in the facts of experience.' Now the use of language, as we saw in the preceding pages, is most certainly one among the many activities of which man is capable. The linguistic philosophers, however, have not, on the whole, been interested in investigating language in its natural context in communicative situations. The two alternative standpoints formulated above have therefore remained isolated from each other in the contemporary philosophical situation.

The existentialist school of philosophy insists that the fundamental datum with which the metaphysician has to begin is the existence of man. Human life becomes the starting point for any philosophical inquiry. Such a shift in interest has happened before in the history of philosophy. Socrates opposed the cosmological guesses of the Ionians with the cry 'Know thyself' and the Stoics can be counted as ancestors of those who would oppose sophistry and dialectical thinking with the category of the existential. Existentialist thinking can claim within its fold cognate authors like St. Augustine, Pascal, Dostoievsky, Berdyaev, Kafka, Camus and the twentieth century school of 'crisis' theologians. Existentialism in its strictly philosophical sense (and the word is unfortunately only too often employed by non-philosophers incorrectly) insists that in the case of man existence is prior to essence. Now the vocabulary of essence and existence has a long and distinguished history. Mediaeval philosophy was concerned with both essence and existence. Essences are definitions or types. The essence of a thing means those qualities without which it would not be what it is. The accidental qualities are those which vary from one member of a class to another. For example the essence of a vase is that it be able to hold water and be able to accommodate flowers, and the accidental qualities of a vase are qualities like shape, colour and size.

An essence, then, it is clear, is a type or universal. An essence need not be actual. We can, for example, state what the essence of a unicorn is (a horse-like creature with a single upstanding horn) although no unicorns actually exist. As long as we are talking only about essences, particularity and actuality are irrelevant. The question of existence is subsidiary to that of essence. Whether any one essence is actually instantiated in the world or not is a contingent matter. Essences are abstractions, whereas existences are concrete. The mediaeval philosophers* believed that all contingent things combine existence and essence, and they were realists enough to hold that we find out what exists and what its characteristics are through experience, and in this respect they were drawing on the empiricist outlook of Aristotle. They believed at the same time that there is one Being about whom the distinction between essence and existence does not obtain for the reason that in His case, the case of God, it *is His essence to exist* and about no other being can the same be said. This was what was meant by the many references to God as a 'necessary Being' that always accompanied rationalist treatments of the existence of God. To interpret this insistence however in merely logical terms, i.e. to say that the statement 'God does not exist' is a formal self-contradiction, is to miss the ontological weight of the Biblical origin of the whole theistic approach, the weight of the sentences 'I am that I am' and 'He who is'.**

Essentialism stresses reason in that we apprehend what essences are through intellection (an intellection, which, it must be remembered, for the mediaevalist, was not counter to sensi-

* The position outlined in what follows is held also by Thomists today.
** Cf. Ch. XV.

bility). Now if the essence of man himself is understood to be reason it follows that the 'essential' activity of man is ratiocinative activity. A contrast with the Divine activity is implicit here. Mediaeval philosophers maintained that only God was 'causa sui' or self-caused, and man's existence was dependent on His Creator. The cognitive enterprises of man were possible because both the world and man himself were created by God, God was Himself in an archetypal sense a rational being, and, if men were made in the image of God as the scriptures taught, the fruitfulness of man's attempts to know were grounded in these circumstances rather than, as Descartes suggested, in an appeal to the Divine veracity. Man by no means exists necessarily. In saying this we are not saying that his non-existence is conceivable, although that is also the case, but we are affirming his finitude, a finitude stemming from his status as a 'creature' i.e. something that has been created, and confirmed in his act of disobedience at the time of the Fall. The non-rational parts of man's 'nature' tended, thanks to the influence of St. Paul rather than to any specific teaching by Christ Himself, to be relegated to the inferior part of man's endowments and even to have an association with the sinful and corrupt. Even so the attributing of emotions to God, even emotions of anger and desire for vengeance, was by no means foreign to the Old Testament. But, on the whole, apart from thinkers like St. Augustine, Pascal, Hume, Shaftesbury and Rousseau there is no doubt that the passional side of man's nature received scant treatment by philosophers.

Apart from the association of essentialism with theology essentialism was also perpetuated by science in the sense that a scientific law is, after all, an abstraction, and as much a 'universal' as the Aristotelian definition had been. The field of what was regarded as intelligible had shifted from the world of quality to that of quantity, but the accidental and the particular were just as much neglected as they had been before. The scientific concern with the objective, however important the role of the spectator may be, inevitably relegated the subjective to a level of unimportance. The rationalism of Hegel and Marx shared the same concern. Instead of laws being found only in the physical world they were found to obtain in the world of society as well. Instead of the universal reign of mechanism we had instead the universal reign of the Zeitgeist, the Absolute at large.

It was explicitly against the Hegelian form of essentialism that Kierkegaard, the founding father of contemporary existentialism, directed his attack. To identify thought and reality as Hegel did, was he said, to maintain something which above all in the case of man's existence was quite untenable. For man existence is precisely the separation of thought and being. A particular existing human being is surely not an idea. To think, is to remain as yet in the realm of the possible. For man it is action which marks the gulf between mere possibility and actuality. Logic is powerless to dictate how man shall act, i.e. what he shall be. No concepts can mediate between possibility and actuality when man as a free being chooses what he will do, and thereby defines in action his essence. In man, therefore, so far from essence being prior to existence, his existence is prior to his essence. We are born into a world, 'thrown' into it, Heidegger says : we exist, that is to say, in space and time, and if we must speak of a 'human nature' we must remember that this can be none other than a capacity, the freedom to carve out our own destinies, an open project in which man cannot lean on any myth concerning his nature as a 'rational animal' but a project in which he is confronted by possibilities between which he has no alternative but to choose.

In this way existentialism throws into prominence the concept of freedom and freedom acquires an importance which is only paralleled in the history of philosophy by the importance it was given by the neo-Kantians and the German romantics in general. The existentialist treatment of freedom (or at least the atheist existentialist treatment of freedom) marks itself off at one pole from the Christian view that 'The truth shall make you free' where freedom is equivalent to spiritual freedom or salvation, and at the other pole from the Marxist conception of social destiny expressed in the slogan 'Freedom is the appreciation of necessity'. Sartre speaks of man as being 'condemmed to be free'. We are alone without excuses and the responsibility of choice cannot be evaded. To evade it is indeed a form of choice. Choice is an experience of risk. There are no moorings.

To be free is to invent. The freedom of man is his condition, and it is of his condition and his situation that we should speak rather than of his nature. At the same time, in virtue of the openness of man's future, man's freedom is his 'nothingness of being', for man *is* not. He only becomes. This is the way in which Sartre speaks of freedom. We may read into his treatment the whole experience of a man who has known the absence of freedom, the experience of a man who was a member of the Resistance Movement in the last war. In his acute sense of the temporality of man's existence we may, moreover, hear the overtones of Bergson's philosophy. But whether Sartre can escape the charge which René Le Senne has levelled against him, the charge that he has replaced the 'idolatry of determinism by the idolatry of the arbitrary', remains to be seen. Sartre does claim in his book on existentialism and humanism that his theory is able to relate satisfactorily the freedom of one man with that of his fellows. This link with others is made a *condition* of freedom by the Catholic existentialist Gabriel Marcel. Instead of freedom being a deprivation, a negation, for Marcel it is an experience of fulness. Instead of self-affirmation we have participation and receptivity. Jaspers too is concerned with uniting our own freedom with the freedom of others. He says 'I must be met by my neighbour's action as well'. If freedom is, as Heidegger puts it, a 'relationship of open resolve', it is certainly a situation in which we are not alone.

Existentialism affirms the centrality of the person as against system, whether the system be that of Hegel or that of Marx, whether that is to say system be interpreted as a theoretical concept like that of the Absolute or whether it be identified with the ideal of collectivism. In their understanding of the word 'person', however, existentialists break away from the main connotations of the term as found in the history of western philosophy, from person understood as substance (consisting of a rational soul and body) as we find it in St. Thomas Aquinas and Boethius, from the Cartesian stress on self-conciousness, and also from the Kantian insistence on man as an imperfectly rational being whose rationality is exhibited in the practical rather than in the theoretical sphere. Now the individual man can be in relation to the world which is both a cognitive and a practical relation, or to his fellow men, or to God. No less important is the fact that he is inevitably in relation to himself. When existentialists talk about the person they are concerned with all the relations we have mentioned except the first. For many of them the relation of the person to his fellows is fraught with difficulties, and for others the relation to God does not arise, that is to say, for those who are atheists. But man cannot avoid being related to himself and this constitutes what may be called his "subjectivity". The Cartesian type of subjectivity had for the most part been geared to man's cognitive adventures. Kant had discerned in the subject certain forms of intuition and rules of understanding which make knowledge possible. In his moral consciousness, however, Kant held that man is the centre of a form-giving activity of a very different kind, an activity which expresses itself in the dictates of practical reason.

The existentialist stress on subjectivity comes as a reaction against the objectivism of science, and, as far as philosophical systems are concerned, as a reaction against the objective idealism of Hegel and his followers. The belief that man has an inward life which cannot be described by using the categories which we use to describe the so-called external world runs as a recognisable theme through the writings of Pascal, Maine de Biran, and the romantics, and comes to a head in the works of Kierkegaard. To Kierkegaard, subjectivity is truth. The truth of which Kierkegaard speaks, it is necessary to remember, is religious truth. The only authentic religion a man can have is one that is deeply felt, in which, perhaps contrary to reason, he attaches himself by faith to Him in whom he believes. In the face of such truth the only question that can arise is whether we are to become a witness to it. The crowd is untruth, and the concept is untruth, because they represent an evasion of this choice that confronts man.

One difficulty which faces the philosopher who wishes to advocate the cruciality of subjectivity is that subjectivity is, in the very nature of things, something which cannot be reduced to the usual categories of description. For this reason Kierkegaard adopts a phenomenological procedure in describing the three stages of life, the aesthetic, the ethical and the religious, the gulf between which, he shows, can only be crossed by a decision. In this way Kierkegaard opposes the Hegelian dialectic of mediation where opposites are sublated in a higher synthesis with his *dialectic of choice*. The existentialists who came after him turned to the developed phenomenological method of Husserl, a method which provides a description of the general modes in which the subject grasps, sees or understands his world. This method lends itself to incorporation in novels and plays and journals, and, less easily, to philosophical disquisitions. In this manner existentialists interpreted life as a field for philosophical investigation by examining the significance of certain key experiences such as anxiety, guilt, nausea and dread, choosing in each case experiences which revealed to the fullest man's 'condition' and his contingency. To the atheist, from such experiences there can be no escape whereas to the theist an experience of fear and trembling is the gateway to faith, to an encounter with 'He who is'.

The conviction that such experiences are self-transcending is shared by all existentialists, and, in so far as they are absorbed with the problem of how man can relate himself to the transcendent, one could say that they are engaged in a traditional metaphysical task. The difference is, and it is a very big difference, that whereas traditional metaphysicians had gone about the task theoretically by exploring the possibility of man's cognising the transcendent, the existentialists are concerned with the problem of how man can find a *practical* point of attachment to the transcendent. How to speak of Being without reducing it to a non-entity is a matter which has occupied generations of philosophers. To contrast it with Nothing, or to refer to it as the 'all-comprehending', is not to throw much light on its nature. In this respect the theist has a very evident advantage.

Religious thinking in general has, one could say, throughout been existentialist, without of course actual bearing this label. Within theology itself we find the protest of inward witness against the demands of system, the standpoint of a St. Bernard as against that of an Abelard. The dramatic conception of human life with its stages of birth, life and death and its experience of conversion is all familiar to religious discourse. The religious thinker has always insisted on the importance of a *metanoia* or change of attitude of mind, a turn to the unconditioned which, in religious terms, becomes a response to the appeal made by God. No wonder then that a theist existentialist like Gabriel Marcel should be able to give positive content to the project of man's attachment to the transcendent. Being is not conceived as anything foreign to man's nature but as an ontological mystery in which man can participate through the human experiences of love, fidelity and hope. Whereas atheistic existentialist thinking is singularly barren of reference to fulfilling experiences, Marcel describes the ways in which our awareness of our own contingency can nonetheless be made instrumental in revealing plenitude. The alienation which for the atheist is absolute can for the theist be overcome through grace. The commitment which is enjoined on us is a project which we are not called upon to tackle single-handed. Above all the relation of man with his fellows, which is the central feature of human life, is shown to be something which bears the seeds of promise, in so far as this and none other is shown to be the very vehicle of man's relation to the transcendent. Man's existence is not absurd but is a progressive response to the demands of his high calling.

If philosophy must necessarily remain within the realm of the strictly logical then what the existentialists have to say must be regarded as falling outside the purview of the strictly philosophical, and so also will much of the work of philosophers like Hume and Rousseau, Bergson and William James. While existentialism has been criticised on the general ground that it belongs more to literature than to philosophy, there have also been more specific points of attack. Those interested in ethics have been dissatisfied with the categories of the authentic and the inauthentic which are substituted for the more orthodox ethical categories. What universal criterion of rightness and wrongness can be extracted out of so subjective a principle, it will be asked. Can even choice, on which existentialists lay so much stress, be done justice to if choice is something merely arbitrary, something in which rational principles have no place? Those who maintain that, *ipso facto*, nothing can be said about the transcendent, will not be attracted by the existentialist attempts to break new ground in this field. Marcel is perhaps the existentialist thinker who has the most original contribution to make here. The challenge presented by the phenomenon of intersubjectivity has been met very differently by the various existentialists themselves. On the one hand we have a state of more or less natural warfare between one person and another as presented by Sartre at least in his main philosophical work, and on the other hand an intersubjectivity grounded in our common relation to God presented by Marcel which revives an approach which is in direct line of descent from the belief of St. Augustine in a God 'in whom we live and move and have our being'.

Existentialism, it could be said, has performed a service in bringing the whole man into the forefront of discussion, something which is definitely neglected if we think of man only as a cogniser, a performer, a behaver, a user of symbols or any other of the other models which are put before us in these times. To raise questions about Being and about Negation out of the context of traditional ontology is again a contribution of value. The categories we employ to investigate nature cannot be appropriate when we turn to the nature of man himself. Man is not a thing, an entity, nor is he a cross-section of behavioral patterns. The relations between persons cannot be explored in terms of the behaviour of the impact of particles or in terms of the more sophisticated field-vocabulary of modern physics. The channels of communication between one person and another are many and not the least of these is the channel of language. Existentialists are as much at fault in ignoring this as the positivists are in treating only of language. Both positivism and existentialism, although in very different ways, make an appeal to experience. Both treat of the meaningful and the meaningless. Both open up approaches to philosophy which each, in diverse fashion, bring back philosophy to reflection on the activities of man and divert it from its overlong absorption with inquiry into the nature of things, a task which, very properly, has been taken over completely by science.

IV The Possibility of Metaphysics

Introduction

PHILOSOPHERS have always found it notoriously difficult to explain what exactly philosophy is about, and, as similar difficulties do not seem to dog the votaries of other disciplines it is not surprising that the sceptically-inclined should have tended to draw the conclusion that there must be something bogus about the whole affair. It is probably even more difficult to try to explain what metaphysics is about and this is serious indeed for metaphysics is pivotal to philosophy in a sense which other branches of philosophy such as logic, epistemology and ethics are not. That this is so becomes evident if we reflect on the fact that it is seldom possible to say anything of importance in these other branches of philosophy without basing what is said on some metaphysical presupposition or other.

It was, at one time, possible to define what metaphysics is by reference to its subject matter. Metaphysics began in ancient Greece as an enquiry into the nature of Being, and by Being was meant 'all that is'. In speaking of 'all that is' the metaphysician was not, of course, concerning himself with an inventory of all the perceptual objects which confronted him in everyday life. On the contrary the metaphysician's reasoning went something like this. Our everyday experience presents us with a changing world, with objects which are not always as they appear, with relativities of perception and with the contrast beween one man's experience and another's. Thought seems to demand that there should be some stable object which is different from the objects of our ordinary perceptual knowledge and which should be the concern of knowledge in another, if not higher sense. This something may be conceived as underlying the world which we are already acquainted with, or it may be regarded as 'other' than this world in some special sense. Such was the way, then, that metaphysicians envisaged their concern with 'reality', meaning by this what was foreign to the usual connotation of that word in our common-or-garden usage.

It is interesting to note, however, that the Ionian philosophers were not immediately able to conceive of metaphysical reality as something supersensible. It was the element in nature which struck them as dominant, be it water, fire or air, that was conceived to be the stuff out of which everything was made. In this respect the work of men like Thales can be deemed as much scientific as philosophical for the procedure of taking a cue from sensible phenomena is after all distinctive of science. Philosophers like Anaximander and Anaxagoras, who formulated the concept of a supersensible principle distinct from the world of sense, were following a method more genuinely philosophical and it is they who were the immediate precursors of the developed concept of a transcendent metaphysical reality which we associate especially with the name of Plato. Central to this developed concept is the assumption of a special object of metaphysical knowledge conceived as unconditioned in contrast to the conditioned world of sense-experience. The faculty whose proper task was the enterprise of ascertaining the nature of this special object was pure reason in contrast to the senses on which we rely for knowledge of the contingent world of sensible objects.

However, the ontological approach to metaphysics, for this is what is was, did not claim to be giving voice to what was merely a demand of thought. The claim, on the other hand, was very definitely a claim that the metaphysician could provide factual information of an order distinct from the factual order which ordinary experience discloses to us. The plausibility of this approach was strengthened by the circumstance that the state of the sciences in ancient Greece was not such as to provide authoritative counter-views to those which the metaphysicians offered. When, later on, the sciences were in a position to provide detailed answers to the question 'what is the nature of that which is?' the answers of high generality provided by the metaphysicians came to be viewed in a different light.

Two major problems, from the start, attended the ontologist's programme, the problem of specifying the nature of the alleged object of metaphysical knowledge, and, what was after all inseparable from it, the problem of explaining how it was to be known. If the object of metaphysical knowledge were as transcendent as seemed to be required, then it was difficult to see how man with his very inadequate faculties could possibly come to know it. A distinguished example of the treatment of this particular dilemma is found in Plato's account of the 'dialectic', the long process through which man may be able to climb out of the cave of ignorance into the full light of *noesis*. If however, the transcendence of the object is done justice to, it seemed inevitable that knowledge of its nature should remain at the level of mere project. The Platonic *noesis* and the Spinozistic knowledge *sub specie aeternitatis* remain immensely attractive as programmes for the employment of speculative reason and the man with a taste for matters philosophical will no doubt have a natural disposition towards this kind of thinking, but the doubt persists if man as he is can, without contradiction, be properly said ever to know anything which is absolute.

Traditional metaphysics tried to present a synoptic view of reality, but, as we have seen, it tried to do this from a vantage-point the attainment of which by man was most problematic. This way of metaphysical thinking is usually known as the *a priori* way, being based as it is on pure reason alone, that is to say, unaided either by experience or by the supernatural infusion of divine grace. The metaphysics of the Middle Ages was built on the ontological foundation laid by Aristotle. There were, however, certain modifications made consequent on the synthesis of Greek and Judaic thought which in fact Christian theology was. The concept of Being was fused with that of Jehovah and the theistic concept of God was the outcome of this fusion. God, moreover, was not merely the object of metaphysical knowledge but was regarded as the Providential ruler of the universe. The projects of reason were not unaided, but, on the one hand, were supplemented by the not wholly rational faculty of faith and, on the other hand, by the beneficent intervention of divine grace. With these reinforcements it can be appreciated that the traditional ontologist's programme seemed far more possible of achievement, and if few voices, if any, were raised against metaphysics in general in the Middle Ages this should occasion no surprise.

It was the combined impact of a gradual decline in religious faith (and this out of a collocation of circumstances most interesting in themselves but into which we cannot enter here) and the rise of scientific method which occasioned disquiet among philosophers and brought about a change in viewpoint leading to an approach to metaphysics which concentrated on method instead of on dogmatic pronouncements as to the nature of what is. In spite of their interest in method, however, the rationalist systems of the seventeenth and eighteenth centuries followed the *a priorism* of the earlier metaphysical systems in many respects. Premisses of metaphysical argument were taken from dogmatic definitions, syllogistic reasoning was allowed to direct the course of arguments, the capacities of reason were not questioned and the gap between the actual world and the world of allegedly intelligible entities was regarded as unfortunate but inevitable. The *a priorism* of Descartes, Leibniz and Spinoza was continued by Hegel in the sense that the speculative capacities of pure reason and the sphere in which reason was regarded as operative were given an even wider interpretation by that philosopher. Further, Hegel extended the scope of metaphysics in several ways, among which perhaps the most interesting were his invention of a logic which was designed to be applicable to the sphere of the dynamic and his view that history, whether of physical nature or of society, had metaphysical significance.

The connotation of 'that which is' in the metaphysician's programme, it can be seen, has had various interpretations. In the long history of the subject certain key concepts like those of Being, God, substance, cause, freedom, mind, matter, system, the Absolute, constantly recur, as a theme constantly recurs in a massive orchestral work. To the metaphysician, however, these concepts were traditionally regarded as being not mere concepts, but as pointing to certain distinctive features of the universe. In making this latter claim the problem was that more was being affirmed than could ever be backed up by experience. Doubts began to be raised as the pronouncements of the metaphysicians were seen to depart more and more from the findings of the scientists. What could be meant, say, by asserting that reality was made up of 'monads' when the scientist could tell us what the specific constitution of water, sodium chloride etc. was? Whether such criticism found its mark we have yet to see. At no time had a metaphysician imagined that he was providing information which was on all fours with the information we obtain through ordinary inductive procedures and the rift between the two sorts of information had always been very patent to metaphysicians themselves right from the time of the Platonic hypotheses of *mimesis* and *mithesis* introduced in order to relate the world of universals and the world of particulars. For, if the claim be made that metaphysics offers information of a special order, then the onus of explanation can lie nowhere else but on the metaphysician.

The limits of our faculties and the limits of language were well appreciated by the mediaeval theologians and it was for this reason that they favoured the method of analogy in metaphysical disquisitions. But their concern was as much theological as philosophical, and for them proofs were but preambles to faith. Now the capacity of pure reason in the spheres of mathematics and the natural sciences was there for all to see in the eighteenth century, the age of the enlightenment. But the achievements of reason in the field of metaphysics were hardly as satisfactory, and this was patent in the conflicting accounts of 'reality' given by the rival dogmatisms of the day. Hence there arose a group of philosophers, who while deeply sympathetic with the impulse which prompts the metaphysician to venture beyond experience, for the first time raised the question as to whether metaphysics as a science was possible at all.

The critical movement

Among the 'critical' philosophers the name of John Locke deserves prime mention. The epistemological standpoint of Locke from the start set him on a path which was in intention counter to that of the traditional metaphysician, for while the heart of the metaphysical procedure is to pronounce concerning the nature of what is and to pronounce dogmatically, the essence of the epistemologist's approach is to postpone the question as to what is, inquiring first into our capacities to know it. The price paid for allowing inquiries to 'wander into those depths where they can find no sure footing' is not only the multiplication of disputes but the encouragement of scepticism. Locke's own work centred on the analysis of what we could properly be said to know and on an insistence that sense experience is the only source from which knowledge is derived. Questions such as whether or not matter can think or the mind be extended he found impossible of answer, and significantly, he denied that any dogmatic answer one way or another could be extracted from definitions in the Cartesian manner. Of the nature of real essences we can say nothing. As to the nature of God, the ontological argument is rejected by him by reason of the empiricist connotation given by him to the word 'idea'. The horizon which is set between what we can and cannot know is determined by the criterion of experienceability and it was Locke's view that there were no elements in experience which could not be traced to some sense-experience or other. To admit any such elements, to the strict empiricist, would amount to opening the door to a host of metaphysical concepts for which no warrant could be found in experience.

Hume's subsequent discovery that there were certain 'ideas' which could not be traced back to any sense impression, therefore, posed a problem. Two alternatives logically presented themselves. Either one could say that the ideas in question were only alleged ideas and not genuine ones at all, or one could modify the initial dictum that every idea is traceable to some preceding impression or other. The latter altenative could only present itself to a philosopher like Kant who recognised that, over and above the role of sensation, concepts too had a part to play in our knowledge of the world. Hume's own procedure was to maintain that in the case of our 'ideas' of space and time (and these could not be traced to any particular impressions) they could be more properly described as the 'manner' in which the sensibles came to us; whereas in the case of our idea of the necessary connection between cause and effect the necessity was but a necessity of feeling based on our habitual perception of uniform sequences; finally, in the case of our 'idea' of the self as an entity, this was none other than a fictitious idea and all we actually had at our disposal was the flux of perceptions which made up our waking life and which in fact constituted the self. In this way Hume avoids saying anything 'metaphysical' about those elements in experience which yet do not appear to have been derived from experience in the sense of being derived from any single perception.

Hume has much to say in his *Enquiries* against what he calls the 'abstruse' philosophy of metaphysics. He speaks of it as 'not only painful and fatiguing, but as the inevitable source of uncertainty and error.' The remedy prescribed (and it is the same remedy that Locke prescribes) is 'to enquire seriously into the nature of human understanding.' We may suppose that it is this enquiry which is acceptable to him as the 'true metaphysics' which is to be cultivated. His stress on 'experimental reasoning' is Newtonian in inspiration and leads inevitably to the rejection of any hypotheses which may be unverifiable. The upshot of Hume's plotting of what he calls 'mental geography' is the strict dichotomy of admissible classes of meaningful statements with which he concludes his First Enquiry :—

> 'If we take in our hand any volume; of divinity or school metaphysics, for instance; let us ask, Does it contain any abstract reasoning concerning quantity or number? No. Does it contain any experimental reasoning concerning matter of fact and existence? No. Commit it then to the flames; for it can contain nothing but sophistry and illusion.'

The inference is that no third category of statement is possible. Sophistry we may perhaps interpret as being a mere playing with words, and illusion as the arriving at false conclusions. At all events no positivist has put the case against transcendent metaphysics with greater forcefulness than has Hume in this purple passage.

The critical movement of which Locke and Hume were pioneers came to full flowering in the work of Kant whose *Critique of Pure Reason* avowedly is an examination of the capacity of reason to undertake the task traditionally assigned to it by metaphysicians. Kant poses the problem in the form of the question 'How are *a priori* synthetic judgements possible?'

An *a priori* judgement may be defined as one which is derived from pure reason i.e. *a priori*, and which yet adds to our information i.e. is synthetic. Now to provide us with such judgements had been the programme of the traditional metaphysician. By using thinking alone he was allegedly able to provide knowledge of a different order from that which we obtain at the level of everyday experience. Plato and Spinoza are notable examples of philosophers who had much to say about this 'higher' kind of knowledge. Christian theology had bequeathed to metaphysics three concepts in particular which it seemed incumbent on the philosopher to discuss, namely the concepts of God, freedom and the immortality of the soul. It would indeed be ultimately detrimental to the cause of religion if philosophers were to be unable to 'prove' that these concepts had a foundation in reality. But the rival accounts given by various metaphysicians convinced Kant that the dogmatic procedure that had hitherto been followed was unwarranted and that the claim that metaphysical statements were genuinely *a priori* and the same time synthetic needed careful scrutiny.

Kant's method is to examine those disciplines in which synthetic *a priori* judgements amount undisputedly to knowledge, that is to say, the disciplines of mathematics and the natural sciences. In drawing attention to the synthetic element in mathematical thinking Kant was saying something new. In his view it had been the wrong account of mathematics given by the rationalists which had encouraged the dogmatic method in philosophizing. Believing that mathematical judgements were analytic, the rationalists had built their systems on definitions and deductions from them. The synthetic principles which underlay the sciences had not hitherto been formulated but Kant believed they were nonetheless to be found as presuppositions in the Newtonian view of mechanics. Kant's analysis of these two classes of judgement provides him with the key to the diagnosis of why metaphysical judgements have not had a parallel success. In the case both of mathematics and the natural sciences we have at our disposal not only concepts but also intuitions and it is this latter element which enables us to 'go beyond' the subject (in a synthetic judgement when I say that 'S is P' I go beyond what is contained in the concept of S) and to make genuinely synthetic judgements. We are now in a position to say why metaphysics has not been able to enter upon the sure path of the sciences. Metaphysics rests on concepts alone, and concepts alone can only tell us what is possible and not what is actual. 'Thoughts without content are empty, intuitions without concepts are blind'.

On Kant's view, then, it is plain that we cannot speak of metaphysical 'knowledge', for in the case of metaphysical statements the one thing without which we cannot speak of knowledge, namely, intuition, is missing. If transcendent metaphysics be impossible is there any other form of metaphysics which may be said to be admissible? On the one hand Kant may be said to have himself provided a 'metaphysic of experience' in showing the legitimate and indispensable role of synthetic *a priori* concepts within experience, and this is what his 'transcendental' philosophy amounts to. On the other hand the Transcendental Dialectic contains the analysis of a different set of concepts, the Ideas of Pure Reason, which our natural disposition towards metaphysics leads us to employ. These Ideas in each case provide Reason with certain projects which lead to the misemployment of the categories, and the joint effect of the employment of an Idea and the relevant misemployment of one of the categories is transcendental illusion i.e. not knowledge at all. However, in spite of the negative character of this conclusion Kant thought that the Ideas had a legitimate heuristic employment, and an employment, moreover, which was of special import in the practical sphere. For example, if we look on the other person as possessing a soul we are less likely to treat him as a means to an end. The concept of God, he thought, can be shown to be a postulate of morality, and the concept of 'system' can act as a stimulus to the scientist in his inductive exploration of the world. In limiting the theoretical role of reason Kant made room for the work of practical reason and for faith, and he believed it to be in the best interests of morality and religion that their basic concepts should be liberated from the ministrations of the speculative philosopher and from the attempts at demonstration which hitherto, as he showed, had been all too unsuccessful.

Logical Positivism

If we look at the history of philosophy we can pick out a number of precursors of what one might call an anti-metaphysical movement. Among these could be mentioned, for example, the nominalist opposition to the substantialist interpretation of universals, Hobbesian materialism, sceptical doubts concerning the capacities of pure reason, and, a big land-mark indeed, the positivism of eighteenth century France. The last of these, especially, was consciously influenced by the advances of the natural sciences and the conviction that those advances were due to the limiting of scientific enquiry to the world of phenomena. If we take experience as our guide, so the positivists held, there is in fact no ground whatsoever for positing any world other than this. The connotation of "phenomena" then lay wholly in emphasis on the 'sensible' and not on any alleged contrast with a 'noumenal' world the existence of which they explicitly denied. Old-style positivism, that is, the positivism of Comte and his contemporaries, was founded on a conviction that the methods of the sciences were the only methods that yielded knowledge, and they were methods which *ipso facto* ruled out any reference to the non-experienceable. The positing of entities was an enterprise which belonged to a pre-scientific stage of thought. The non-verifiable could be no concern of the scientifically-minded. There seemed no limit to the applicability of scientific method, and indeed it should be possible to discover the operation of laws not only in physical nature but also in society. In this respect the naturalism of Comte was to be developed still further by Karl Marx.

The importance of Hume's distinction between propositions concerning relations of ideas and propositions concerning matters of fact and its influence on later positivists cannot be exaggerated. In the long run too, the pragmatic insistence on the cash-value of ideas and Pavlov's stress on the observable (implicit in the technique of conditioning) have made their mark. Logical positivists in Britain, in addition, drew inspiration from certain aspect of the work of Russell and Moore, however far the work of these two philosophers may be, in the remaining aspects, from the general position held by the positivists. Russell's theory of descriptions showed how apparently substantival expressions can be substituted by descriptive expressions, thus doing much to counter the whole tendency to assume that nouns correspond to entities, a tendency which had been in large part the legacy of Aristotelianism. The application of Occam's razor could prune away much metaphysical undergrowth although, as Wisdom wittily remarked, even after reductionist operations had been completed there still lingered a peculiar smell from the fictional entities which remained.* Russell's advocacy of the piecemeal method was in itself a direct attempt to 'make philosophy more scientific'. Whether his own philosophy of logical atomism could escape the charge of being highly metaphysical fortunately does not concern us here. Moore's own work, especially in ethics, was certainly metaphysical. And yet his attachment to commonsense and to ordinary language provided a very definite alternative to the oracles beloved of traditional metaphysicians. The piecemeal analysis of particular philosophical puzzles would surely act as a deterrent to those anxious to embark on over-all theorising.

Logical positivism in its pure and unadulterated form was not (from the British point of view) an indigenous product, Hume notwithstanding. The Vienna Circle, represented by Carnap, Schlick, Neurath and others was its founder. Their point of view is typified in an article which Carnap published in 1932, entitled 'The elimination of metaphysics through the logical analysis of language.' The point was not, he said, whether metaphysics was false, uncertain or sterile, but that metaphysical statements had strictly no meaning. Following Hume's 'great divide', only two classes of propositions could be admitted, *a priori* ones which were tautologous and where the question was whether or no the putative propositions were valid or invalid, and empirical ones where the question was whether the putative propositions were verifiable or not.

From the start the main problem facing the verificationists was that of formulating the so-called 'Verification Principle' so that it would exclude the propositions dubbed as metaphysical and yet make room for the propositions of science. Kant had

* Metaphysics and Verification, *Mind*, 1938, p. 460.

already drawn the attention of philosophers to the fact that, if going 'beyond' experience were the mark of metaphysics, science also, we must not forget, goes beyond experience. What makes the one procedure inadmissable and the other admissable is the lack of anchorage in experience which is the characteristic of metaphysics, whereas the statements of the scientist are rooted in a starting-point in the perceptual world. For Kant, then, the crux of the difference between the two lay in the reference to intuition, a reference which was integral to science but which was woefully lacking in the groping among mere concepts which was the fate of metaphysics. The logical positivists, however, approached the problem of demarcating the difference, not from the point of view of what can and cannot be known (as in the case of Kant), but from the point of view of what can and cannot be said. The various distinctions which Ayer draws between practical verifiability and verifiability in principle and strong and weak verification are all attempts to formulate the connotation of 'literal significance', for only a literally significant statement can, on the positivist view, be said to be meaningful.

One type of proposition which seemed to provide a paradigm of verifiability was the 'basic proposition'. Neurath had defined a 'protocol proposition' as one which contains the name or description of an observer and reference to an act of observation. It was difficult, however, to give a clear example of any single basic proposition, or to expunge the taint of subjectivity from the putative ones. It could be doubted, in the first instance, whether any empirical proposition could properly be said to be incorrigible. Any empirical proposition was, after all, more in the nature of a hypothesis which could always be corrected on the basis of subsequent observations. Linguistically, moreover, the formulation of such propositions depended on convention. Could a sentence ever adequately record an experience, and were there in fact sentences which were not, in part at least, vague? The problem of 'stoppers', or termini of the verification process, was, it was evident, hedged in with difficulties. If the termini were mere experiences, that is to say, if they were unverbalised, then we were *ipso facto* beyond the range of language. If the termini were some type of proposition we were up against the admitted corrigibility of all empirical propositions, a corrigibility stemming on the one hand from the conventional nature of language, and, on the other hand, from the possibility of falsification arising from further observations. Ayer had to admit that, whether or no basic propositions are possible, the vast majority of empirical propositions are not basic and that what is required for verification is the occurrence of no particular sense-contents but the occurrence of one or other sense-content within a certain range. The controversy concerning basic propositions is of interest, however, in so far as it is a symptom of something which has attracted the Continental positivists especially and, in U. K.. Bertrand Russell, namely the project of founding a calculus of propositions where the basic 'terms' represent units of experience. In the earlier work of Wittgenstein and in that of Russell* the programme is definitely metaphysical —the metaphysic of logical atomism. In the case of a philosopher like Carnap the concern is more a linguistic one. Both approaches, however, stem from Leibniz' project of constructing a perfect language. The piecemeal approach to language leads in a very different direction, that of the recognition of the 'unclear' character of much of empirical discourse, and, at the same time, the recognition of its fertility.

Ayer's final formulation of direct and indirect verifiability was designed to clear up the ambiguous status of scientific propositions and to make room for the presence of a certain number of analytic statements which are likely to be there in the field of pure theory. The claim was made that, in so formulating the verification principle, all metaphysical discussion concerning, say, the reality or unreality of the world of sense experience, how many substances there were, and the like, would be at one blow eliminated. Now that the tumult and the shouting has some what died down it is more easy to see the work of the positivists in perspective. Much of their work had roots in earlier stages in the history of philosophy, as we have seen. The distance of the work of the late nineteenth century idealists from the findings of commonsense and from science undoubtedly encouraged a movement of reaction, and, as with all reaction

* Vide *Our knowledge of the external world.*

movements, the immediate impact seemed to wipe away all that had gone before.

Whether the original programme of the positivists—the elimination of metaphysics—has been carried out, remains to be seen. The verification principle itself, it was pointed out by many critics, was itself of doubtful lineage. If the only admissible types of proposition were to be tautologies on the one hand, and empirical propositions on the other, the verification principle could by no means be accommodated in either basket. For the linchpin of the whole scheme to come under suspicion in this way was indeed a challenge to the positivists themselves. At the end of the *Tractatus* Wittgenstein had spoken of his own propositions as 'elucidatory'. 'He who understands me finally recognises them as senseless, when he has climbed out through them, on them, over them. (He must so to speak throw away the ladder, after he has climbed up on it). He must surmount these propositions; then he sees the world rightly.' This ascent into mysticism was not, however, appreciated by all the positivists. Ayer has spoken of the verification principle as a 'convention'. The bulk of the positivist programme, he maintains, was descriptive and it tallied moreover with common usage regarding empirical sentences. The prescriptive part of the programme, that no third category of sentence could be admitted as meaningful, has not been altogether carried out. What has been established, on the contrary, is that metaphysical statements do not fall into the same category as the statements of logic, history, science or commonsense, and this, we may comment, is something of which traditional metaphysicians had always been aware. As R.M. Hare has said, the verification principle provides a criterion of 'empiricality' and that is about all. Metaphysical statements may be neither true nor false. They may even be misleading. From another point of view they may be suggestive, fertile, or important (in Dorothy Emmet's sense of the term). But this will not be the same as saying that they are meaningless.

The positivists were not singular in looking upon experience as a promised land. The idealist Bradley, and the existentialists, for example, have tried to found philosophies on experience, and with no less enthusiasm, although certainly they have understood by the word "experience" very different things. Positivism, however, shared with the empiricist tradition in general an insistence that the only proper connotation of the word 'experience' was 'sense experience'. That this should be so was taken for granted by the philosophic heirs of Locke and Comte. That experience was itself something that called for analysis was appreciated most fully only by Kant. That there can be no simple appeal to the 'facts of experience' was realised in this century by those who concerned themselves with the logic of science. It could be pointed out by others, especially those who were not particularly interested in the nature of perception, that there were many kinds of experience apart from sense experience. In aesthetic experience we were, for example, aware of something which could not be exhausted in the bare perceptual data given to us. In moral experience we had an example of something which was admittedly not experience of an 'object' but which nonetheless deserved the title of 'experience'. Religious experience likewise, we are told by those who claim to be familiar with it, is certainly experience of something. In these ways, then, the narrow connotation given by the positivists to experience came in for criticism.

Even more damaging charges could be framed from within the fold of science itself. Sense experience by itself cannot establish any scientific theory. The facts yield themselves up, not to unsophisticated observation, but to controlled experiment in the laboratory, a procedure in which the role of hypotheses is most crucial. In formulating his hypothesis the scientist goes beyond experience, although the end process of his investigation is rooted in the verifiable. The entities which the scientist posits are in principle unobservable for the reason that they are in essence conceptual in nature. The demand that an electron or proton be observable is therefore in the nature of things impossible to satisfy. The natural laws discovered by the scientist are likewise unobservable, although instances on the basis of which the laws are formulated can of course be encountered in experience. It was again Kant who saw the uncanny resemblance between the procedure of induction and the procedure of the metaphysician. The legitimacy of the former stems from the appeal to intuition which for the scientist is always the ultimate anchorage for theorising. The infertility of speculative metaphysics stems from the absence of this one vital condition. The logic of science has developed much since the controversy between the standpoints of Poincaré and Mach. If the role of hypotheses in the natural sciences be done justice to, it becomes no less urgent to recognise the role of concepts in our everyday perceptual experience. To do this, however, is to admit that the terminus of the process of verification is a theoretical limit which we must presuppose rather than something which is actually given in sense experience.

If all our knowledge transcends the immediately given the positivist quest for the incorrigible is a bootless one. What is behind this quest, however, is an interesting hangover from the legacy of rationalism. It amounts to the search for an analogue in experience to the axiomatic. One key assumption presupposed here is that there is a systematic coherence among the data of experience, a coherence analogous to the internal coherence of deductive systems, an assumption which, although it may be a demand of the understanding, is not backed up by the data of experience themselves. The positivists thus tend to veer between a hankering after system (represented more by the Continental thinkers than by the British) and an appeal to the simple facts of sense experience. The inherent difficulty of the latter appeal was reflected in the giving up of the quest for ostensive definitions, for these could either be so ostensive that they would be unverbalised and therefore not 'definitions' at all, or they would be basic propositions the demand for whose verification would in turn have to be made. The appeal to sense experience was moreover constantly dogged by the bogey of solipsism. Various improvements were made on Neurath's initial definition of a protocol proposition as a proposition containing the name or description of an observer and reference to an act of observation. What was necessary for verification, it was later said, was not the occurrence of any particular sense experience but the occurrence of certain sense contents falling within a certain range (Berkeley had said much the same thing long before). The neutral language of 'event' was a still further improvement which did something to exercise the bogey of solipsism.

Historically the positivist movement gave way to linguistic analysis which can be described as a 'movement' provided justice is done to the considerable diversity of approach accomodated within its fold. It was realised that the verification principle needed to be supplemented by a detailed examination of particular metaphysical arguments, and, further, that the types of sentence which had been excluded by Hume's rigid dichotomy called for analysis instead of condemnation. If in science there was sometimes an obliqueness of relation between a piece of theory and a perception deemed to be relevant to its substantiation, why should not the same indulgence be granted to the metaphysician ? If Bergson could appeal to the eye of the Pecten mollusc as evidence in favour of the hypothesis of divergent lines of evolution a theist may also appeal to it as evidence of the Divine intelligence. Scientific methodology shows how concepts enter into the very constitution of fact. It also shows how alternative concepts can be utilised to illuminate a single range of data. The perception of resemblance which stimulates the transfer of a hypothesis from one field to another is a perception which stimulates the philosopher to speak of analogy. Much of the sting is removed from the positivist programme when we reflect that the project of making philosophy more scientific carries with it inevitably a vindication of the role of concepts and a vindication of the legitimacy of alternative vocabularies which is most encouraging to those who have a natural disposition for metaphysical thinking.

PART TWO: THE NATURE OF KNOWLEDGE

v Theories of Knowledge

Introduction

It has often been said, and rightly, that preoccupation with epistemology, rather than ontology, has been the dominant characteristic of modern philosophy. Now in our everyday life we employ the word 'know' quite freely, and without misgiving, in a large number of contexts. We say 'Jane knows her six times table', 'Mrs. Jones knows that you were at home yesterday', 'We know that there is no such thing as a unicorn', 'You know you ought not to tell lies', 'Mrs. Smith says she knows there is life after death'. The examples could be multiplied indefinitely. We speak of 'knowing more' and 'knowing better', of 'knowing once upon a time and not knowing now'. Much of what the philosopher talks about under the title of epistemology may, at first sight, seem to have little to do with such ordinary usages. The plain man never speaks of 'knowing the table' but when he opens a book on perception he will find that tables (and chairs and inkpots) are favourite cognitive objects. How did philosophers begin to talk about knowledge in the first place ?

With the exception of a few philosophers among whom Protagaras was the most influential, in the ancient world theory of knowledge was on the whole subordinate to metaphysics. Plato, however, was impressed by what seemed to him to amount to a difference in status between our various cognitive operations. Imagination seemed merely imitative compared with perception. In turn the objects of mathematical knowledge were of a very different order in comparison with the objects of ordinary perception. Now it seemed to Plato that the object of the highest form of knowledge should in the nature of things possess even more fixity than the objects of mathematical knowledge, and, being ideal, should not be merely an object of intellect but should possess value as well. Thanks to this fourfold division of the possible objects of cognitive operations philosophers were inclined to concentrate on the last of these types and indeed to regard it as the chief business of the philosopher to deal with a very special and rarified sort of subject matter. Perceptual knowledge, on such a view, was of a lower order than mathematical knowledge and its inferior status was evident in the shifting nature of the objects of the perceptible world. The Platonic tradition, fortified as it was by Pythagoreanism, did a lot towards diverting the attention of 'rationalist' philosophers from the interesting and varied world which the senses reveal to us. The objects of knowledge in the strict sense were, according to this tradition, entities of a special kind which only pure reason could perceive clearly and distinctly. Aristotle, however, being inspired more by the practical temper of the scientist than by the speculative abstractions of the mathematician, was not willing to divorce the objects of knowledge from the world of sense. Even so, the philosophies of both Plato and Aristotle are looked on as ontological (rather than epistemological) by reason of their dominantly metaphysical concern. It would, at the same time, be a mistake to overlook the very weighty contributions made by Plato in particular to theory of knowledge.

The Aristotelian way of ontologising was further developed by the mainstream of scholasticism and the treatment of knowledge tended to become still further removed from the world of commonsense in that the main field of interest for the Schoolmen was, very understandably (for they were churchmen), our knowledge of God. With the gradual growth of science it became increasingly noticeable that philosophy was not keeping in step with the new discoveries. The 'external' world, that is to say, not the inner world of man's desires and aspirations, nor the transcendent world of God and His angels (the philosophers of the Middle Ages had quite a lot to say about angels), was not something that could be ignored. Man lives in the world of space and time and this is the world of fact. no matter if he may, at the same time, be a denizen of a very different and most hierarchical order represented in the religious cosmology of heaven, hell and limbo. Scientists were not only 'knowing' the sensible world but the fruits of their knowledge in the shape of the prediction and control of natural phenomena were there for all to see. To reconcile this new 'knowledge' with the old became the pressing philosophical problem of the day in the seventeenth century. The problem of knowledge *par excellence*, for the first time in the history of philosophy, was identified with the problem of perception. Instead of merely comparing perception unfavourably with the pure science of mathematics philosophers became interested in the actual processes of perception for their own sake. New discoveries about the nature of light and sound showed that there was a causal aspect to the phenomenon of perception. The technique of experiment showed that the discovery of nature was by no means a passive process. Maybe perception too was not so passive as some people had thought.

If it was the impact of science which converted the philosopher's problem of knowledge into the specific problem of perception, and this right up to the present day, it was only to be expected that many philosophers should be loath to abandon the older interpretation of knowledge as concerning in the first place the clear and distinct objects of mathematics and logic and that they should be equally loath to abandon the traditional philosophical claim to a super-knowledge which should be the special prerogative of the metaphysician. The bulk of this part of the book, however, will concern the development of the theme of our knowledge of the external world, that is, the various theories of perception, for this is modern epistemology proper. This is followed by a treatment of *a priori* knowledge which, as has been seen, is knowledge in its traditional sense. Finally propositional knowledge is considered under the heading of "Theories of truth".

Representationism

One might imagine that the easiest way to approach the problem of knowledge would be to start from the commonsense assumption that we perceive things for the most part as they are and that when we do so it is because they are there. The word 'because' here does not indicate causal transaction, but just a matter of commonsense. But it would be possible to show that this naive theory will not do because often we seem to perceive things that are not there, or we perceive them erroneously. Some kind of analysis of exactly what the object of knowledge is, therefore, would seem to be called for. Such an analysis, however, would not necessarily lead to the hypothesis that the object of knowledge is never 'out there' in the common world but is in some sense or other a subjective content. A critique of naive realism, would not inevitably have led the history of epistemology on the path that it did in fact follow.

As it happens we find that the bulk of the problems which modern philosophers set out to tackle—and some of these may strike us as highly artificial—arose out of the circumstance that it was Descartes who first found something problematic about our knowledge of the external world. Indeed the philosophers before Descartes had not been particularly troubled by the 'externality' of the world, for it came naturally to the scholastic thinkers (however much maligned they may have been) to think of man as a creature living in space and time, being himself a substantial unity of body and soul, able to know the world thanks to the providential congruence of the world to man's capacities of knowing it, a congruence which stemmed from the goodness of God. The break which Descartes made with this way of looking at things was really quite far-reaching. For whereas to the schoolmen 'intellectus' was not merely a discursive faculty, Descartes made of pure reason a faculty which was only at home in the realm of symbolic operations, and it was only the contingent circumstance of the extraordinary applicability of the Euclidean type of geometry to the actual world which enabled him to conclude that the nature of the 'real' world was in fact the abstraction called 'extension'. (There was, however, it must be recognised, another strand of thought in mediaeval philosophy which, drawing on the Aristotelian view that reason was the essence of man and the Pauline stress on the dualism of the spirit and the flesh, could be interpreted as advocating a rift between man and nature.) At any rate it suited Descartes, mathematician as he was, to find in clear and distinct perceptions the proper employment of thought. The dualism for which he is notorious, and about which he appeared to be convinced even before enunciating the Cogito, was in fact the fount and origin of the representative theory of perception which is our immediate concern here.

Descartes seems to have taken for granted the idealist (and ultimately Platonic) view that knowledge is not possible unless there be some kinship between the subject and object of knowledge. If the subject of knowledge be mind, as indeed it must, then it follows that the object of knowledge must also in some way or other be mental. Now in the project of knowing the physical world we are trying to know something which is extended, something that is, which is alien to mind as 'res cogitans'. Such a world, then, can only be known *via* the media of 'ideas' thanks to whose representative agency the mind can become acquainted with the 'external' world. Now the ideas which come to us in this way (and the transaction was regarded by Descartes as a causal one) are of two kinds, ideas of primary qualities (that is to say measurable qualities, or quantities) which he reckoned were true copies of the qualities, and secondary qualities which are subjective ones depending on the position, state, etc. of our sense organs. Two problems immediately arise from such a theory. In order to know that the representations are faithful one would need to see the originals. But if one *did* see the originals the representations would become superfluous. Moreover it is unjustifiable to speak of the ideas as 'copies' at all if the ideas are all that we have. To use a simple illustration, to speak of some of our ideas as true copies would be like pronouncing a photograph to be a good likeness of X when we have never seen X. Locke, who agreed with Descartes' theory and himself spoke of ideas as 'the pictures of things' seems also to have been aware of the difficulties which attend it, for in examining Malebranche's philosophy he comments "How can I know that the picture of anything is like that thing, when I never see that which it represents."

The unfortunate vocabulary of "ideas" introduced into epistemology by Descartes subjectivised the object of knowledge and made our empirical propositions in principle unverifiable. Two species of perceptions seemed to lend some support to the Cartesian theory, first of all relative perceptions (like the appearance of a penny as elliptical from a certain angle), and illusory perceptions (like seeing pink rats which are not there). Now it could be argued, and wrongly, that since the elliptical penny and the pink rats were not in fact 'out there' they must be somewhere, and where else can they be put 'in the mind'. The mind could be looked on (as Ryle has scathingly described) as a convenient receptacle for awkward cognitive objects which could not be tenanted elsewhere. Now the argument from illusion has been, for the most part, not only amalgamated with the argument from the relativity of perception, and this unwarrantedly, but wrong inferences have been made from the phenomenon of what one might loosely call 'deviations' from standard perceptions. To take the first, whereas both you and I see the penny as elliptical from this particular angle and in fact the elliptical penny can be regarded as one of the many 'perspectives' of the penny, the pink rats are only seen by the man who is in an inebriated condition. The elliptical penny coheres with our own experience of other 'angles' on the penny (if, say, we gradually turn round), and also 'coheres' with the corroborations provided by other people, whereas the pink rats neither cohere with the drunkard's experiences at other times nor with those of his sober friends. There is a simple way we can bring in due mention of the phenomena under discussion. We can say 'The penny *looks* elliptical from this angle', 'I thought I saw a snake', 'The pencil seemed to be broken'. In this way the subject, verb and object form of sentence is not allowed to dictate the positing of a whole collection of dubious mental entities, but the status of these 'deviation' experiences (and we have already pointed out how different in kind they are) is made quite clear through the verbs 'looks', 'seems' etc.

The representative theory of perception, from the above considerations, would seem to have little to recommend it. In positing a *tertium quid* between mind and its object Descartes (and his followers) fostered a whole host of problems for his successors. To begin with, it was misleading to look upon the knowing relation in terms of a causal transaction between two types of substance on the analogy of transactions within the physical order. The vocabulary of ideas, moreover, was an atomistic vocabulary counterpart to the chemist's vocabulary of atoms and molecules. In making the object of knowledge completely mental it was thought by many that the whole nature of knowing as revelatory of an 'other' had been destroyed. It was no wonder, then, that the representative theory of perception should have been directly responsible for a series of rebound philosophies which came after it—subjectivism, scepticism and realism in particular. One thing, perhaps, which the theory did, was to sharpen the issue, to make clear what exactly the problem of perception was—namely, the problem of specifying the subject and object of knowledge. The term 'idea' was, for the time being, to obscure this distinction, for, as Moore pointed out later, the term 'idea' serves to straddle it. The epistemological approach was more marked in Locke than in Descartes in that Locke thought that the question of the sources, certainty and extent of our knowledge could be best investigated through an examination of our cognitive equipment. Whereas Berkeley tried to be equally informative about the subject and object of knowledge, Hume remained in the last analysis sceptical as to the *what* of our knowledge of things although he was in no doubt *that* things existed. Kant's approach was unique in that, instead of trying to isolate the quiddity of the object of knowledge, he initiated an entirely new approach—that of laying bare the *conditions* of knowledge from the side of the subject. Some of these subsequent approaches will concern us in what follows.

Subjective Idealism

The subjectivist theory of knowledge is usually associated with the name of Berkeley, although not always justly, as there is much in Berkeley which is not subjectivist at all. As Mabbott and others have pointed out, the viewpoint expressed in his later works is definitely objectivist. Nor can the later-day charge of solipsism be correctly levelled against even the Berkeley of the *Principles*, for it is evident that he is enough of a scholastic to take as his starting point a common world in which there is a plurality of finite beings or spirits. Berkeley's main purpose throughout is theological. He wants to combat atheism, and he thinks that the belief that our perceptions come about through the efficacy of matter will lead the ordinary man to believe in the self-sufficiency of nature, a belief which is contrary to the theist's conviction that all depends on God. To say, moreover, as Locke did, that substance existed although it was a 'something we know not what' was to invite scepticism, and this too is contrary to the Divine intention that we should have confidence in our God-given faculties. Whatever subjectivism there be in Berkeley is different in temper from that of Descartes, for, in the case of the latter, resort is made to subjectivity subsequent on the methodological doubt of the *poêle*. In Berkeley's mind there is not the least element of doubt whatsoever. The subjective idealist part of Berkeley's philosophy is the direct and logical working out of the view put forward by both Descartes and Locke, that the immediate objects of knowledge are ideas. If the Lockean thesis be correct, and Berkeley does not doubt for a moment that it is, we have no ground for inferring to the existence of unobserved entities. As good Occamists we should not multiply entities unnecessarily, and, as contemporaries of Sir Isaac Newton, we should not fall a victim to the fascination of unverifiable hypotheses. Bearing in mind, then, that some of Berkeley's theological presuppositions protect him in some degree from some of the strongest objections against subjectivism we can proceed to see what exactly his theory of perception amounts to.

Berkeley points out, to begin with, the inherent contradiction in representationism. How can we speak of X as representing Y when all we have is X? And here what Berkeley has to say is surely incontrovertible. Unfortunately, however, he inherits the Cartesian vocabulary of ideas, so that the conclusion inevitably follows that things are immediately perceived by us as 'states of our own consciousness'. Ideas cannot be anywhere else but in minds. They cannot exist unperceived. Since the objects of our knowledge are ideas it is evident that these objects have a relative existence, for ideas are relative to minds. To speak of ideas as copies of anything non-mental is to speak without meaning, for an idea can only be like another idea. As for Locke's distinction between primary and secondary qualities, this ignores the fact that the former are as relative to our position and state as the latter. The concept of material substance in Locke has become so tenuous (what does 'support' mean, for example?) that it can well be left out. There is evidence for material substance neither from reason nor from sense. There is certainly, however, a causal question to be answered, for our ideas of sense come to us involuntarily and therefore they must have been caused by some power other than ourselves. In ourselves we are aware of the causal agency of spirit in contrast to the passivity of sense and so we have good reason to believe that some spirit other than ourselves is responsible for causing ideas in us. When we look around us and see the wise disposition of all phenomena, their order and utility, we are led to the conclusion that the cause of our ideas can be none other than God.

The details of the arguments Berkeley uses to come to this conclusion and the way in which he defends himself against anticipated objections are to be found in his *Principles of Human Knowledge*. The issues that are at stake between the 'minute philosophers' and the theologian on the nature of explanation are laid bare in that work. Whether there be need of matter in natural philosophy is as pertinent a question in our own day as it was in Berkeley's. The idealist part of Berkeley's thesis associates it definitely with idealist theories of somewhat different brands, namely, his view that to make of knowledge a relation between mind and something foreign to mind is to make the knowledge relation 'unintelligible'. There can be no compromise possible between the philosopher who thinks that the immediate object of knowledge must be something mental and the philosopher who thinks that this is precisely the negation of knowledge. Existence is always relative to thought—this is the typical idealist position. Any philosopher who speaks of existence out of the context of reference to actual and possible experience must be prepared to say what he means. In speaking of the existence of God are we using the word 'exist' in a different tone of voice? On Berkeley's own terms are we entitled to speak of the *absolute* existence even of God? Once more, only an understanding of Berkeley's reliance on scholastic procedures of analogy can enable his meaning to become clear. Whether on his view of the univocal meaning of the concept of existence he is entitled to speak of Infinite Spirit as he does is an interesting question, but not one which is immediately tied up with the treatment of subjective idealism.

The subjectivist theory of perception has not been slow in sparking off a varied barrage of criticism. Indeed, stated in an extreme form and shorn of the many presuppositions which, as we have tried to show, attended it in the works of Berkeley, it is easy to criticise it. For all that Berkeley thought that his view of the existence of things did in fact square better with actual scientific procedure than the "residual" view of substance ('something we know not what') retained by Locke, one may wonder whether in fact the subjectivist can ever do justice to the concept of "thinghood". Can the concept of 'thing' be cashed completely into that of a congeries of ideas, even if, with modern phenomenalism, we give up the old-fashioned vocabulary of ideas in favour of the more neutral language of sense data? By a thing we normally mean a seat of active and passive powers such as impenetrability (seen wisely by Locke), inertia and the like. Moreover there seems to be a significant difference between the various data themselves. Sounds, smells and tastes seem to emanate from, and visual and tactual data seem to be a part of an object. Can the word 'idea' reflect this difference?

Four other (historically most important) lines of criticism were made by Perry, Moore, Whitehead and Kant. These are not in chronological order, but the Kantian criticism is the most far reaching and its pertinency will appeal most after the other objections have been mentioned. Perry maintained that the slogan of 'Nothing exists but my ideas' involved what he styled the 'ego-centric predicament', and he held that Berkeley could be accused of advocating what in fact amounted to solipsism. How could a 'common' world be 'constructed' out of the helter-skelter world of private data? That some such dilemma did beset the empiricist can be seen in Russell's book *Our knowledge of the external world*. 'Idea' language, and even sensedatum language, does seem suspiciously private. In the case of Berkeley Perry's criticism is probably not too damaging, for, as has been indicated earlier, Berkeley does begin with the ontological assumption of a plurality of finite spirits. He does, moreover, say in Section 48 of the *Principles* that

'Whenever bodies are said to have no existence without the mind, I would not be understood to mean this or that particular mind, but all minds whatsoever.'

Moore's criticism centres on the ambiguity of the word 'idea'.* He agrees with Berkeley, against Locke, that knowledge is a two-termed relation and not a three-termed relation. Berkeley is right in having abolished the 'outer circle' (unperceived substantial entities) but the term "idea" hardly does justice to the difference between the subject and object, a difference without which the very nature of knowledge is destroyed. We need, Moore thought, to make a clear distinction between the act and the object of knowledge. Now as to the 'act' of knowing, Moore, no less than Berkeley, is vague. 'Transparency' and 'diaphaneity' are not too unlike Berkeley's 'immediacy'. In saying that there is no intermediary between the mind and its object Berkeley is in agreement with the realists. Berkeley does realise that an experience has to be an experience to someone. But an adequate theory of perception requires an analysis not only of the perceptual object but also of the percipient, and in this respect both Moore and Berkeley have far less to say than Kant.

Whitehead's criticism, in which he is joined by Thomas Reid, Berkeley's contemporary, takes its starting point in our experience of action. Now without looking on the will as in some mysterious ontological sense a centre of agency, a view which Hume sought to show was untenable at least on experiential grounds, we do in action come up against an experience of resistance on the part of objects. For example, in opening a recalcitrant lock I have just such an experience. Often the experience is the opposite of that of resistance as when I press a soft and resilient surface. Such experiences surely constitute direct evidence, Whitehead says, of the externality and 'otherness' of the physical world. One might even wonder how it was that Berkeley did not reach some such conclusion himself in view of his fresh analysis of tactual experience in his work on vision.

* Moore's later viewpoint on this question differed considerably from his original "refutation". Vide Preface to his *Philosophical Studies* pp. vii-viii.

None of these criticisms, however, are as damaging to Berkeley's position as the critique given by Kant in his 'Refutation of Idealism' in the *Critique of Pure Reason*. The basis of idealism, Kant says, is the assumption of the primacy of inner experience. Now if we examine the character of our inner experience, that is to say, the character of the data of inner sense, we find that the very essence of these data is their temporal nature. But if we proceed, in the transcendental manner, to ask how the perception of a temporal series be possible, we find that the presupposition of perceiving a temporal series is the awareness of something permanent, for change can only be perceived in contrast with something that is not changing. Now we know, following Hume, that there is nothing permanent to be found in the subjective succession of our experiences. It follows, then, that the 'perception of this permanent is possible only through a thing outside me and not throughout the mere representation of a thing outside me; and consequently the determination of my existence in time is possible only through the existence of actual things which I perceive outside me.' In this way Kant turns the tables against idealism in a most skilful manner, for, so far from the inner being the condition of the outer, it is the outer which is the condition of the inner. There are two things that are of interest in this connection. The first is that it was not until the work of Hume that the attention of philosophers was drawn to the temporal character of our experience, and Kant's whole argument is based on what must be presupposed by the temporal character of that experience. The second thing to note is the way in which Kant apparently abandons his own 'critical' standpoint in maintaining in his *Refutation* that we have an "immediate consciousness of the existence of outer things". Finally, in understanding Kant's own position, it is necessary to examine in what ways 'transcendental' idealism differs from the idealism that he has been concerned to criticise.

Transcendental Idealism

It is very misleading to assess Kant's transcendental idealism, as it is sometimes assessed, as being in some way, a 'reconciliation' of rationalism and empiricism. We shall see shortly that the central contribution of Kant to epistemology is something that cannot in any sense be extracted out of the main tenets of either rationalism or empiricism. One way of approaching the analysis of the meaning of 'transcendental' idealism is to compare it with other types of idealism. This comparison Kant has in part provided himself. The idealism of Descartes Kant styles 'problematic'. He explains this as follows in his Refutation of Idealism. Problematic idealism 'merely pleads incapacity to prove, through immediate experience, any existence except our own'. Only the existence of the self, on this view, is certain, and the existence of objects in space is 'doubtful and indemonstrable'. Elsewhere Kant calls this kind of idealism 'sceptical'.

The second type of idealism Kant refers to is that of Berkeley. This he calls 'dogmatic idealism' and he interprets it as holding that 'space, with all the things of which it is the inseparable condition, is something which is in itself impossible', and that Berkeley 'regards the things in space as merely imaginary entities.' This way of putting subjective idealism (as it is usually called) is perhaps a little unfair to Berkeley. In some ways Berkeley's account of the various sensible spaces in his *New Theory of Vision* is more complete than Kant's. Probably no idealist, of whatever brand, can do full justice to the 'externality' of physical things, without either, like Berkeley, regarding God as the ultimate (and presumably, proximate) cause of our ideas, or as Kant surprisingly does, positing things, 'outside' me, the perception of which makes possible consciousness of my own existence as determined in time. As to how outer intuition itself is possible Kant has something interesting to say in the First Edition of the Paralogisms. He says '. . . this is a question which no human being can possible answer. This gap in our knowledge can never be filled.' Kant's main objection against Berkeley arises from what he sought to show in his Transcendental Aesthetic. Kant believes that space is neither an entity (as Newton thought), nor something purely relational (as Leibniz thought), nor something which we 'construct' through amalgamating the various sensible spaces (as Berkeley thought), but that it is the 'form' of our outer intuition without which we would not have awareness of anything spatial at all.

The third comparison, which cannot be found in Kant, for it concerns a theory which came after Kant's time, is the comparison with objective idealism. To the objective idealist the objects of knowledge are conditioned by mind, but mind in the sense of "universal" mind, that is to say, not this or that particular mind, but mind in general. One might simplify the difference between the subjective, transcendental and objective types of idealism in the following way. They differ precisely in respect of the role given to the mind in knowledge. To the subjective idealist both the subject and the object of knowledge are mental. To the transcendentalist the object of knowledge is partly conditioned by mind, but not completely so, for Kant showed that, in order for there to be knowledge, there must needs be a manifold which is *given* to mind. To the objective idealist the object of knowledge is completely determined by mind, but mind is looked upon as an impersonal power at work in the universe and the universe is in fact its objectivification. It remains now to see what Kant himself understood by 'transcendental' idealism.

In the introduction to the *Critique of Pure Reason* Kant says 'I entitle *transcendental* all knowledge which is occupied not so much with objects as with the mode of our knowledge of objects in so far as this mode of knowledge is to be possible *a priori*.' Elsewhere he speaks of transcendental idealism as 'formal' idealism in order to contrast it with 'material' idealism. It deals with the formal aspect of our knowledge and Kant believed this formal aspect of our knowledge to be twofold. We have, in the first place, forms of intuition and these are the forms of space and time, that is the formal aspect of our outer and inner sense, and then we have forms of thought or the categories which enable sense-given material to be thought through. In each case the transcendental procedure consists in showing that the formal *a priori* element in question is a condition of the possibility of experience. That which is *a priori* means that which is universal and necessary, and it is the uniqueness of Kant's procedure that he should find universal and necessary elements not only in the field of pure thought (where after all these are to be expected) but in sensibility as well.

Kant's treatment of transcendental idealism when he is concerned with sensibility is bound to be somewhat different from when he is concerned with pure concepts of the understanding. In writing about space and time the main adversaries that Kant has in mind are Newton and Leibniz, for whereas the one made the mistake (on Kant's view) of looking on space and time as absolute, that is, as things in themselves, the other thought that we derived our notions of space and time from our perception of spatial and temporal relations between phenomena. Kant believed, as against both these views, that if sensibility were regarded on its own we would find it necessary to presuppose certain forms of intuition without which it would be impossible for us to perceive sensible objects at all. In saying this (and Kant gives a detailed explanation in his Transcendental Aesthetic) Kant was departing as far from rationalism as he was departing from empiricism. Leibniz had connected the ideas of space and time with perception, but, as Kant points out in the *Critique of Pure Reason,** he 'intellectualised' them, leaving to the senses 'nothing but the despicable task of confusing and distorting' our representations of objects. The empiricists had taken a purely inductive view of the origin of such ideas and in any case they believed that sensing was a passive process and never considered the possibility that there could be an *a priori* element in sensation. The nearest that any empiricist came to seeing that our notions of space and time were in some sense a puzzle was Hume's guess that the distinctive thing about our ideas of space and time was the 'manner' in which the simples were arranged. As far as Kant's account of the transcendental ideality of space and time is concerned, then, we can see that there is no occasion for describing Kant's work as in any sense whatsoever a reconciliation of rationalism and empiricism. Kant's treatment of the transcendental ideality of space and time constitutes the first stage of his project to establish that we can only know appearances. All sensible objects are perceived in space and

* Vide Section on The Amphiboly of Concepts of Reflection. Kemp Edition p. 332.

time. This is to say that what we perceive is conditioned by our forms of intuition. To demand that we should know what falls outside the framework of space and time would be to demand that we should know what is unconditioned. The account of space and time, it can be seen, has great importance in plotting the initial limits within which we can legitimately speak of what "exists". To speak, as the rationalist theologian does, of the existence of a Being outside space and time, is to speak of something which is outside the limits of our experience. Beyond the limits of space and time we have no means of distinguishing between the possible and the actual.

The second set of conditions which, Kant believed, determine the object of knowledge, is intellectual. There are certain *a priori* forms of thought, he said, which operate in our perception of physical things. Since they operate in giving us information about nature and are at the same intellectual rules or categories, they deserve the title of 'synthetic a priori' concepts. In explaining how these rules function in our experience Kant faced a somewhat different problem from the one he faced in explaining the transcendental role of our forms of intuition. The forms of intuition are the very condition of our receiving any sensible impressions whatsoever, and since they are themselves sensible in nature the formal and the material in their case are both of the same kind. In explaining the transcendental role of the concepts of understanding, however, we are concerned with relating something intellectual to a manifold which is non-intellectual. For this reason it is necessary for Kant to give a transcendental 'deduction' of the categories. The categories themselves Kant takes over from the traditional Aristotelian table, converting what was for Aristotle an ontological table of categories into a table of forms of thought. In the Transcendental Deduction Kant's purpose is to show how our forms of thought can relate *a priori* to objects, how they can have objective validity. The most important part of this deduction is the Kantian account of 'synthesis' and indeed it would be correct to say that the most distinctive feature of the transcendental kind of idealism is precisely this account. It is also this aspect of Kant's treatment of perception which was most objected to by the realists. It is not possible here to give a full account of the meaning of synthesis. For this Kant himself is the best source. It can be appreciated, however, that in giving to thought a role in perception Kant was doing something unique. It is important to remember that the synthetic activity of mind is treated by Kant in a transcendental and not a psychological manner. Further, Kant insists that the synthetic function of understanding is only productive of knowledge when the understanding is confronted by a sensible manifold.

The transcendental approach, unique as it is in the history of philosophy, carries certain consequences with it. To say that our perceptual objects are conditioned by our ways of knowing them is to say that we never know things in themselves. It means, moreover, that the proper (and indeed the only) object of our cognitive enterprise is the world as revealed in perception. Throughout the Critique Kant seeks to link transcendental idealism with empirical realism. There are passages, most notably in the Refutation of Idealism and also in the Paralogisms, where Kant's realism seems uppermost, and in such passages his realism may not always seem easily reconcilable with his critical standpoint. His main intention, however, it seems clear, is to counter those who would make of our knowledge of nature a matter of hazardous inference. To say that the objects of knowledge are conditioned is not in any way to put the existence of those objects into question. The world we know is a world of appearances but only in the sense that to ask for knowledge of a world of things in themselves would be to ask for knowledge of things other than as they are known which is obviously self-contradictory. The world that we know is for us the real world, and, moreover, it is the world that science investigates. This, then, is what Kant means when he says in the Paralogisms :—'The transcendental idealist is, therefore, an empirical realist, and allows to matter, as appearance, a reality which does not permit of being inferred, but is immediately perceived'.* The transcendental viewpoint, therefore, affirms the fact of knowledge, analyses the conditions of knowledge, and finally sets limits to knowledge. The last of these is set forth initially in Kant's distinction between thinking and knowing and most

* Vide *Critique of Pure Reason*. A371.

fully of all in the Dialectic. The former distinction provides him with a criterion whose utility becomes patent in the Dialectic, namely, the criterion that without the possessing of some intuition or other we cannot speak of knowledge. The failure of the three projects of pure reason which Kant diagnoses in the Dialectic are all attributable to the absence of intuition in those three projects.

To conclude somewhat summarily one might say that the transcendentalist analysis of perception is the only one which takes account of both the a *priori* and the empirical elements in perception. In so doing it restricts our knowledge to knowledge of appearances. At the same time the transcendental idealist is keenly aware that the mind tends to seek an object of knowledge which goes beyond the perceptual order. The utmost however that can be ceded in this direction is to say that the concepts of understanding have a problematic extension beyond the realm of the sensible—an extension which, try as we may, can never yield knowledge.

Objective Idealism

We have up to now noticed the derivation of much of idealist vocabulary in the modern period from the Cartesian language of ideas. This language, in turn, was traceable to Cartesian dualism, the apparently uncompromising nature of which seemed to make inevitable the positing of a *tertium quid* between the mind and its object. The logical outcome of this line of thought we found in Berkeley's restricting of knowledge to the ideas themselves. Some may discern in Berkeley another form of dualism, that of ideas and spirits. But the latter do at least possess the common character of being of the nature of mind and so whatever dualism there may be is considerably tempered by this circumstance. The subjectivist trend implicit in the *Cogito* in a sense has its culmination in Hume's strong awareness of the successive nature of our subjective experiences. In another sense his theory of belief can be interpreted as a break away from subjectivism. It also most definitely amounts to a clear-sighted recognition of the inability of the empiricist tradition to provide an account of existence

6

within the framework of Locke's formula of the agreement and disagreement of ideas. One could even say that implicit in Hume's theory of belief is a budding recognition that the vocabulary of 'ideas' was played out. The official obsequies were presided over by Kant. The 'physiological' procedure, of which the vocabulary of ideas was an integral part, is entirely foreign to Kant's methodology. Even when he is treating of the empirical self he feels no need to resurrect the old empiricist vocabulary. Kant's own form of idealism, as has been shown, was unique in many respects. If there be an aspect of dualism in it, it was a noetic dualism, a dualism of the twin conditions of knowing to be found in sense and understanding respectively. Those who came after Kant followed him in not resurrecting 'idea' language. But the distinctive flavour of the objective brand of idealism is probably best approached by examining the many Kantian caveats which were found irksome by the post-Kantian idealists and which they disregarded one by one.

One of the distinctions which was most vital to the critical approach was Kant's distinction between phenomena and noumena. Phenomena were the only objects of our knowledge, and the concept of noumena plotted, as it were, the boundary between what we could know and what we could not know. This was a distinction which objective idealism reacted to in various ways. Kant's linking of the noumenal order with the moral realm was objectified by Fichte into one type of absolutism. To others the difference between appearance and reality became a matter of degree, and Kant's stress on the identification of phenomena with empirical reality was thrown overboard. Kant's distinction between thinking and knowing, which, as we saw, has to be understood in connection with the distinction between phenomena and noumena, was likewise discarded. If to think and to know are the same then we cut adrift from the anchorage which was provided by Kant's reference to the "manifold". Form and matter, instead of being disparate, are regarded as differing in degree. In this way a return was effected to a framework of thought belonging to Aristotle on the one hand, and, in more recent history, to the philosopher whom Kant had ever been concerned to criticise—Leibniz.

Kant's distinction between understanding and reason was

amply backed up by the difference in the employment of the categories and the Ideas which he was at pains to make clear in the Analytic and the Dialectic—the difference, that is, between principles which are constitutive and those which are regulative in their use. Centainly in his pre-critical works Kant had not made use of these two terms, (understanding and reason), but in attempting to answer the question whether there could be a 'real use' as distinct from a merely 'logical use' of reason Kant had already realised that the combining role of the mind in perception and scientific knowledge should be distinguished from the projective function of reason in its speculative employment. In the *Critique of Pure Reason* it was his view that, for purposes of clarity, and especially in order that there be no doubt when the categories are being properly employed and when they are being misemployed, it is better to keep two separate terms, understanding and reason. The Hegelians' use of the word 'spirit' marks their concern with the speculative use of thought and their abandonment of the Kantian viewpoint that there is a proper and an improper use of the categories. Likewise, for Kant it is possible, and indeed essential, to distinguish between the real and the rational. The empirically real world is a world which is 'given' to us, although, at the same time, it is a world which is susceptible to our forms of intuition and our categories of thought. The rational, that is, that which is demanded by pure reason, cannot always be met with in experience. The rational demand, for example, that the soul be substantial, is not a demand that can be satisfied in experience. To Kant, then, the real and the rational are not identical. Indeed the strongest weapon he has against Leibniz and the Wolffians is his conviction that by merely consulting concepts we have no means of distinguishing between the possible (i.e. the rational) and the actual (i.e. the real).

Kant was never afraid of living with unresolved dichotomies. At the close of the Introduction to the *Critique of Pure Reason* he says:—"By way of introduction or anticipation we need only say that there are two stems of human knowledge, namely, sensibility and understanding, which perhaps spring from a common, but to us unknown, root."* Similarly the Antinomies

* A15 B29

which he posits in the Dialectic remain unresolved. It is for this reason that the Ideal of Pure Reason, which after all is the highest project of speculative thought, remains for Kant mere project, a mere projected unity. Now of all the concepts put forward by Kant there was none more fascinating to those who came after him than this concept of 'system'. It was Kant's anticipation of this fascination that led him to insist that the search for systematic unity was set us as a task, that the Ideas of pure reason are heuristic and not ostensive concepts. The attraction of the idea of the purposive unity of things is also something of which the Kant of all three Critiques was well aware. He says in the Dialectic :—

"This highest formal unity, which rests solely on concepts of reason, is the purposive unity of things. The speculative interest of reason makes it necessary to regard all order in the world as if it originated in the purpose of a supreme reason."* The heart of Kant's intention is centred in the words 'as if'. To ignore this is to hypostatise what was for Kant a mere project of pure reason. Enough has perhaps been said to trace the seeds of objective idealism to a divergence from some of the essential teachings of Kant, so that, although without the Kantian Dialectic it is doubtful if objective idealism would have ever been born, there can be no doubt that Hegel and his followers departed far indeed from the work of a philosopher whose life-work it was to provide a 'Critique' of pure reason.

The most stringent limit set by Kant to the operations of pure reason was his view that thinking and knowing are not the same thing. To gain knowledge we need to have not only concepts but intuitions and in the case of perceptual and scientific knowledge (as distinct from our geometrical knowledge where we are concerned with pure intuitions) these intuitions can be none other than sensible. It follows then that, if thought has no material to work on, thought must work on itself, and if thought works on itself we arrrive at a new sort of logic, not the pure general logic of which Kant had spoken, nor indeed even the transcendental logic which was his own unique creation,

* A687 B715

but the triadic logic of Hegel. It is this logic which provides the framework of the idealist theory of knowledge. It takes its starting point from the presence of dichotomy, but goes on to say that thought cannot rest content with mere dichotomy and must move on to its resolution. The simplest example—and also a key one for Hegel—is the example of the dichotomy of Being and non-Being. A thing cannot both be and not be. This had been one of the corner-stones of Aristotelian logic, something which we needed to assume in syllogistic reasoning. Hegel says, however, that the thesis Being and the antithesis non-Being can be sublated in a third term, namely, Becoming. In this way Hegel gives an entirely new turn to the discussion of the problem of being and change, a problem which had been answered in such different ways by Heraclitus, Parmenides and Plato. We can illustrate the sort of thing Hegel has in mind when he says that Being plus non-Being gives us Becoming. A child is a man and not a man. It is *becoming* a man. The triadic logic, it can be seen from this example, is a logic of development. Although Aristotelian metaphysics had certainly given a dynamic interpretation of reality with its theory of substances each endowed with a nisus, developing from potentiality to actuality, Aristotelian logic somehow had stopped short with a static analysis of the function of concepts and this Hegel thought he had remedied in his new logic. Hegel's debt both to Aristotle and to Leibniz is great, but Hegel had an advantage which they did not have, the advantage of writing at a time when an entirely new concept was gaining currency in the thought of the day, a concept which was to carry the notion of development further than it had ever been carried before, that is the concept of evolution. Thus, if the logic of Aristotle was essentially a logic of classification, the logic of Hegel was the logic of developing forms, the logic of the organic concept, the logic of becoming, where one species turns into another, is cancelled out, yet raised to something higher. Or to put it another way, Hegelian logic is not the denial of Antinomies but the denial of the finality of Antinomies.

Philosophers from Descartes to Kant had taken their cue largely from science and mathematics. The desire to show that nature is a coherent rational system is something that we associate, and rightly, with the rationalist philosophers. It must be remembered also that exactly the same motive is to be found in the work of Newton himself. At the same time the rootedness of the scientific enterprise in the data of perception is something which was all along stressed by the empiricists. No philosophy which is inspired by science can for long ignore the pull of fact. But a philosophy which is inspired by a very different field of interest can very easily come to the conclusion that the perceptual world is not the main concern of the philosopher. All the accounts of knowledge with which we have been concerned up till now shared the common characteristic of regarding the perceptible world as the proper object of knowledge. The objective idealist theory of knowledge departs from this and it is not difficult to see why if we remember that the inspiration of the idealist philosophers was not the study of science but the study of history. In the writing up of the results of experiments in the laboratory we are concerned with perceptual data or at least with something which is related to perceptual data. In writing history our data are in the past. Our material has to be 'reconstructed'. The core of fact itself, around which a historical narrative is written, is not 'out there' in the sense in which the brute facts of the sensible world are 'out there' (even this of course is a simplification if we regard the mind as having a transcendental role to perform in perception). The writing of history is a highly selective and interpretative business. If we bear all this in mind we can understand the stimulus behind the a *priorism* of the Hegelians, the methodology of thought working on itself, the immanentist view of thought as inherent in reality. Kant had showed the thread of mind running through the fabric of nature. In the story of society (which history is) the very warp and woof is the work of mind.

Up to now it has been sought to show that it was the inspiration of actual work done in historical studies which convinced the idealists that the proper object of knowledge is something which is far indeed from the perceptual order. This plus the triadic logic which Hegel called the 'dialectic' was epitomised in the slogan 'the real is the rational'. Hegel, although in this he was not followed by all his successors, agreed with Kant in holding that the role of thought is discursive. Yet by reason of his dialectical view of the movement of thought he understood by the term "discursive" something very different from Kant. Hegel believed that through the dialectical use of concepts thought could proceed progressively towards what he called the 'Absolute'. To the objective idealist the Absolute is the object of knowledge *par excellence*. But the Absolute can only be approached through the teleological movement of thought. It is, perhaps one should say, the *goal* of thought rather than the object of thought. In stressing the teleological movement of thought the idealists aligned themselves against the associationists who, to their way of thinking, had distorted thought by first regarding the contents of mind in an atomic manner and then by regarding these contents as related to each other in a mechanical way. Now Kant had already protested against the associationists in his insistence on the 'spontaneity' of understanding. Kant had also spoken very sympathetically of the 'demands' of pure reason, but it was very far from his intention to suggest that the demands of thought must in the nature of things be fulfilled. The idealist Absolute was Kant's 'system'—a mere project of pure reason—hypostatised. Not only was it beyond perception, but, as the idealists themselves admitted, it was also beyond thought, which was, after all, what Kant had said in the first place. It was no wonder that some idealists should have turned to some faculty other than reason as a vehicle for approaching the Absolute, and this was in fact what, in different ways, Schelling and Bradley did.

The object of knowledge, to the idealists we have been considering, was an object of a very special kind—the Absolute. Such an object could only be approached speculatively. Now the notion that the proper object of knowledge in the strict sense should be something which lies beyond sense perception was not in itself new to philosophy by any means. Plato had spoken of *noesis* which he had regarded as the crown and summit of the cognitive enterprise.* Theologians had for centuries spoken of the 'knowledge' of God and discussed to what extent

* *Noesis* was contrasted with *eikasis* (imagination) and with *pistis* (perception) by Plato.

reason may be an adequate instrument for attaining such knowledge and whether perhaps the supplementary work of faith may not need to be invoked to make such knowledge a practical possibility. Spinoza had written about what he called *scientia intuitiva*, a kind of knowledge which could only be aspired to when the other lower rungs of the ladder had been scaled. The whole possibility of what Aristotle had called in his *Posterior Analytics* a '*metabasis eis allo genos*', literally a turn to a category of a different kind, had been subjected to a searching analysis by Kant in the second part of his *Critique of Pure Reason*. Was there in fact a 'higher' kind of knowledge which deserved the title of metaphysical knowledge? This was the crucial question. In reviving the claims of speculative thought, the objective idealists were answering this question in the affirmative. Only it is important to note that, instead of following the Platonic tradition of regarding the object of this knowledge as transcendent, they on the other hand were insisting that its object was in fact immanent to thought.

This metaphysic of immanence depended on the axiom of internal relations which can be understood as the exact contrary of the axiom of external relations on which the metaphysic of realism depended. According to the axiom of internal relations two terms are said to be internally related when each modifies the other and neither would be what it is apart from its relation to the other. An example will make this clear. The lungs and the heart are internally related in the sense that neither organ can function without the other. On reflection we can see that the various organs of the body are all related in this way. The axiom was especially germane to the analysis of 'organic wholes', for in living things the relation between part and whole is such that no single part can survive without the rest (speaking broadly). Now if A and B and C etc. are so intimately related that the 'nature' of each is determined by the nature of the others we do not really have the right to speak of their having independent 'natures' at all. We should speak of their all constituting one organic whole. In this way, then, the axiom of internal relations leads to monism—the view that reality is one. Apply the axiom of internal relations specifically to the relation between subject and object and you get the conclusion that mind and its object modify each other in the knowing relation—that is, you get an immanentist view of the relation between thought and reality. Now many philosophers have thought dualism to be unsatisfactory, for the demand for a concept of 'ultimate reality' seems to be the demand for a concept of a single reality. The monist has to look upon all evidences of diversity and discord as internal to reality for to him nothing can fall outside reality. Appearances will not be contrasted with reality, as if they were external to reality, but appearances will be regarded as a part of reality. The concept of reality will be an all-inclusive concept, capable of development and capable of embracing not only the world of man's experiences, the history of man, but even God.

Within the framework of a general idealist position, as might be expected, there was room for a considerable variety of metaphysical viewpoints. With Fichte it was the moral nature of the Absolute which was of prime concern. Schelling's approach owed more to Kant's treatment of imagination. Royce's form of idealism was almost personalistic. In the work of T. H. Green idealism was grafted on to the British Liberal tradition. Bradley's idealism was governed more by logic than by any concern with the philosophy of history. Even so, the critics of objective idealism regarded the various forms of absolutism in much the same light and all were classed by William James, qua forms of monism, as examples of 'tender-minded' philosophies. It was to be expected that critics of objective idealism would be found in the empiricist camp. No advocate of a pluralistic universe could find the "block universe" of the monist congenial. In more irreverent vein Bertrand Russell likened the idealist universe to a big blancmange. Karel Capek satirised the whole approach in a book called *The Absolute at Large* and a nonsense number of *Mind* appeared with a 'picture' of the Absolute as a frontispiece. The 'picture' consisted of a piece of pink tissue paper. The ignoring of perceptual data and the methodology of science on the one hand and the association of Hegel with a kind of étatism unpalatable to the Anglo-Saxon world contributed to the gradual discrediting of the absolutist viewpoint, so that when the verificationists of this century ridiculed some of the wilder statements made by idealists at the turn of the century they were flogging a horse that was already dead.

The objective idealist viewpoint, however, deserves a more sympathetic treatment than is at present fashionable. It is no longer considered good form to recognise, as Kant most surely did, the natural disposition of the philosopher towards metaphysics. However that may be there is no doubt that the difficulties which beset the idealists were almost insuperable. Only a few of these can be mentioned here. The Kantian line of criticism is evident from what we have said earlier. Once the discursive nature of thought is admitted there can be no transition possible to knowledge of things in themselves. If the relational view of thought is accepted another consequence follows, moreover. Discursive thought cannot embrace the particular, and this is true in the case of the particulars which sense reveals to us and in the arch example of the claim that there is a unique particular of an entirely different order—God. The world of sense perception, therefore, inevitably slips through the net of pure thought, and this, to a generation inspired by the progress of scientific discovery, was in itself sufficient to damn the objective idealist theory of knowledge. The religious-minded were unhappy about the relation of God to the Absolute according to idealism, for either God would be a little lower than the Absolute, or, being identified with the Absolute, His personal character would be swallowed up in an impersonal undifferentiated unity. The particularity of the human individual likewise seemed to receive scant recognition in the block universe of the Absolute. What room was there for human freedom unless there were chinks in the system? The practical example of the Prussian state was there for all to see and the prospect was not encouraging.

As the present century advanced there was increasing criticism of the use made of logic by metaphysicians of the old school. Russell detected an adherence to an out-of-date subject-predicate logic in Hegel and Bradley and, in spite of his own employment of logic in a more or less metaphysical manner in his theory of 'logical atomism', he regarded the idealist dependence on the older logic as thoroughly sinister for the reason that no form of subject-predicate logic, on his view, could do justice to relational language, a language which was above all integral to mathematics. The axiom of internal relations came under fire in the writings and classroom sallies of G. E. Moore, and, in spite of the very interesting departures made from Continental idealism by men like McTaggart in England and Howison in America, the reaction had set in and realism became the dominant epistemology of this century, so that when the verificationists of our own times resurrect an occasional diatribe against the idealist theories of earlier in the century the whole controversy sounds with the ring of battles fought long ago.

Realism

Realism, which may perhaps be more correctly described as a movement rather than as a theory, reacted against the various theories of perception which have been under review. There were some differences in points of detail between the realists themselves, but their theory of knowledge is best understood as a specific, and indeed the key application of the axiom of external relations which formed the basis of their system of metaphysics. According to this axiom A and B are said to be externally related when neither modifies the nature of the other. For example the pen on this table is externally related to the table, because, in spite of the pen being on the table, the pen remains what it is and the table also remains what it is. The axiom is well illustrated in the well-known words of Butler, cited by Moore in the beginning of his *Principia Ethica*—'Everything is what it is and not another thing'. This presupposes a pluralist metaphysic where each of the terms is independent of the rest. Perry, in fact, speaks of realism in general as a 'theory of independence'. In enunciating the axiom of external relations the realists were considerably influenced by what they discerned to be the distinguishing character of logical and mathematical terms. It is not possible in logic to speak of the relation between A and B and C unless these are independent terms. Similarly in mathematics it is not possible to construct a series unless you have discreteness of the terms. Physical objects too, they thought, possess an analogous discreteness. Thus the realist theory of knowledge becomes the crowning example of the principle of external relations, for, according to the realists, the subject and the object of knowledge are externally related. This is to say, in the knowing-relation neither object nor subject are in any wise altered in the process. 'Experiencing makes no difference to the facts'.

The realists were equally opposed to Lockean representationism,* scepticism and transcendentalism. What they have to say about each of these may briefly be noted. Historically the first critic of representationism was Arnauld who, in spite of his Cartesianism, yet saw the untenability of regarding the object of knowledge as a "representation" of something other than itself. Years later Thomas Reid saw the mistake of positing a *tertium quid* between the knower and the known, for such a procedure would make the verification of our empirical sentences in principle impossible. There was no need to posit any intermediary whatsoever between the mind and its object. The most authoritative realist criticism of subjectivism was given by Moore in his famous 'Refutation of Idealism' to which reference has been already made.** Moore argues that the relation of 'being aware' of something is an original kind of relation. It is *sui generis* (he says the same thing about the nature of 'good'), and, moreover, *what* we know is not the same as our knowing it. Further criticism of Berkeley's esse is *percipi* was made about the same time by Russell in his *Problems of Philosophy*. Any spokesman of the view that knowledge is not only possible but is a fact would understandably be opposed to any form of scepticism. Hume had, however, been wise enough to take as his starting point Berkeley's rejection of representationism and he had at the same time allied himself with the commonsense view when he said:—

"We may well ask 'What induces us to believe in the existence of body?' but 'tis vain to ask, 'Whether there be body or not? That is a point which we must take for granted

* Laird speaks of our perceiving data which are full of "meaning". Broad speaks of sense data as "symbolising" objects, but such phraseology is not to be confused with 'representation' in the Cartesian sense.

** Vide p. 74.

in all our reasonings." Perhaps, for this reason, Hume for the most part escapes specific criticism at the hands of the realists.

Transcendentalism, however, came in for a long and detailed attack by Prichard in his book entitled *Kant's theory of knowledge*. 'This or that object is known' was not at all to be interpreted as 'This or that object is conditioned by knowing'. So to interpret it was to give a merely psychological account of knowing. Prichard's well-known charge of 'manufacture' against Kant made out that the theory of 'synthesis' which constitutes the heart of the Transcendental Deduction of the Categories amounted to nothing more or less than pure 'constructionism'. Now to look on knowledge as a process of construction was to destroy its very nature, for knowing is discovery, finding, and not making. In this way Prichard erodes the notion of synthesis, overlooking the fact that that there can be no synthesis without material to be synthesised and that Kant's stress on a manifold which is synthesizable absolves him from the charge of crude "manufacture".

What then do the realists have to say positively about our knowledge? To begin with it is important to remember that to them the physical object is the object of knowledge par *excellence* and this can by no means be said of all theories of knowledge. For this reason the realists' theory of knowledge is to be identified with their theory of perception. The subject has an immediate intuitive awareness of sensible data. This sensible kind of intuition was called "acquaintance" by Russell in his historically most important chapter on 'Knowledge by acquaintance and knowledge by description' in the work already mentioned.* It was necessary, however, to make quite clear what exactly we were acquainted with. The realist answer was contained in the sense datum theory, a theory which in itself has a chequered history. We were not acquainted with material objects, Russell said, but we were acquainted with sense data. The objects could be regarded, he explained in his later work *Our knowledge of the external world*, as "logical constructions" out of sense data. From this it can be seen that sense

* *Problems of Philosophy*, ch. V.

data were conceived as atomic in character. Each was a sensible particular, intuitable *via* an act of acquaintance. It therefore followed that since things are what they seem, 'relative' and illusory data (say, bent pencils and the drunkard's rats respectively) are also to be included within the fold of sense data. The advantages of the sense datum theory seemed, to those who propounded it, to be great. Instead of the suspiciously subjective vocabulary of 'ideas', they had introduced a conveniently 'neutral' vocabulary in its place. Our knowledge of the external world was not to be regarded as a matter of hazardous inference. After all, to know is to know, and if we could never at any time say with conviction 'I know' we would have no means of distinguishing between truth and error. The theory, then, at least had the merit (and one to which increasing importance has been attached) of according with our ordinary everyday experience. Instead of contrasting, in a somewhat problematic manner, the world we were acquainted with and a noumenal world which we are by definition excluded from knowing, the realists could comfort us by saying that the world we know was the real world and the only world that there was. Knowing is a species of confrontation and not a species of construction, still less a species of penetration. The goal of knowledge is the discovery of fact, precisely that which the advocates of an 'organic' theory of knowledge did scant justice to. And if realism stresses in an uncompromising way the 'brute' character of fact at least it offers the solace of putting knowledge within our reach. One final big advantage seemed to be offered by realism. The realist theory of knowledge, in centring all on perception, kept in line with the procedures of science, for science too, starts with the data given by perception.

Gradually, however, cracks appeared in the theory and it is these which stimulated a constant reformulating of the basic tenets of realism in what is by now a very vast amount of philosophical literature. The core of the theory was the notion of acquaintance as formulated most clearly by Russell. Did we, in fact, ever have any such moments of acquaintance or should we regard them as theoretical limits which are to be presupposed? Is the act of knowing as simple as the realists make out? The Kantian notion of synthesis* does not fit in too badly with the account given by psychology of the processes of selection and combination involved in perception. On the other hand some may say that the theory of synthesis presupposes as atomic an account of the data of knowledge as the theory of acquaintance. Even so, the word 'acquaintance' poses the problem rather than solves it. The vocabulary of sense data has been subjected to a succession of criticisms. Are sense data universal or particular? Are they genuine data or rather limits which we approach asymptotically? Being sensible are they not still uncomfortably subjective in character? The criticism at this point spills over into the criticism of phenomenalism in general which we shall be considering shortly.

If every act of acquaintance has an object, objective status must be given to elliptical pennies and to pink rats. How then are we to distinguish between our veridical and non-veridical perceptions? Surely these should not be given the same status? Erroneous and relative perceptions, moreover, could hardly be classed together. The extreme example of the realist dilemma was found in Meinong's endowing of even round squares with objective status, an absurdity which played some part in leading Russell to the formulation of his theory of descriptions. The model of discrete terms to be found in mathematics and logic was not ultimately something for which there is an analogue in the world of process. The most elaborately worked out attempt to apply this model to the world of perception is found in Russell's *Our knowledge of the external world*. But again, the atomicity of the data which, in the nature of things, demand a 'construction', is something of which we need first to be convinced.

The distinction between act and object has been regarded by some philosophers as being as objectionable as the older distinction between form and matter. Act and object language savours too much of a 'transaction', a model which, after all, may be proper, indeed essential, within chemistry, but which is out of place in epistemology. It is the distinction between act and object which is responsible for the realist mistaken

* Kant's synthesis is, however, transcendental not psychological.

analysis of erroneous and also of relative perception. Adverbial language may in some cases be more illuminating, or, as we saw, (vide supra p. 69) words like "seem" can obviate the necessity of positing spurious objects such as pink rats and the like. In any case, the understanding of mind in terms of a series of atomic operations is far too simple a model to satisfy. If, as was hinted earlier, an adequate theory of perception must do justice to the percipient as well as to the perceived, a full-fledged account of perception will need to have something to say about the self, a matter on which the realists are conspicuously silent.

The various types of realism such as New Realism, Neo-Realism, Commonsense Realism and Critical Realism, to mention a few, have tried to analyse the relation between sense data and perceptual objects. But perhaps the most interesting challenge to realism in recent years is the increasingly symbolic character of scientific vocabulary. The end process of verification can hardly any longer be conceived of as a simple confrontation with 'the facts'. As Einstein and Heisenberg have shown, knowing *does* make a difference to the facts. Science is no longer glorified commonsense. The scientific world is a world of theoretic constructions. The approach of a Copernicus, a Kant or a Poincaré is vindicated in our own century more than in any other. The world does not simply confront the mind of man. The particular speculative instruments we use in no small part shape what we discover. In conclusion it must be admitted in this connection that more recent formulations of 'scientific realism' do try to come to terms with recent changes in the status of physical objeets, the constitution of 'matter' and the conception of scientific 'law'.

Modern Phenomenalism

There are various types of phenomenalist theory but all agree in maintaining that our knowledge is confined to appearances. The earlier positivists discerned in the method of scientific discovery what we nowadays call the phenomenalistic approach. Science investigates the invariant relations which reveal themselves in the phenomenal world. Locke had said that as to the 'real essences' of things we were ultimately ignorant, and

Berkeley thought that in saying that in perception what we do is to become aware of the order of appearances he was at the same time giving a description of what the scientist does in a more thorough way. An example of phenomenalist writing which was influenced by Comte and the Continental positivists is to be found in Mill's *Examination of Hamilton's Philosophy*. In talking about 'permanent possibilities of sensation' Mill anticipated the later-day vocabulary of actual and possible sense data, and some may think that, in so far as he was free from our twentieth century sense datum language, he was at an advantage.

It is necessary, however, at this stage to stress that there is one big dividing issue between phenomenalists which is of the utmost importance—that is the issue between those who speak of phenomena in contrast to noumena and those who speak only in terms of phenomena. The first position is represented by one philosopher, Kant. Logically enough, Kant takes the view that if we speak of phenomena we need also to speak of that which appears, i.e. noumena. Now the word 'noumenon' means literally an object knowable by 'nous' or pure reason. Noumena are, etymologically, intelligible objects. Kant believed that our knowledge was confined to phenomena, that is, to the world of appearances i.e. sensible objects. This knowledge was endowed with objectivity no doubt, but this objectivity was conditioned by our own categories of thought. Our knowledge of appearances is therefore conditioned. But this should not lead us to imagine that there is anything unreal about the objects of our ordinary perceptual knowledge. On the contrary what we are acquainted with in our perceptual knowledge is most certainly empirical reality. Since this is all that we may know, the concept of 'noumenon' for Kant takes on a special significance. It is a 'limiting' concept, telling us negatively what we may not know, and positively what we may 'think'. There can be no question of our knowing noumena, because the only sort of intuition we possess is a sensible intuition, and in order to know an intelligible object we would need to possess an intellectual intuition which is just what we are denied. The concept of noumenon, therefore, is very important in Kant's philosophy in that in his Critique it provides a transition to the Dialectic, that is to say, a transition to that part of his work where he is concerned with the limits of knowledge. It is precisely this limit which the post-Kantian German idealist philosophers were unwilling to accept. They found the positing of a noumenal world most tantalising and thought that through their own special brand of logic they could override the distinction which Kant had so carefully laid down.

Apart from the philosophy of Kant, however, the main line of development of the phenomenalist tradition belonged to empiricism, to those philosophers for whom the noumenal world held no special fascination. The case of Berkeley, however, needs special mention. In paragraph three of his *Principles* we find one of the clearest statements of the phenomenalist thesis. In discussing what is meant by saying that the table exists he writes :—

"...... if I were out of my study I should say it existed, meaning thereby that if I was in my study I might perceive it, or that some other spirit actually does perceive it". This is Berkeley's most authoritative answer to the puzzle of the existence of things unperceived, this rather than the answer satirised in the well-known limerick. An atheist Berkeleyan, if one could for the moment imagine such a self-contradictory being, would be able to account for the existence of things unperceived in the way Berkeley has indicated above. Whether of course he could give any account of how our perceptions were 'caused' is a very different question. The peculiarity of Berkeley's phenomenalism is the manner in which it has been combined with idealism and it was this of course which prevented his contemporaries from realising the novelty of what he had to say. But, as we have seen, inheriting the Cartesian vocabulary of ideas as he did, Berkeley was bound to state his phenomenalist thesis in the way he did. Phenomenalism is an entirely different theory from that of idealism,. and it is in fact only Berkeley who happened to combine the two theories in one. If it was Berkeley who introduced the language of 'collection' and 'congeries' it was Hume who introduced the language of series into phenomenalist writing. Hume extended the application of the phenomenalist theory from the analysis of material objects to the analysis of selves as well. Hume's exposition of the theory, moreover, made most clear just what it was that phenomenalism stood for—the substitution of the concept of relation for that of substance. Hume's particular contribution was to point out the temporal nature of the relations between our perceptions. Both the phenomena of matter and mind were to be understood not in terms of their relation to a core, but (respectively) in terms of their relation to each other. This was in fact the substitution of the language of law for the language of entities.

The phenomenalism of this century differs from all the kinds that have been mentioned so far in being avowedly a linguistic thesis. The theory has been expounded by Russell, Ayer, Price and others and its central thesis can be put as follows: Every material object sentence can in principle be translated without loss of meaning into a series of sense datum sentences. Whereas the older theory talked in terms of 'things' being constituted of sense qualities, it can be seen that the current theory, in keeping with the linguism of the times, is a theory about language and its possible translation. It is significant that the formulation only says 'in principle'. In practice it would be difficult to translate even a sentence as simple as 'the cat sat on the mat' into a series of sentences which only contained descriptive words. The motives which inspired the new formulation were perhaps even more anti-metaphysical than those which inspired the earlier formulations had been. Russell's theory of descriptions had made philosophers suspicious of nouns. Adjectives and adverbs seemed to be relatively emancipated from the dangerous concept of substance and if we were called upon to say what our empirical sentences 'meant' it was safer to answer in terms of these less harmful parts of speech. The theory was, it can be seen, not merely a development of the empiricism of the old school but had close affiliations with what we now call logical empiricism, the motive of both phenomenalism and logical empiricism being to protect us from 'nonsense' statements. Full use was made of the new logic, and phenomenalist philosophers extended the theory to take in not only the analysis of ordinary perception but also the analysis of scientific language. The piece of theorising which illustrates all these tendencies the most clearly is Russell's account of logical constructions in his book Our *knowledge of the external world*.

Rumblings of disquiet, however, soon made themselves heard. A whole barrage of criticism was directed against the sense datum vocabulary with which phenomenalism was associated. Even when the atomicity implied in this vocabulary was done away with by substituting the language of sense fields, there was still a lot of discussion as to what exactly the 'data' were. That no complete translation of a material object sentence according to the prescribed programme had ever been made seemed to be a considerable stumbling block in the path of the theory. The existence of unsensed objects was not too grave a problem, for, as Berkeley had already shown, these could be spoken of in hypothetical terms. In order to supplement the theory on this particular point, C. D. Broad introduced the phrase 'unsensed sensibilia' and this in turn, after all, had been partly anticipated by Mill. It was objected by some, particularly in view of the language of perspectivism as used by both Russell and Price, that the theory was too much wedded to the data of visual experience. Berkeley, for all his faults, had appreciated the considerable difference between the various data themselves. Logicians felt uneasy about the projected translation of categorical sentences into hypothetical ones (no matter how long the series). Could any finite number of hypothetical sentences ever be regarded as 'equivalent') to a categorical sentence? Price at one time suggested that an existential premiss would be needed at some stage (e.g. '..... and there is one such') in order to effect the translation 'without loss of meaning'. Doubts were raised as to whether the phenomenalist could do justice to the dynamic element in nature. What could be said about the causal efficacy of things? Could the 'unity' of things be satisfactorily accounted for? The phenomenalist theory of the self, especially, was weak and was open to all the objections usually levelled against empiricist theories of the self. The latest form of the theory expressed in near-behaviourist terminology, by Ayer, is perhaps the extremest limit yet reached by phenomenalism.

In spite of the project to expunge material object words from the proposed translation many such words crept back in an adjectival form (e.g. a "bookish" object, a "cattish" animal). A brave attempt was made by some phenomenalists to employ adverbial expressions, but this, after all, was, not always possible. Russell had spoken of 'referring' sense data to things. But what exactly was this act of referring? It sounded something like the third moment of the Kantian synthesis. At all events it opened up the question of the role of mind in perception, a question which the realists had thought was safely interred. The scare of subjectivism continued to make itself felt. Could phenomenalism account for a common world? In spite of his earlier answer to this question given in the theory of logical constructions, Russell tackled the problem afresh in his book on human knowledge, bringing in something not too unlike the notion of the synthetic a *priori* with the addition of the postulates of quasi-permanence, continuity, similarity and causality. Phenomenalism, in other words, was coming in for significant modification. Differences between veridical and non-veridical perception, it was realised, could only be accounted for, on the phenomenalist view, by some sort of coherence theory. This again fitted in oddly with the empiricist-realist tradition of which phenomenalism was after all an extension. The problem of the relation of ordinary perception to the constructs of science is in process of continued analysis by phenomenalists. The culmination of the verification process in physics especially does not terminate in anything that could properly be described as sense data *simpliciter*. However, the phenomenalist will always insist that his general analysis is correct in the sense that a material object sentence to the verification of which no sense experience was at all relevant would have no meaning, and at this point the connection between phenomenalism and verificationism in general comes into the open.

VI A Priori Knowledge

The Problem

MOST philosophers have agreed that a distinction should be drawn between two sorts of objects that we may be said to know, those which belong to the world of sense perception and those which cannot be shown to belong to that world. The philosophical problem connected with the first of these is the problem of perception, and the problem connected with the second is that of specifying the nature and extent of our *a priori* knowledge. Propositions like 'A thing cannot both be and not be 'and' 2 + 2 = 4' are universal and necessary. They are universal in the sense that they hold good of any term we may substitute for 'thing' and any pair of couples we may substitute for '2 + 2.' The necessity of the first is logical necessity as expressed by the law of contradiction. As to whether the necessity of mathematical propositions can be accounted for in quite the same way we shall see shortly.

It is with respect to the propositions of logic and mathematics, then, that the problem of *a priori* knowledge arises, and the problem is a twofold one, concerning both the origin of these propositions (they do not seem to be derived from experience) and concerning the peculiar circumstance that we seem nervertheless to be able to *apply* them to the actual world. One of the earliest solutions to the first of these puzzles is set forth in Plato's *Meno*. Socrates asks Meno to call a slave boy and then proceeds to question him concerning certain problems in geometry. By dint of persistent questioning Socrates succeeds in eliciting answers from the boy. Where can he have obtained these answers from? No alternative seems to present itself other than to say that it is thanks to recollection, recollection of knowledge brought by the soul from an earlier existence, that the correct answers have been given. In this theory the phrase '*a priori*' is interpreted literally. We are said to be endowed with knowledge prior to experience and this knowledge is derived from the faculty of reason itself. The question as to how our a *priori* knowledge happens to be applicable to the world of experienced things in Plato's philosophy takes the form of the problem of the relation between universals and particulars, a problem which Plato tackles by having recourse to the notions of imitation and participation. This, it can be seen, is a somewhat roundabout and metaphysical way of explaining how we are able to say that any ten marbles and five marbles amount together to fifteen marbles.

The conviction that the truths of logic and mathematics are in a separate class, distinct from our ordinary sensible knowledge, and that they constitute knowledge in a paradigmatic sense, was handed down from Plato to the rationalists of the eighteenth century. Centuries had passed by, centuries marked by a general lack of interest in mathematics on the part of philosophers, this being an understandable concomitant of the scholastic preoccupation with theological matters. Whereas the scholastic philosophers had found various *theological* propositions 'self-evident', the title of self-evidence was bestowed by Descartes and his successors on those truths which reason could perceive clearly and distinctly, namely the truths of logic and mathematics. In the latter class most notably were to be found the propositions set out by Euclid. It is inconceivable that the external angle of a triangle should not be equal to the sum of the interior opposite angles, inconceivable in the sense that given the definition of a triangle (and a straight line) the proposition concerning the external angle follows. The criterion of conceivability, which was, after all, a logical criterion, was combined with what sounded suspiciously like a subjective consideration, the notion of 'certainty'.

Now Descartes inherited (among other things) the scholastic doctrine that the mind was invested with innate ideas, a doctrine which owed much to the Stoic theory of *prolepses* or principles which the soul contains originally. Leibniz too thought it not unreasonable to suppose that our knowledge of necessary truths was evidence of 'something divine and eternal' in us. The motive of those philosophers who supported the theory of innate ideas was as much theological as epistemological.

Leibniz, amazingly enough, links up the theory with a passage in Romans, Ch. ii v. 15, where St. Paul says that the law of God is written in men's hearts. St. Paul was most certainly not referring to epistemology when he said these words. There is no doubt, however, that the requirements of theory of knowledge had become confused with theological exigencies. Innate priciples were said to constitute a 'distinct sort of truth' and this as much because they were believed to have been 'imprinted' on the mind by God as to mark their difference from our sense perceptions. The innate principles advocated by Lord Herbert of Cherbury included exhortations such as 'Men must repent of their sins' which belonged properly to the pulpit. The doctrine of innate ideas, as Locke pointed out, thus tended to degenerate into a cloak for dogmas and a means for affirming their sacrosanct character.

The strictly philosophical issue which lay behind all this however, was put best by Leibniz in his *New Essays on the Human Understanding* which was intended as a rejoinder to Locke's polemic against innate ideas. The question was, Leibniz says, "whether the soul itself is entirely void, like a tablet whereon nothing has yet been written", or whether it is originally endowed with certain germinal notions. From this arose also another question "whether all truths depend on experience, that is to say on induction and on instances, or whether there are some which have another basis also." Leibniz' figure of the block of veined marble and its contrast with a wholly uniform block presents the first of these two questions admirably. Leibniz says:—'For if the soul were like these blank tablets, truths would be in us in the same way as the figure of Hercules is in a block of marble, when the marble is completely indifferent whether it receive this or some other figure. But if there are veins in the stone which marked out the figure of Hercules rather than other figures this stone would be predetermined thereto, and Hercules would as it were in some manner be innate in it, although labour would be needed to uncover those veins, and to clear them by polishing, and by cutting away what prevents them from appearing.' In this way Leibniz insists that there can be 'virtual' knowledge, something which, by reason of his empiricist principles, Locke could not admit.

as in the case of empirical knowledge we have propositions concerning matters of fact. In Hume's view mathematical propositions are analytic, that is to say, in every such proposition the predicate is contained in the subject so that to affirm the subject and deny the predicate would be to contradict oneself. To say that mathematical propositions were analytic was to say that they were a *priori*, meaning by this that they were derived from reason itself and did not require any reference to experience for their validation. In Hume's view analytic propositions were to be contrasted with synthetic ones which were formulated on the basis of sense experience and which could therefore be spoken of as a *posteriori*. In Hume's view mathematical propositions (and logical propositions also, about which, by reason of his opposition to Leibniz, Hume had less to say) and empirical propositions exhausted between them the universe of meaningful propositions.

Hume's formulation of the distinction, however, was not very satisfactory. In mathematical propositions we were concerned, he said, with 'relations which depend entirely on the ideas which we compared together.' But at the same time he maintained that all our ideas were derived from impressions, making it difficult to see how the distinction between relations of ideas and matters of fact could be justified. Moreover Hume's ground for regarding geometry to be inferior in exactness to arithmetic and algebra is based on curious reasoning. He thought that algebra and arithmetic were 'the only sciences in which we can carry on a chain of reasoning to any degree of intricacy and yet preserve a perfect exactness and certainty.' In the case of geometry we were hampered because we could never be certain of the truth of its axioms. Hume could appreciate that geometry was applicable to nature, but he seemed to have confused this with a wrong identification of mathematical points and *minima visibilia*, an understandable mistake, however, if one starts off, as he did, with a conviction that all our ideas were ultimately traceable to some sense impression or other. What Hume did in the case of geometry was, it can be seen, to accept the applicability of its concepts to nature, but at the cost of consistency. The fact that no existent line can be perfectly straight and no existent surface perfectly plain he interprets as a defect in the method of demonstration, and so confused the question of the nature of actual measurement and that of the cogency of demonstration. To say that mathematical propositions are analytic is to make their applicability to nature unintelligible. Either one could affirm the analytic nature of mathematics and deny its applicability, or look upon it as a synthetic a *posteriori* science in which case the universality and necessity of its judgements would be sacrificed completely.

Kant's treatment of a priori knowledge

The difficulties into which Hume was led by his division of judgements into analytic a *priori* judgements on the one hand and synthetic a *posteriori* judgements on the other, led Kant to consider afresh the whole question of the nature and extent of our a *priori* knowledge. Rationalist philosophers had assumed that there were three classes of *a priori* propositions, those to be found in logic, those to be found in mathematics and those to be found in metaphysics itself. As to the first of these Kant had no fault to find with the rationalists. The truths of logic were universal and necessary and undisputedly a *priori*. There was no occasion for surprise at this for in logic pure reason deals only with itself and abstracts from consideration of any object. The nature of logic is purely formal and it does not serve to extend our knowledge whatsoever. To employ logic to extend our knowledge was, in Kant's view, to misuse logic and to misunderstand its function. It followed, from Kant's view of logic, that the deductive method of philosophizing amounted to an improper employment of logical concepts, since logic could not (by reason of its analytic nature) tell us anything about reality. In respect of the second class of a *priori* propositions i.e. mathematical propositions, Kant, however, considered that both Hume and the rationalists were mistaken in thinking that mathematical truths were analytic. If we take the proposition $7+5=12$ we find that the concept of 12 is not contained in the concepts of 7 and 5. The concepts of 7 and 5 have to be *added together* before we can arrive at the concept of 12. To say that the above arithmetical proposition is analytic would be to say that it is the same in type as the proposition "All bodies are extended," which is surely not the case.

Kant's own formulation of the distinction between analytic and synthetic judgements was as follows. In an analytic judgement the predicate is contained in the subject or is part of the meaning of the subject, as in the proposition 'All bodies are extended'. Such judgements are a *priori* and are based on the principle of identity or non-contradiction. On the other hand a judgement is synthetic if its predicate is not contained in the subject as in, say, the judgement 'All bodies are heavy', because the concept of weight is no part of the meaning of a body. Kant was, however, not saying that the meaning of a term was to be identified with whatever be associated with it in the mind of this or that individual, that is, he was not talking about "subjective intension" as some contemporary critics like to imagine he was. The meaning of a term is the common scientific meaning which is the same for all individuals. In a synthetic judgement we make an addition to what is contained in the subject. Synthetic judgements are, as he put it, ampliative, while analytic judgements are merely explicative.

In Kant's view the rationalists, and Hume too, had wrongly diagnosed mathematical judgements as analytic. Not only in the case of arithmetical propositions like $7+5=12$ but also in the case of geometrical propositions like "a straight line is the shortest distance between two points" we have examples of a "going beyond" what we started with in our original concepts, i.e. the concepts of 7 and 5 and the concept of 'straight line' respectively. Before, it had been thought, by the empiricists, that the only basis on which we could 'go beyond' what was contained in the subject of a proposition was by an appeal to sense experience. That this could not be the case as far as mathematical propositions were concerned Kant was convinced of, for this would be to purge them of their undoubted universality and necessity. How then were the synthetic judgements of mathematics possible? Kant answered this challenge by insisting that they were founded on pure intuition, the pure intuitions of space and time, the nature of which had been misunderstood by rationalists and empiricists alike. In geometry we had construction in pure intuition and in arithmetic the intuition of, say, referring to our five fingers or five points and the operation of combining them. The mistake that, according to Kant, had been made by preceding philosophers was that they wrongly looked upon pure intuitions as bare concepts, for mathematical inferences certainly do involve concepts later on, but we must realise that the foundation of mathematics itself is intuitional nonetheless.

Kant's investigation into mathematical knowledge provides him with the first example of his theory that there can be, and indeed is, knowledge which is both *a priori* and at the same time synthetic. It provides the first illustration of his explanation of how such knowledge can be possible. Kant finds that, not only in mathematics, but in the natural sciences too, we have examples of synthetic *a priori* judgements as principles. The proposition 'Every event has a cause' is the most important of these principles, and Kant believed that Hume, in reducing it to an empirical principle, would have to deny that scientific judgments were universal and necessary, a consequence which seemed serious indeed at a time when the deterministic model of Newtonian mechanics was taken to be literally true. The 'going beyond' what was contained in the subject, which we saw was integral to all synthetic judgements, could be found to hold good of the synthetic *a priori* judgements of science too. In their case the going beyond was not provided by pure intuition as in the case of mathematical judgements, but was occasioned by empirical intuition, for, as everyone knows, science cannot proceed without recourse to observation. In saying this Kant completed his diagnosis of how synthetic *a priori* judgements were possible. In the case of both mathematical and scientific judgements we have found an intuitional element to be present and this gives us the key. Synthetic *a priori* knowledge is possible in relation to objects of experience and it is only with regard to such objects that we can be said to have knowledge.

The way is now clear for Kant to examine the credentials of the third class of *a priori* propositions put forward by the rationalists, the propositions to be found in works of speculative metaphysics. These have most certainly claimed to constitute a class of judgements which were both synthetic i.e.

they served to extend our information, indeed to provide us with knowledge of a supposedly high order, and at the same time a *priori*, i.e. they were derived from the operation of pure reason unaided by any appeal to sense experience. The contradictory and inconsequential nature of the accounts given by speculative philosophers of matters like the existence of God, freedom and the immortality of the soul can now been elucidated. In so far as such accounts rest on mere concepts—for we have no intuition of God, the soul, or freedom—they are doomed to failure. They constitute a dialectic of illusion and do not provide us with knowledge at all. Metaphysical judgements are only spuriously synthetic and now we know why. Kant's discovery of synthetic a priori knowledge in the spheres we have considered at the same time serves him with the means of denying the title of synthetic a *priori* knowledge to the sphere in which it had been assumed by traditional metaphysicians to have undisputed sway. It is important to realise that on his showing, in the case of our mathematical and scientific knowledge, the question arises as to how synthetic a *priori* judgements are possible in these sciences. In the case of putative metaphysical knowledge the question is a different one, the question not as to *how* but as to *whether* genuine synthetic judgements are to be found here at all. Kant's contribution to the investigation of our a *priori* knowledge is a unique one, amounting, as it does, to an entire investigation into the legitimate and illegitimate uses of thought, the discovery of the synthetic a *priori* concepts presupposed in our everyday knowledge, and containing a warning as to the limited sphere in which such concepts can be found fruitful, the sphere of possible experience.

The "Conventionalistic" theory of a priori propositions

The view that all necessary propositions are tautologies was put forward by Wittgenstein in his *Tractatus* and adopted by all the logical positivists. In a sense it provided a neat solution to the puzzle of providing a satisfactory account of logic and mathematics within the framework of a general empiricist theory. For what were the alternatives? One could say, with Mill, that the propositions of logic and mathematics are inductive generalisations in which case not only would their universality and necessity be lost, but one would be making the mistake of confusing the question of how we come to discover the truth of such propositions with the question as to the nature of their status. To say that we can know some truths about the world independent of experience, that is, to admit the synthetic *a priori*, would be to say that thought can be an independent source of knowledge, and this would be to stage a comeback for metaphysics. To say that logic can be used for metaphysical purposes would be to undo the work done by Hume. If *a priori* propositions are tautologies their universality and necessity is saved and at the same time their absence of factual content is made patent.

Several factors are behind the formulation of the conventionalistic theory. The formalization of logic brought about through the contributions of Boole, Russell and Whitehead served to emancipate it on the one hand from considerations concerning men's minds, i.e. from the idealist logic of 'judgement', and, on the other hand, from attachment to things, i.e. from the ontological affiliations of Aristotle's syllogistic logic. Tautologies were not to be regarded as synonymous with trifling propositions like 'a house is a house'. On the contrary, to appreciate the tautological character of logical and mathematical propositions, lengthy processes of symbolic transformation are required. An omniscient being would immediately be able to see all the implications of any particular proposition of this type. The discovery of geometries alternative to Euclidean geometry made it clear that the applicability of any particular geometric system was based on pragmatic considerations and not on the *a priori* 'fit' of any one particular system. That mathematics *per se*, has no factual content, could be illustrated even from arithmetic, a branch of mathematics which otherwise seems to have more relation to the actual world than any other branch. Surds and recurring decimals are not to be encountered in the actual world.

According to the conventionalistic theory, then, we say that a proposition is analytic when (*pace* Ayer) 'its validity depends solely on the definitions of the symbols it contains'.

The validity of the proposition 'Either some ants are parasitic or none are' is an analytic proposition in this sense. Such propositions, although they do not give us knowledge, illuminate the way in which we use certain symbols. They call attention to our linguistic usage. Instead of saying, with Hume, that logic and mathematics are to do with relations of ideas, we are to say that they are to do with relations between symbols.

To understand logic and mathematics in this way, however, is to invite several difficulties. There is something paradoxical, to begin with, in holding that the proposition $7 + 5 = 12$ is of the same type as 'an oculist is an eye-Doctor'. Whereas for 'oculist' we can substitute only 'eye-Doctor', for 12 we can substitute a host of expressions e.g. $11+1$, 4×3, $6+6$, $36\div 3$, etc, and each of these involves a different mathematical 'operation'. We might do worse than to appeal to this diversity of possible substitutions in favour of the view that, in addition to the law of contradiction there is also another law—the law of synthesis. Whether or not we are convinced by the way in which Kant works this out, we cannot avoid being struck by the type-difference set out above. Then again it is certainly true that logic and mathematics make use of symbols. But this does not show that these two disciplines have no other content. The symbols do not operate themselves. It is we who operate *with* the symbols. To say that a *priori* propositions are completely divorced from the world of fact is to make their applicability a matter of surprise—a situation encountered earlier in the history of philosophy by David Hume. By founding his account of mathematics on the pure intuitions of space and time Kant is at least able to make intelligible the applicability of mathematics to nature, and if we are not so happy about the linking of arithmetic with time (something about which Kant himself was not altogether clear) it is more easy to see an intimate connection between the basic concepts of Euclidean geometry (which was after all the only geometry with which Kant was concerned), and our notions of space, i.e. our notions of side-by-sideness and distance.

The conventionalistic theory has come under fire from yet another quarter. Quine has raised the whole question of the legitimacy of the analytic-synthetic distinction. Any statement, he says, is analysable into a linguistic and a non-linguistic component. In some statements the factual component may be nil, but, even so, it is not possible for us to draw a clear boundary between the two. The usual understanding of analycity has been in terms of synonymy, and this in turn was interpreted to mean, 'interchangeability'. But synonyms may not always be interchangeable in all sentence-frames. For example the phrase 'unmarried man' is not substitutable for 'bachelor' in the sentence " 'Bachelor' has less than ten letters". Together with Whorf and Cassirer, Quine is of the opinion that words cannot be divorced from their contexts, and this fits in well with Wittgenstein's later teaching, namely, that language is part of life. To speak of 'conventions' drives us back to linguistic behaviour, and so it would seem, oddly enough, that the linguistic approach to necessary truths leads back to the original terrain, that of the world of experience, from which it was so anxious to emancipate logic and mathematics.

VII Theories of Truth

The problem

In putting our knowledge into propositional form we always lay ourselves open to the verdict of critical scrutiny. If I make the statement 'X knows how to type' my statement can be shown to be true or false according to whether or not X acquits himself well when confronted with a typewriter. If I say 'There is a cat in the bathroom' this is a statement which is corrigible, for, if I find, on investigation, that there is no cat in the bathroom, then my statement will be shown to be false. If I say 'The three angles of a triangle are equal to two right angles' we would all agree that this statement was true and we would do so, not on the basis of an appeal to facts, but on the basis of the axioms propounded by Euclid. If someone says 'Napoleon was holidaying in the south of France in 1812' we would say that this statement was false because we know that he was retreating from Moscow in that year. If someone finally produces the well-worn syllogism about Socrates (All men are mortal, Socrates is a man, therefore Socrates is mortal) we should say that the statement made in the conclusion was true.

Now although the statements we have taken as examples are all of varied types we can see that each statement can be validated or invalidated. Sometimes the method of validation or invalidation involves referring to 'facts'. In some cases getting to know the facts is a relatively easy matter as in the case where a straightforward act of observation will put us right, e.g. looking in the bathroom to see if the cat is there. In the case of checking on a historical statement we still need to get at the facts. But here we are in a different position in that historical statements are about the past and the past is over and done with. We refer to historical facts by consulting records, seeing if our various pieces of information cohere with each other and so on. Here we see that the very concept of fact becomes a matter of investigation. In the examples from logic and mathematics we seem to be on rather different ground. These statements do not demand 'verification'. We judge them to be true or false depending on whether or not there is internal consistency between the various parts of our statement. For example, if I say that the external angle of a triangle is not equal to the sum of the two interior opposite angles this is not consistent with the definition of a straight line as consisting of two right angles together with the definition of a triangle as likewise consisting of two right angles. The statement I made does not cohere with the basic axioms of Euclidean geometry (It may of course cohere with some other geometric system). Our question, then, is this:—What is meant by saying that any particular statement is true or false? We have already noticed a considerable difference in kind between the various sorts of statement that we make. Even so philosophers have tried to give a general answer to the question we have just posed and their answers are contained in the various theories of truth. Whether there can ever be a general criterion of truth which can cover all the different examples is something we can decide later.

The Correspondence theory of Truth

The correspondence theory of truth is held by the realists. The theory maintains that truth is to be defined by reference to the facts. Truth depends on a relation between a proposition and a fact, and this relation is called the relation of correspondence. Russell puts it as follows :—'True propositions have a certain correspondence with complex facts, while false propositions have a different correspondence.' The correspondence of a proposition with a fact can be further analysed into a correspondence of the various elements of the one with the various elements of the other. How are we to ascertain what the facts are? We are to ascertain them by an act of acquaintance. To quote Russell again :—'We can only be assured of the truth of our judgement in virtue of something with which we are acquainted.' Lest the word "judgement" should lead us astray, Russell warns us that he regards judgement as consisting of "an occurrence whose constituents are a mind and certain objects, particulars or universals." Such a view presupposes the axiom of external relations on which, as we saw earlier,* the realist theory of knowledge is based. This axiom involves a metaphysic of pluralism. Apply this to the particular problem we have in hand and you have the view that truths are multiple, each truth is independent of the rest. Facts are atomic in nature and the propositions made about them are likewise atomic. In this way the realist account of truth links up the concepts of correspondence, acquaintance and independence. Facts are out there to be discovered. Experience makes no difference to them. To take the example we had earlier, the statement 'There is a cat in the bathroom' is to be verified by a simple act of sense perception. If the statement is found to 'correspond' with the facts, i.e. if there is a cat there, then my statement can be said to be true. If there is a lack of correspondence then my statement is false. The theory in itself sounds simple and close to commonsense. But from what we have already seen of the realist approach to knowledge it is evident that it is based on many metaphysical presuppositions. The idealist criticism of the correspondence theory did in fact centre round an analysis of the three main theses which we have seen to be upheld by it—namely, the notion of correspondence itself, the concept of acquaintance and the concept of independence.

What is meant, first of all, by saying that a statement 'corresponds' to the facts? We have been told that correspondence does not mean 'copy' or 'resemblance'. If there is to be a one to one correspondence between elements of both proposition and fact this rests on a metaphysic of atomism the truth of which we have first to be convinced. In any case does a proposition consist of elements which are externally related, even a proposition as simple as 'There is a cat in the bathroom'? The nouns 'cat' and 'bathroom' may conceivably be said to correspond to the things indicated by those words, but what do the words 'there', 'is', 'a' and 'the' correspond to? The sentence would not be a sentence at all without these words. There has been, in this century, an increasing realisation of

* Vide p. 91.

the importance of words other than substantives, and in this respect the work of Russell has been perhaps the most significant. Verbs and prepositions, especially, cannot be regarded as corresponding to anything which is 'external' *simpliciter*. The idealists, represented authoritatively by Joachim, point to the linguistic data we have been mentioning as evidence that judgement cannot be looked upon as a mere amalgam of elements at all. Judgement, they say, means a holding together of the various elements in a unity by the mind, and this is something which only by a wilful distortion can be spoken of as 'acquaintance'. Facts are not 'out there' to be corresponded to or not corresponded to. The discovery of facts is an enterprise undertaken by the mind. Experiencing makes a difference to the facts in the sense that the facts only reveal themselves to the inquiring mind.

How is the concept 'fact' to be defined? A fact is that through reference to which the truth or falsity of a proposition is determined. Events happen, but facts are reckoned to be timeless. Are facts out of relation to each other? The fact that there is a pen on this table is related to the fact that there is a table here. The one fact is not completely independent of the other. The fact that the grass is green seems on the other hand to be unrelated to the fact that the plague in London was followed by the Great Fire. The correspondence theory is connected with the realist metaphysic of pluralism, with the theory that the world is made up of a multiplicity of atomic facts. What is an atomic fact? The limits of reducibility, that is to say, the atomic elements, are supposed to be sensibles. But what is a sensible out of relation to a possible mind capable of sensing it? Those who talk in terms of sensible experience are the least able to eliminate reference to actual and possible experience. It would seem to follow, then, that one fact may not be completely independent of all other facts and that facts cannot be conceived out of relation to some mind or other.

The correspondence theory of truth, as has been seen, is linked up with the realist theory of acquaintance which was criticised earlier in another context.* The terminal points in

* Vide Ch. v. p. 93ff.

the process of verification are regarded as moments of acquaintance when the cognising subject is brought, as it were, face to face with the clinching data. Whether there are in fact any such atomic moments of acquaintance is one consideration to give us pause. But there is another difficulty. According to the theory of acquaintance the data of sense experience in themselves offer no criterion of the distinction between veridical and erroneous perception. The moment of acquaintance in itself, then, does not provide knock-down evidence of the truth or falsity of whatever proposition we are trying to verify. We need to appeal to the rest of our experience, to the criterion of whether the moment of acquaintance in question coheres with the rest of our normal or 'standard' perceptions.

Critics of the criterion of correspondence have further drawn attention to certain categories of sentence to which the criterion seems difficult to apply. If I say 'The next time you do that you will be punished' the *verificandum* and the process of verification both lie in the future. There is no fact with which the proposition can be immediately compared. Past conditionals are on a similar footing. We would normally say that the proposition 'If it had rained you would have got wet' was true. Here again the reference is to a point in time which is outside the present. Moreover this example illustrates another class of awkward sentences vis-à-vis the theory—the case of hypotheticals.

On yet another track it would be true to say that the analysis of the meaning of historical sentences is something that deserves more attention at the hands of philosophers. If I say 'Charles I died in his bed' we would say that the statement was false because it does not correspond with the facts. But what is the nature of these facts? They seem to be of a different order from the experience of furry and caterwauling data which constitutes evidence for the verification of the statement 'There is a cat in the bathroom'. But what exactly is the difference? At the core of the verificatory process in the case of historical sentences there seems to be an irreducible reference to what, extending the phenomenalist thesis, one might style past possible and past actual experience. But the criterion of correspondence is surely not enough. In assessing the causes of a war, for example, there are no easily accessible facts to which there can be a simple correspondence or lack of correspondence.

The correspondence theory may, in its defence, refer us to a different class of data—the data of introspection. Statements made by us about how we feel, it may be claimed, are true because they 'correspond' with the actual state of affairs. Now the data of introspection have come under fire from many quarters in recent years. The data given are after all retrospective data and therefore fallible by reason of the fallibility of memory; self deception is very possible; subjective data are not 'luminous' as the Cartesians had thought and so on. Probably, however, the most pertinent point of criticism for our purpose is the consideration that statements about subjective states of affairs should not be looked on as descriptions but should be looked on as 'expressions' which are themselves parts of the states of affairs. To try to compare a statement about a subjective state of affairs with that state of affairs is probably an incorrect procedure. There is no question of the 'verification' of statements made about introspective data. What may arise is a question of a very different order, the question as to the *authenticity* of these statements.

That correspondence as a criterion of truth is inapplicable to the propositions of logic and mathematics would be admitted by the realists themselves. Realism shares the empiricist insight into the essential difference between propositions which concern matters of fact and those which concern relations of ideas, to use the Humean terminology. But the question of the determining of the truth of scientific propositions requires some reflection. To show that atoms are built up from three smaller particles—the proton, the electron and the neutron, as Lord Rutherford showed—is not to show something which can in any simple one-to-one way be regarded as 'corresponding' to the facts. The criteria of coherence and pragmatic success are, in a way, more relevant. As in the case of verifying statements about the past, one might say that there seems to be, at some stage, reference to an irreducible minimum of perceptual data (in the case of the past, possible past data) which, as it were, set the limits within which the verificatory process takes place. At the same time one must remember that the statement which appears to correspond to experience may be false. If I say 'The pencil is bent' my statement apparently corresponds to the phenomenon before me. The Ptolemaic theory (according to which the sun revolved round the earth) seemed to correspond to common experience, but the theory was subsequently proved false. The progressive discovery that the appeal to experience is not in itself a source of knock-down evidence constitutes a departure from old style empiricism. That much of experience has to be discounted, or at least 'weighted', comes as a challenge to the pure empiricist. The realisation that the observer may be in better position to make objective statements than the experient is something which modern psychology especially has to take in its stride. All such developments, however, serve to swell the criticism of the simplified model on which the correspondence notion of 'fact' depends.

The most pertinent criticism of the correspondence theory is to be found in Kant's *Critique of Pure Reason.* The nominal definition of truth, Kant says, is that it is the agreement of knowledge with its object. But the proper demand is not that we should have a 'general criterion' of truth but that we should be able to determine the general conditions of the objectivity of our statements. Such conditions he gives in the Analytic and these provide a logic of truth as against the logic of illusion which is to be found in the Dialectic. The novelty of Kant's approach is that truth and falsity become distinctions to be deployed within the sphere of the experienceable. Fact is not something external to mind, something alien to which mind must conform. The conditions imposed by mind, that is, the forms of intuitions on the one hand and the categories on the other, constitute the framework within which we are able to distinguish between true and false. Outside that framework we are not able to discriminate between our statements. We cannot say, for example, whether it is true to say that the world has a beginning in time or not. To say that the world *has* a beginning in time may be true or it may be false. We have no means of deciding. Correspondence would have been the criterion of truth had our knowledge been a matter of intuition only. But since concepts too play a part in knowledge, the demand for a 'correspondence' of our knowledge with its objects is an improper demand. In this way Kant makes the concept of fact relative to the investigating mind. The facts we discover are relative to the questions we ask, and in this respect Kant's treatment of truth is far closer to the scientific notion of truth than that of any other philosopher. What we discover is relative to what we are looking for. At the same time there is a hard core which may be described as the 'material' of intuitions, the manifold which is given to mind. This is not, however, something to which our empirical statements are in any way called upon to conform. In such a way, then, Kant replaces the notion of fact conceived as external to mind by an analysis of the conditions under which we are able to make the distinction between truth and falsity in our empirical judgements.

The Coherence theory of Truth

The coherence theory of truth forms part of idealist epistemology and metaphysics* and it is important to remember this, otherwise, when for example Brand Blanshard says 'Truth is the approximation of thought to reality' the statement may seem unintelligible. The coherence theory defines truth in relation to thought. Any proposition is said to be true if it is both self-consistent and coherently connected with our system of propositions as a whole. The truth of the proposition which states that the external angle of a triangle is equal to the sum of the interior opposite angles consists in the coherence of this proposition with other propositions concerning the definition of a straight line and the definition of a triangle. The conclusion of a syllogism coheres with the major and minor premisses and this is what constitutes the validity of the conclusion. That there is a tree outside coheres with my experience of shade and the sound of rustling leaves. That Hitler died during the fall of Berlin coheres with what we know of the other happenings of those days. What is important, then, on this analysis of truth, is not the relation of a proposition to a fact but the relation of a proposition to other propositions.

The metaphysical view behind this theory is the one which

* Vide Ch. v. p. 81ff.

we found to be behind the objective idealist account of knowledge. The coherence theory is a special application of the axiom of internal relations. One judgement is not external to another judgement. Judgements stand or fall together. The shift from the language of proposition to that of judgement is significant. A "proposition" suggests the *that* of what is stated. A "judgement" suggests the very movement of thought itself. There is certainly a certain amount of ambiguity about just what the idealists mean by judgement, but at all events they are very much against the realist understanding of jugement in terms of an amalgam of atomic elements. Judgement, they say, cannot be divorced from the process of judging. The movement of thought is such that its moments are not a mere temporal series but are internally related to each other. At this point the category of unity assumes a key importance for the idealists. The unity of thought is something that defies dissection. This unity is to be seen not only in the single judgement but in reality as a whole. The unity of reality satisfies the demand of thought for a coherent system, something whose internal consistency is fulfilled completely only in the Absolute. Reality and thought are not to be regarded as opposites. The objective reality that we call the universe is the counterpart of mind. It is mind's own objectification. If this be so it follows that any single judgement can do scant justice to the concrete unity which reality is. But first the idealist use of the word 'concrete' needs some elucidation.

Idealists posit the term 'concrete universal' against that of the term 'abstract universal'. The abstract universal is the same as scientific law—"abstract" because any scientific law gives us highly selective information, and "universal" because the law is said to hold necessarily under certain specified conditions. But the abstract universal fails to give the concrete fullness of things. The individuality of a thing is thereby sacrificed to the general type. An individual is an 'identity in diversity', something which the abstracting activity of the discursive understanding cannot encompass. Only the speculative mind in its teleological progress can do justice to the concrete individuality which reality as a whole constitutes. But what is meant by reality 'as a whole'? If the axiom of internal relations is taken seriously then all terms will be internal to each other. Nothing will be what it is apart from its relation to other things (and this is the direct converse of the maxim given by Butler* which we cited as typifying the attitude of realism). On such a view reality constitutes a single term and this single term is what is meant by reality 'as a whole'.

To return to the coherence theory as such, it can be seen that, on the basis of the metaphysical view as outlined above, no single judgement can, strictly speaking, stand on its own. No single judgement can be completely true. A single judgement will be partly true and partly false. Truth in its ideal form is to be found only in the Absolute. For the rest we have degrees of truth. The more consistent and coherent with the rest of the body of judgements our judgement is the more true it is. An erroneous judgement is a matter of degree. Joachim definies error as 'that form of thinking that claims to express truth unqualified'. On such a view, however, an erroneous judgement is not completely false but partly true. If we take examples of erroneous empirical judgements the coherence theory seems difficult to maintain. The statement 'There is an elephant in the drawing room' we would say was completely false. But if we take a statement like 'The Second World war was caused by Hitler's ambitions' the coherence account begins to appear intelligible. Such a statement is true up to a point, and yet untrue if we insist on taking it in an unqualified manner. In assessing the causes of a war the fuller and more consistent our account is the more likely it is to be true. A completely true account is, in a sense, for the historian, an impossibility. For that we would need to know more than we can ever know. Now the concept of system is one that a philosopher could derive either from the inspiration of geometry and logic or from the study of history. The rationalist systems which derived from Descartes were inspired by the former. The idealist systems which derived from Hegel were inspired by the latter. In the study of history context is enormously important. The weighting of evidence, the determination of relevance, are all determined by reference to context. Historical knowledge grows. It does

* Vide p. 91.

not proceed mechanically by the mere accumulation of data. Small wonder then that philosophers who remembered the work of Herder and Grimm should stress the importance of coherence. Truth, on such a view, remains an ideal, something to be gradually approximated to; individual truths are to be subordinated to the ideal of truth in this absolute sense.

Those who did not always bear in mind the original historical origin of the theory did not find it hard to pick the coherence theory to pieces. The very style of idealist writing, as Brand Blanshard, (himself one of the most distinguished exponents of the idealist standpoint today) has remarked, is bound to rouse opposition in those who are of an empiricist temper. To say that reality itself is coherent can only be maintained on the basis of some previously conceived logical methodology. There seems to be a genuine surd element in reality, an element which does not amount merely to a confession of our ignorance, but which is deeply engrained in the nature of things. Only by confusing logic and reality, it may be said, could a philosopher imagine that reality was coherent. The notion of experience 'as a whole' likewise, it may be urged, signifies nothing. Experiences are centred, to use the vocabulary of the idealists themselves, in finite centres of consciousness. The notion of an experience which is not centred in anyone in particular is not something to which we can give any content. The very word 'judgement', on which the whole theory rests is full of ambiguity. Judgement may mean the act of judging or it may mean what is judged. Are all acts of judging internal to each other or are the contents of all judgements internal to each other? We should, it may be objected, know which is meant.

The notion of system, as we saw, owed much to historical studies. But the concept of one over-all system may appear as an illegitimate extension of what otherwise is a legitimate working concept. Even in historical writing, unless we are philosophizing about history or trying to construct a theory about the rise and fall of civilisations, we work with a restricted view of "systems". If I am working on the causes of the Industrial Revolution in eighteenth and nineteenth century England I need not concern myself with Genghis Khan and his hordes. In science again, unless he is working in the field of over-all theory, the researcher operates with the assumption of the isolation of systems. There is an irreducible difference between some of the systems themselves. Physics and mathematics are on a very different footing in that physics has ultimately to conform to sense perception. In physics the pull of the world of sense data provides the terminus of the process of verification. In mathematics there can be no question of the coherence of some of the systems with others. For example Euclidean and Riemannian geometries cannot cohere with each other for the reason that the basic axioms of each are different. Within a particular field the research worker may be guided by the thought of the coherence of the different discoveries he is making. As against this the discovery of something new is so often sparked off by the finding of something which does *not* cohere. Without the shock of finding something that did not cohere there would have been no discovery of radium and penicillin.

The notion of consistency with which the coherence theory is connected (truth consists in the coherence of consistent prepositions) has also come in for criticism. Ideas can be consistent and yet untrue. A child can give a consistent and coherent account of the period of his truancy from school and yet the child will not be speaking the truth. Can reference to the facts be completely eliminated? If we modify the theory and say 'cohere with the facts' or 'cohere with experience' are we not really admitting the element of correspondence? Joachim speaks of correspondence as a 'symptom' of the truth. Even to say this, of course, will still leave the notion of correspondence itself in need of analysis. Sometimes, conversely, coherence may be a symptom of the truth. We distinguish illusions from veridical perceptions in no small part through coherence with 'standard' perceptions. For example, my perception of the bent pencil does not cohere with the smooth 'feel' of it when I put my hands in the water. My perception of pink rats running up and down the counterpane does not cohere with the perception of an unperturbed cat sitting in the same room (not that this incongruity may strike me at the time).

Some truths seem to be independent and among these we

have notably truths discovered on the basis of sense experience (that the grass is green is independent of 2×2 being equal to 4), propositions in logic (which although they are relevant to a system are not relevant to what is outside it), the data of self-consciousness (which seem to bear an immediate authenticity), the data revealed by memory, and the coherence principle itself. And yet no matter how 'atomic' an empirical proposition may be it is not wholly divorced from what might be described, in a rather hackneyed way, as a 'universe of discourse'. For example, even if I make a statement about a patch of colour (and these are usually regarded by epistemologists as being simple statements) what I say is related to the standard vocabulary of colour classification and presupposes a world where there are many colours which can be compared. No empirical statement is 'independent' to the extent that the correspondence advocate would have us believe. As to the independence of the propositions of logic and mathematics we have seen that this is only a relative independence. Arithmetical statements form part of a corpus of propositions concerning previously laid-down operational procedures. One plus one equals two in virtue of what we have ourselves decided with regard to the series of simple cardinal numbers.

Turning to the data of self-consciousness first we have to clear a muddle. Only propositions can be said to be true or false. Facts cannot be true or false and data cannot be true or false. If I express in a sentence form something that I am feeling, for example, if I say 'I am feeling hot', some theorists would urge that there was no sense in anyone protesting that the sentence was false. Such sentences, it may be urged, are inevitably true, and are so independently of reference to anything else, whether fact or proposition. But those who analyse language point to the irrelevance of the distinction between truth and falsity in certain classes of sentences. Some logicians would prefer, for example, to keep the terms 'valid and 'invalid' for the discourse of logic and mathematics, and reserve the terms 'true' and 'false' for empirical discourse. Imperatives and emotive expressions, we have learnt these days, are neither true nor false. Statements made about oneself, one is inclined to think, bear the character of testimony and so the words true and false used in this particular context bear a special connotation. The existentialists certainly use the word 'truth' in a sense which is foreign to logic. In any case the data of self-conscious experience are probably not unrelated to phenomena like organic sensations, and if we have learnt the lesson of Kant's Refutation of Idealism correctly, these data are related no less to our perception of an 'external' world. The data revealed by memory are likewise of the nature of testimony. As in the case of historical statements there is a parallel problem here to that of the determining of what the 'facts' are since the *referenda* are in the past. In the case of memory there is in addition (and this is probably the most distinctive thing about memory) the feeling of pastness about what is remembered. The statements we make about our memories are surely related to our temporal awareness of ourselves, that is, to our sense of before and after. An isolated memory unrelated in any way to my other experiences, would hardly be a memory. Our memories cohere with each other. And yet unless a memory 'corresponds' in some way (and how this comes about needs analysis) with the happening of which it is a memory, we would not be justified in using the word 'memory' at all.

But apart from the above considerations, some of which concern very specific problems in epistemology, we have yet to evaluate the alleged independence of the coherence principle itself. Here there is a parallel problem to that which besets the verificationist. What is the status of the coherence principle itself (just as what is the status of the verification principle itself?)? Does this principle itself cohere with other propositions? To ask this question is immediately to see the 'metaphysical' character of the coherence principle. The principle of coherence is part and parcel of the whole absolutist metaphysic. But how are we to know whether a particular proposition coheres or not? This cannot be known by an appear to coherence itself. We can only judge whether a particular proposition coheres by an act of intuition. Does this mean that the coherence theory needs at some point to admit a non-discursive capacity of the mind? The mediaeval schoolmen were probably better able to make room for such a capacity that the post-Kantians with their insistence on the combining role of the mind.

The logician will be likely to find fault with the coherence theory on rather different grounds. To speak of a proposition as being partly true and partly false seems to posit a form of judgement half-way between assertion and denial. Once more the kind of qualified judgements which are native to historical writing may seem to fall outside the bounds of logic in the strict sense. The philosopher, like the historian, makes use of the criterion of coherence in his critical work of reflection. But it seems difficult to avoid the conclusion that without the shock of reference to 'facts' the criterion of coherence by itself is not adequate once we are outside the sphere of purely symbolic systems. The stimulus of the concept of 'system' is a very powerful one to the speculative mind and no one realised its attraction more than Kant. However, reality is in many ways impervious to the demand for a single system.

The contribution of the coherence theory to the discussion of the problem of truth is considerable. It reminds us of a problem which is almost Platonic in design—that of the relation of truths to Truth, and secondly it reminds us that the concept of fact is relative to the questions posed by the inquiring mind. As for the latter reminder, its importance is immediately evident if we reflect on the concept of 'historical fact'—a concept which incidentally had been left out of the empiricist and realist treatment of fact. But the logic of question and answer, as Collingwood saw, is relevant even beyond this sphere, and, what is important for the metaphysically minded, it constitutes the spring of the movement of philosophic reflection, a movement which is wedded to the concept of truth in a manner which cannot rest content with the view that the relation between thought and reality is that of mere correspondence.

The Pragmatist theory of Truth

The pragmatist approach to philosophy, associated as it is for the most part with the work of American philosophers, can also be traced back to the positivism and phenomenalism of the eighteenth century. The empiricist tradition owed much to the scientific use of experimentation. Now an experiment is a special form of observation, observation under controlled conditions. The leading role played by hypotheses in directing the precise way in which the conditions should be controlled led Kant to generalise this procedure as being the key not only to the scientist's discovery of causal lines in nature, but also as being the key to the analysis of the problem of knowledge as such. Just as the scientist approaches nature with certain questions in his mind, the questions we call hypotheses —so also, even in ordinary perception, the mind approaches nature with certain forms of thought or rules of procedure. If we reflect on the actual process of experiment, however, we can see that the hypothesis by itself does not lead to the wresting of nature's secrets. The hypothesis has to be applied, it has to be put into the crucible of actual testing, and this testing is in fact what an experiment is. The technique of experimentation fathered three quite different philosophical standpoints. The scientist's use of numerals for measurement confirmed the rationalists in their choice of mathematical models for philosophizing. The scientific use of observation stimulated the whole movement which we call empiricism. The scientific appeal to practice fathered the movement called pragmatism.

Behind William James' dubbing of acquaintance as a 'dumb' way of knowing was his conviction that there was no analogue to acquaintance in the concrete practice of the scientist in his laboratory. In order to discover the truth something has to be done. James defines the true as 'the expedient in the way of thinking'. The test of the truth of a proposition is to be found in its practical consequences. The true proposition is the one which works. That this is a chair before me is verified not only by the perception of certain visible and other sense-data, but by its being sittable on. True propositions have a 'cash-value', a term which later-day phenomenalists incorporated into their own vocabulary. A true proposition has a cash-value in the sense that just as a valid cheque can be exchanged for cash at a bank a true proposition is backed up by the perception of relevant sense data. Empirical propositions predict that under such and such conditions such and such sense-data will be experienced. The concept of verity gives way to that of verification. The 'working' of the true proposition consists in the fulfilling of the predictions made by the proposition. In his book *Pragmatism* James adds another criterion as well. The true proposition is one which coheres with the other things we believe. William James further extended the application of the pragmatist analysis to religious phenomena as well. The criterion of religious truth, no less than that of truth in other spheres, was to be determined by how 'satisfactory' religious belief was to the believer.

Reference to belief also comes into John Dewey's formulation of the theory. The quest for truth is always preceded by doubt. Just as biological need stimulates adjustment, so also, in the process of inquiry, doubt leads on to belief. But a belief has no unequivocal truth or falsity. A belief can only have 'warranted assertibility' in relation to a particular inquiry and a particular stage in the history of thought. Inquiry takes place in the time series and it is a progressive procedure. Thought is an instrument of adjustment, and this is why Dewey calls his form of pragmatism 'instrumentalism'. The humanistic aspect of the theory comes about through the implications of the view that the true is that which is practical and satisfactory. The implication is that 'true' means not 'true for me' but 'true for all'. Schiller, James and Dewey all claim that in making truth relative to human enterprises they are propounding a form of humanism, a humanism moreover which is consistent with the practical service which science renders to man. The tentative nature of our discoveries is reflected in Vaihinger's variant of the theory—the view that we should act 'as if' our ideas were true.

From our examination of earlier theories it has been evident that it is difficult to find a criterion of truth which can be applicable to all kinds of propositions. The pragmatist theory has been found to have perhaps an even more restricted applicability than either the correspondence or coherence theories. In the first place many propositions do not have 'practical consequences'. The pragmatists, on the strict interpretation of their theory, had to reject necessary truths. An extreme, and humorous, example of this is found in the view expressed that even $2+2=4$ is conditional, for, if we are summing lions and lambs $2+2$ will equal 2, and furthermore $2+2$ drops of water will not result in anything numerable at all. These are *reductio ad absurdum* examples. If the theory cannot account for the propositions of logic and mathematics it is likewise unable to account for historical propositions other than those which concern the simple record of events (which could presumably be expressed in terms of past conditionals).

The introduction of biological criteria by some of the pragmatists complicated the issue. The theory of evolution had made much of the notion of adjustment. The pragmatists adopted this notion when they said that the true proposition was the one which was useful for adjustment. Moreover, just as no stage of evolution can be regarded as final, so also any single proposition is but a temporary halting place in the progressive discovery of truth. But what is experimentally true might at the same time be biologically useless for adjustment. In such a case would we say the proposition concerned 'worked' or not? The notion of 'working' is too vague and ambiguous. Untrue ideas so often work. This century is abundant in evidence of this. The 'working' of the falsehoods told about the Jews by the Nazis is a matter of recent history. The working of propaganda is often in inverse ratio to its truth. This shows that the statement 'All true propositions work' cannot be converted. Many propositions which work are not true. This shows, *inter alia*, that the notions of truth and utility are not synonymous. (Cf. a similar line of argument by G. E. Moore, that if the pleasurable is sometimes not good then the good and the pleasurable mean different things.) The concept of 'that which works', moreover, has been criticised on the ground of its involving relativism. Even if we speak of 'social' pragmatism the question can legitimately be raised as to *which* society we have in mind. As in the case of the coherence theory, the pragmatist account involves the notion of 'partial' truth. Dewey's formula of 'warranted assertibility', for example, seems to involve this. The pragmatist acquiesces too easily in agnosticism about metaphysical truth. The pragmatists had an animus against what they called the 'useless' knowledge of the idealists, but in having this animus they rejected the ideal character of truth altogether. To the pragmatist there is no such thing as "the" truth.

The concept of 'working', then, is as beset with difficulties as that of correspondence or that of coherence. Yet the virtue of the pragmatists' treatment of truth undoubtedly lies in their insight that the quest for truth is an enterprise which demands active effort. We need to distinguish between the will to find truth and the actual discovery of truth. So much of human activity is project rather than achievement and this the pragmatists saw. Our working hypotheses have a certain utility. There can be no finality in the discovery of truth. In science, most certainly, our formulations have to be constantly open to modification in the light of new evidence. Truth in such contexts is closely related to our purposes at the time. The pragmatist agrees with the Marxist in his conviction that our actions can change the facts. Man need not forever acquiesce in the face of 'reality'. Reality is in a sense "in the making" and so also is truth. Such a humanistic approach is far both from the realist's acceptance of 'brute' fact and from the objective idealist's acquiescence in the march of the *Zeitgeist*.

Each approach perhaps supplements that of the other. In mathematics if we wish to retain the notions of truth and falsity (and many philosophers would wish to exclude these terms from both logic and mathematics) we must recognise that they amount to no more and no less than the rightness and wrongness of our calculations. The scientific concept of law incorporates elements from all three theories. The scientist tries to discover the facts, but the facts reveal themselves to the active enterprise of experiment, and the theoretical framework which guides the investigation forms (although in a restricted sense) a system. As to the idea of truth in an ideal sense, in these commonsensical days the concept of the Absolute seems to be sound and fury signifying nothing. It would be unwise, however, to underestimate the regulative role which the idea of a unified system may play in the thinking of the philosopher and, as Kant thought, such an idea may also have a directive influence on the work of the scientific intellect as well.

PART THREE: MAN AND NATURE

VIII Matter

Introduction

THE notion that there is a 'stuff' or ultimate material out of which everything is made seems to have been a very familiar one to the Greek mind. The concept of an artefact is that of something which is made out of pre-existing material, as, say, a table is made from wood, a statue from marble and a vase from clay. If we generalise this procedure we arrive at the question 'What is everything made of, not just this table, this statue, this vase, but everything that exists?' It is out of such thinking that the concept of 'matter' was born. The search for something ultimate is certainly a genuinely metaphysical quest. But it might just as convincingly be maintained that the search for an underlying substrate of change is a genuinely scientific task. If we try to answer the question 'What is it which underlies all change?' speculatively we are metaphysicians. If we try to answer it making use of the experimental method we call ourselves scientists. As it happens, when the early Ionian philosophers thought of air or water as the substrate of changing phenomena they picked on something which to our mind may not strike us as particularly 'material', air and water being lacking in the element of "pushiness" which we associate with matter.

The main problem which attends such theorising had, however, emerged in the fifth century before the Christian era. It may be metaphysically satisfying to have come to a conclusion regarding the nature of what things are made of, but in the finding of an identical substrate in all things the problem still remains why there should be differences at all, and why there should not be 'just one big thing'. In this respect the atomic theories of Leucippus and Democritus were a considerable advance on those of their predecessors, for they came to the conclusion that the differences between things could be none other than differences of quantity and arrangement, and thus they anticipated most remarkably the modern substitution of quantity for quality, which, since the seventeenth century, has been characteristic of the sciences. The atomic theory which they advanced also contained the germ of another aspect of what we now take to be the typically scientific way of viewing phenomena, the method of breaking down things into their ultimate constituents in order to find out the secret of their organisation. This was the technique which bore fruit first in chemistry where its application was obvious, and later in the other natural sciences as well.

What Leucippus and Democritus had to say, however, was eclipsed in the ancient world largely owing to the influence of Aristotle whose way of looking at nature concentrated on its qualitative rather than on its quantitative aspects. The Aristotelian metaphysics of nature, according to which there was a plurality of substances each having an essence and accidents, was not conducive to the growth of a world-view which one might call 'relational'. Not only were qualitative differences considered to be accessible to perception but causal transactions were conceived to obtain between what were after all *entities*, and such a view was far from what we now regard to be the characteristic of causal transactions—the way in which their operation makes of any property essentially something relational. The teleological bias of Aristotelianism, moreover, ran completely counter to the mechanistic approach which had been uppermost in the works of the two earlier philosophers. Aristotle did, it is true, speak of 'materia prima', but not only was this concept not fully worked out, but by reason of his notion of a 'nisus' its very materiality was called into question. Aristotle settled for the most part for a view of form and matter where the difference between them was merely qualitative, so that 'materia prima' was regarded as something undeveloped instead of as something intractable which resisted change. There can be no doubt that it was Aristotle's absorption in biology which was behind his dealing with matter in this way. Much of what he said would not be altogether unacceptable to workers in the field of bio-chemistry to this day. It was the influence of Aristotelianism coupled with the other-worldly concerns of mediaeval philosophy that were jointly responsible for the absence of any advance made in the treatment of the concept of matter for many centuries to come. Of prime importance during those centuries was the concept not of matter but of substance, and this in turn included both the concept of Divine substance, i.e. God, and finite substances, namely created things, among whom certainly man had a privileged status.

A germinal approach to what was later to become the scientific method *par excellence* was found in the work of the mediaeval alchemists who were fascinated by the project of turning one substance into another, in particular turning dross metals into gold. One might well consider that pioneer work in the field of weighing and compounding was undertaken by them. Not that there had been no trace of the experimental method in the history of Greek science. But Greek thinkers tended to be interested in astronomy above all, and when they thought of the concept of order it was the order of the heavenly bodies that came first to mind, and it is easy to see that, although it is possible to observe the heavenly bodies to a certain extent, astronomy is not a science in which one can make experiments. The concept of matter, we have been trying to suggest, was nurtured by these early blundering attempts at chemistry made by the alchemists. The other source was mathematics, for in the technique of measurement mathematics was put to work, and the world of qualities, in submitting to the operations of being weighed compounded and transmuted, was seen as a world to which numbers could be applied.

It was in the work of a mathematician-philosopher, Descartes, that the concept of matter was to receive its next most authoritative formulation. Matter was defined by him as *res extensa*, or extended thing. The real world was the world capable of measurement and space was what Euclid described in his geometry. For the first time matter could be regarded *de more geometrico*. Descartes' view of matter was enormously influential in the seventeenth and eighteenth centuries. The geometric method seemed to offer what philosophers had been looking for, a way of demonstrating propositions about the actual world. The criteria of substantiality, that is to say, independence and permanence, seemed to be admirably satisfied in the concept of *res extensa*. The Pythagorean approach in western philosophy seemed at last to have come into its own. In spite of the initial enthusiasm which the geometric method aroused, Descartes himself was by no means unaware of some of the difficulties which attended it. Was the extended world something which could be properly said to 'exist'? How much could our definition after all tell us. We could say it was 'non-thinking' by formulating the contrary of the definition of mind. The nature of the world—even of its essence—did not seem to be exhausted in the characteristic of extension. Much later it was to be pointed out that the circumstance of the applicability of Euclidean geometry to the physical world was something contingent, that there can be other geometries and that geometry as such is not 'descriptive' of any thing at all. To speak of geometric concepts as 'substantial' was, therefore, to speak incorrectly. In all fairness to Descartes, however, it can be appreciated that, in the world as we know it, there is little enough to which the scholastic category of substance seems applicable, and it seemed to him that in the sphere of mathematics there was to hand a world of entities to which the category was eminently suited. In our own day the attraction of the world of Pythagorean numbers has been testified to by no less a philosopher than Bertrand Russell.

Post-Cartesian philosophers reacted variously to what Descartes had said about matter. In Leibniz' view it was a mistake to speak of the extended world as substantial, for extension was divisible, and one of the essential features of substantiality was its indivisibility. While the work of Descartes was consonant with the practical experiments of a Kepler or a Galileo, Leibniz' exclusion of extension from the sphere of substantiality made the scientists' activity difficult to explain. The obvious solution, that is, to drop the notion of substance as an entity altogether, is not a solution that could occur to any rationalist philosopher. In making thought and extension both attributes of one substance, namely God, Spinoza avoided the dualism which Descartes had found so unbridgeable. But by this time the extent of the departure of the philosophical treatment of materiality from the commonsense view of things existing in space and time was patent.

Empiricist philosophers did much to emancipate the concept of matter from that of substance, although, such was the influence of Cartesianism, the task was not an easy one. Their contribution may best be assessed by an examination of the controversy concerning primary and secondary qualities.

Primary and secondary qualities

The involvement of this distinction with the representative theory of perception has already been noted elsewhere.* We are to consider it here as marking an important landmark in the weaning away of empiricistically-inclined philosophers from the vocabulary of scholasticism, and as contributing to the scientific conception of matter. The Aristotelian language of quality was employed by Locke, and he defines a quality as 'the power to produce any idea in our mind'. In this respect he is saying something very similar to the scholastic view that things possess an efficacy which brings about changes in other things. Primary qualities are reckoned to be 'utterly inseparable from the body, in what estate soever it be' and they are listed as the characteristics of solidity, extension, figure, motion or rest, and number. The qualities which belong to a substance were looked upon as belonging to it 'in itself' and to be 'always in them.' This leads Locke to say that it is the primary qualities which are the 'real qualities'. He says of them that our 'ideas of primary qualities are resemblances of them and their patterns do really exist in the bodies themselves'. In speaking of 'really existing' it is clear that Locke still holds the ontological assumption of independence as the distinguishing characteristic of what is 'real'. It was not difficult for Berkeley to spot the weakness in his formulation of the theory and to point out that extension and all the rest are not ascertainable out of relation to an observer, thus bearing witness to a "Copernican" way of thinking which even to this day the strict empiricist finds uncomfortable.

It is the primary qualities which, for Kepler, Galileo, Descartes and Locke provide the definition of materiality. This generalisation, however, needs to be qualified in the case of

* Vide p. 68.

Locke. Locke's inclusion of 'solidity' among the primary qualities is a most interesting departure from Cartesianism and amounts to a very considerable concession to the commonsense standpoint. It is the characteristic of solidity which we associate most of all with thinghood, the pushiness of things which most of all makes us speak of them as material. In including this characteristic (which is something which we learn a *posteriori* about things) Locke is, strictly speaking, denying that one can properly speak of a 'definition' of matter at all. It is because, on his view, it is not possible for us to know real essences (and this is clear because he says that we know only *ideas* of the primary qualities which he thinks are copies of them and not the qualities themselves) that he makes the amazing observation that we cannot say dogmatically that mind cannot be extended or that matter cannot think. This aside of Locke's would have involved him in serious controversy with the clerical world had it caught their attention.

Locke's departure from Cartesianism in this respect aligned him closer than Descartes had ever been with Boyle and the other scientists of his day. The real 'definition' of matter is not with reference to extension. Geometry alone cannot inform us about the physical world. Primary qualities can only be found out through experience, albeit experience in a special sense—the observation under controlled conditions which experiment is. That the scientist's concern is with quantities Locke has no doubt. It is only quantities which are public and therefore objective. The secondary qualities we are informed of even more indirectly in the sense that there are more conditioning factors in their case than in the case of our 'ideas' of the primary ones. Given that, say, the perception of colour is dependent on the transmission of light and the condition of the relevant sense organ, there is some point in saying that secondary qualities are 'subjective' in a sense in which primary qualities are not.

What is of special interest in Locke's account is the way in which it brings out the inherent clash between scholastic language and actual scientific practice. If the language of qualities is retained, the word 'substance' must also find a place, for qualities must inhere in something. The scientists, however, in using the language of quantity not quality, were under no such obligation, and for them the word 'substance' was already one of those superfluous hypotheses, which, as good Newtonians, it was incumbent on them to discard. Locke, however, did not go far enough. In realising that science did not deal with the inner natures of things but with properties, he failed to realise at the same time that those properties were relational. In saying that salt is soluble I am attributing a relational property to salt for I am stating what happens when salt is brought into relation with water. Although Locke does not reach this conclusion, and although he does not succeed in freeing himself from the concept of substance, his own achievement is nonetheless considerable. The concept of material substance as an entity is retained by him as an exigency arising from the adoption of quality language. What individual substances are is to be disclosed only through experience. In eliminating the subjective from the real world he lays the foundation for the 'materialism' of the centuries which succeeded his own. That the distinction between primary and secondary qualities could not long be maintained is evident once we reflect on the fact that extension, figure and the like are not 'out there' but are only ascertained by the active participation of an observer using an instrument of measurement. Our knowledge of the 'material' world, Locke wishes to tell us, is neither as much as we had hoped, nor as little as we had feared.

When Berkeley points out the redundancy of the concept of material substance in the form in which Locke had retained it, he was doing something which was consonant with what Newton had prescribed. His polemic against the "minute" philosophers is designed to stress the 'phenomenal' character of the data with which scientists deal. There is no transcendent order of materiality with which science can claim to deal. That science is concerned, above all, with the discovery of *laws*, is something which both Berkeley and Kant saw more clearly than Locke had. By the end of the eighteenth century philosophers were more reconciled to admitting that 'matter' was properly the concern of the scientists rather than of the philosophers. Society and its history was proving itself to be as interesting a field as physical nature for speculation, with the advantage too that it was a virgin field for the philosophic mind to explore. In France the alternative attractions of nature and society as offering scope for the speculative intellect were very evident in the work of the Encyclopedists. It was the latter who laid the theoretical foundations of what was later known as materialism. Germany had first to go through Hegelianism, a movement in which interest shifted abruptly from speculative concern with nature to speculative concern with history. But this in its turn fathered materialism, respectively the materialism of Feuerbach and Karl Marx. In the meantime science furthered knowledge of the material world beyond all expectation and it was not long before theoreticians had to hand in the concept of 'events' something which seemed happily free from all taint of subjectivity. That it was this very concept which was destined to rob the material world of its brute 'materiality' was something which could not possibly be foreseen.

Materialism

The ancestry of the philosophic movement known as materialism is, as we can already see, diverse. Hobbes, in the seventeenth century, sums up the main thesis of the movement in his dictum 'All that exists is body, all that occurs motion'. Nineteenth century materialism, as far as strictly philosophical considerations are concerned, was mainly a reaction against post-Kantian idealism. The vogue it enjoyed was comparable to that of realism in the early twentieth century, a vogue following on the speculations of Bradley, Bosanquet and others. The Hobbesian thesis had even more plausibility in the nineteenth century than in Hobbes's own. The growth of the physical sciences had been spectacular. Knowledge about matter had led to control over nature, exhibited in the invention of machines and the rapid industrialisation of the Victorian era. The refined may shy away from the kingdom of this world (the other-worldliness of the Tractarians is so interpreted by the unsympathetic), but the majority of Victorians were all for it, being only too convinced of the practical potential of science and the further possibility of material progress. Far more was known about matter than about mind, which seemed to point to the preferability of a metaphysic based on "the devil we know". Materialism certainly had the advantage of being in tune with the ethos of the times.

The theoretic foundation of materialism was to be found in classical Newtonian mechanics, in the theory known as *mechanism*. A mechanical system is one consisting of solid particles of matter moving in a fixed frame of space and time as the result of the push and pull of various forces. Any single event can be given a determinate position in this frame of reference. The theory is also spoken of as deterministic because it holds that the laws of nature are such that if we could ascertain the whole state of the physical world during a finite time we would be able to infer its state at any past or future time. Any given event takes place as a consequence of the occurrence of certain antecedent events. Everything in nature is explicable by reference to uniform laws and these laws follow a simple deterministic pattern. In order to explain a complex phenomenon all that is necessary is to break it down into its constituent elements and these elements will be found to follow the same uniform laws. It is because natural laws are so uniform that we are able to predict with a high degree of probability what will happen in the future.

The mechanistic hypothesis soon came under fire from many quarters. Considering that the hypothesis of mechanism was, when all is said and done, a hypothesis within science itself, it was only proper that criticism should arise from within the ranks of the scientists. With the rejection of the Newtonian conception of space and time (that they are absolute frameworks, ontological in status) a serious blow was given to the theory. A piece of matter was no longer regarded as a persistent thing within a fixed frame but a system of inter-related events. In quantum mechanics the "pushiness" of matter has apparently gone. All scientific laws are not found to be as simple in pattern as Newton's law of gravitation. Our observations are always subject to inaccuracy and many physical phenomena for the time being elude our attempts to reduce them to any pattern of law. Heisenberg's principle of "indeterminacy" confirms the pertinence of what Kant had said more than a century and a half earlier—that it is impossible to specify the nature of the object without taking into account the role of the spectator. Certain micro-particles are such that the very observation of them, for this is a process dependent on light, deflects them from their course. The much vaunted 'objectivity' of scientific laws is thus seen to be inveterately infected with subjectivity. In the meantime some biologists were not at all sure that mechanical principles of explanation were sufficient to account for all phenomena in the organic world. The vitalists, harking back to a way of approach reminiscent of Aristotle, believed that there was such a thing as the principle of 'entelechy' operative in the organic world and that mechanism by itself left many phenomena unexplained.

The philosophers supplemented these criticisms with some of their own. The central technique behind materialism was described by Comte as that of explaining the higher by the lower and this was taken by many to be a fault. Bergson, in criticising roundly both mechanism and teleology, was of the opinion that the problems of the relation of mind and body, matter and life, determinism and choice, still remained unsolved. Bacon had spoken of the teleological principle in no uncertain terms as an obstacle to the explanation of natural phenomena. He had said :—'the handling of final causes mixed with the rest in physical enquiries, hath intercepted the severe and diligent inquiry of all real and physical causes.' The critics, however, could raise the crucial question whether purposeful action could be interpreted as being merely the outcome of the push and pull of impersonal physical forces. In Bergson's view the teleologist's affirmation of the pull of the future was as deterministic as mechanism, the difference being that the determinism was from in front instead of from behind.

The teleologists did have the advantage of offering a principle which seemed specially geared to the explanation of individual phenomena, especially the phenomena of the living world. The prototype of teleological activities was alleged to be found in God and it was understandable that the 'materialists' should find sturdy critics among the theologians. To insist on the empire of deterministic laws was to deny the existence of the transcendent. It was to deny the possibility of miracles, for while to the religious man a miracle amounts to the direct intervention of God in the course of nature's everyday performances, to the scientist a 'miracle' means an event for which the natural explanation has not yet been found. The metaphysic of materialism was prophetically seen, by the religious-minded, to usher in an age of secularism. The universal sway of causal laws seemed to leave no room for moral action, for if we could not do otherwise what point was there in blaming us for what we did? The latter argument betrayed some muddled thinking for moral action would surely be equally impossible if there were no order in the natural world, and if say, a bullet sometimes hit its target and sometimes pursued a zigzag path.

Those who were keen on vindicating the reality of the unperceivable hailed with approbation developments in twentieth century physics, for if protons and electrons were unperceivable why should not the existence of other unperceivable 'entities' of a spiritual nature be admitted too? The slogan that the world is more like a thought than a machine seemed to encourage such hopes. Here again there was some muddled thinking. The pushiness of the Democritean atoms has certainly gone, but the procedure of the sciences remains, basically, what it was. The secret of the complex is to be found in the infinitesimal, only instead of the infinitesimals being taken 'literally', their highly conceptual nature is, in this century, being done justice to. Whether the fringe of the unknown is to be regarded as something eventually tractable to the enquiring mind or whether recourse is to be had to the invasion of a separate principle of explanation is what is really at stake between the 'materialist' and his adversary.

IX Space and Time

Introduction

EVERYONE would agree that our human existence is a spatio-temporal one, although we may not, except in our reflective moments, and if we are not philosophically-minded, put it quite like this. We experience spatial distance between things in that we see things to be apart from each other and tactual experience also reveals them to be such. We appreciate distance in a still more forcible way when we pace out the distance between places and find them to be further away than we thought. We experience temporal 'distance' between events when we compare the felt pastness of what happened yesterday with the vividness of what is happening right now, or when, in watching a race, we observe events taking place in succession. We are also familiar with the fact that there is a subjective aspect to our experience of the spatial and the temporal for our mile-long constitutional seems long or short according to our physical condition, and an hour-long lecture may seem twice its length thanks to certain factors in ourselves or in the lecture.

But immediately we begin to reflect on all this we rightly raise the question 'What is space and what is time'? It will not do to offer the simple answer 'space is what the surveyors measure and time is what the clocks measure', for units of spatial and temporal measurement are clearly conventional; we could, if we so desired, define a foot as sixteen inches instead of twelve and define a year as five times 365 days which would make our numerical ages much less than they are now although our 'actual' age would not be altered in the least. There can be no simple answer to the question what space and time are for we never perceive space and time on their own. We perceive objects side by side and events in the relation of before and after. The problem of space and time is, therefore, a 'metaphysical' problem like the problem of matter (we perceive tables and chairs, but not 'matter') and the problem of causation (we perceive the marble hit against another marble, but we do not perceive the 'cause').

From the above it would seem that the problem of space and time is deeply rooted in experience and this indeed it is. But the problem is tied up not only with the analysis of perceptual experience but also with geometry, for the subject-matter of geometry is extension, and with the natural sciences, for the natural sciences investigate the spatio-temporal world. Psychologists too have had their say concerning this problem, for a genetic account of our awareness of space and time is no less possible than the analytic accounts which physicists and philosophers may give. Theories of space and time, then, tend to be of three types, psychological, metaphysical and scientific, and sometimes there are examples of puzzling amalgams of two or more of these. We shall be in the main concerned with theories belonging to the second category, the metaphysical.

The Greek cosmogonies had quite a lot to say about space and time, although of course, in a speculative way. The atomists of the fifth century before Christ were convinced that a Parmenidean model of the universe could, quite literally, make no room for motion and change. The discussion took the form of a controversy concerning the concepts of 'plenum' and the 'void'. There could be no motion in a plenum or in what James called a 'block universe', whereas, if we had a pluralistic world with empty space between the atoms, motion could be accounted for. Whether motion was to be conceived as being the original endowment of the atoms themselves or imparted *ab extra*, was, of course, a further problem that the atomists, and also subsequent philosophers, had to contend with. The atomistic account, however, strikes us as far more in line with modern thinking than, say, the imaginative account provided by Plato in his *Timaeus*. There Plato speaks of time as the moving image or shadow of Eternity; both space and time are regarded as links between the sensible and the ideal or eternal world. In so far as they are to do with particularity and individuation they are imperfect, and the world of Forms is regarded, by contrast, as non-spatial and non-temporal.

Aristotle's treatment of space and time falls within the

framework of his doctrine of the categories, for place and time are two of the ten Aristotelian categories. In the course of his *Metaphysics* Aristotle was concerned with change only in so far as the category of quality was applicable to it, for it was in qualitative and not quantitative terms that he envisaged the world of substances. Changes occur thanks to the unfolding of the potential into the actual. Such an account of change is concerned with development no doubt, but it certainly ignores the temporal aspect of change. In his *Physics*, however, Aristotle deals with change of quantity and change of place and it is here that he has something to say which is more comparable to 'modern' treatments of space and time. The same place can be occupied by different objects at different times and this would suggest that space is not to be confused with objects; not, however, that we should posit a void lying between objects, for this hypothesis Aristotle specifically rejects. Events, according to him, are ordered in an objective sequence and it is possible for certain events to occur at the same time. Moreover Aristotle realised that if space and time were interpreted in a corpuscular way it would be impossible to make the notion of continuity intelligible, and in this respect his views were in advance of those of the atomists. In spite of this, however, the historical influence of Aristotelianism centred far more on his metaphysical terminology of potentiality and actuality than on the scientific view given in the *Physics*, and the outcome of the use of this terminology was undoubtedly to detemporalize the concept of change and to substitute for time, the notion of a purely qualitative process.

Christian theologians were hard put to it to give an account of space and time which would be acceptable to those brought up in the shadow of Aristotelianism and yet which would do justice to the strong historicity of Christian belief. St. Augustine confesses quite frankly 'What is time? If no one asks me, I know; if I wish to explain it to one that asketh, I know not.' Christians, no less than Plato, saw time against the background of eternity, and, again like Plato, often spoke as if the temporal in some way 'participated' in eternity, the difference being that whereas the project of full participation in the eternal was for Plato a cognitive (and at the same time an ethical) project, for the Christian it was associated with regenerate man, that is man spiritually reborn through the experience of conversion. The "turn to the unconditioned" of which Plato had spoken in philosophical language was spoken of by the Christian in religious language. The spatio-temporal order of existence was a finite one, and yet it was into this very world that Christ had come, thus transforming the merely contingent, the merely 'accidental', in so far as the human, that is, what is inherently bounded in space and time, becomes the vehicle for the exemplification of the Divine nature. Christian thinking had to hand in the notion of a history governed by Providence a notion no less potent in its capacity to straddle the space-time dichotomy that had dominated philosophizing on this subject in the ancient world than the contemporary space-time concept with which physics operates today. For history, no less than the natural sciences, deals with events, that is to say with what happens at a place and at a time.

The terms in which the mediaevalists treated space and time may strike us as altogether 'unscientific'. They were, for example, much preoccupied with the question of the beginning and the end of time, that is, with creation and with eschatology. Reformists among Christian theologians have struggled against the crude thinking which would reserve 'eternal life' for some future state and which would discover for heaven a remote spatial location. Space and time were the dimensions against which the drama of human life was plotted out, not, as we tend to regard them today (barring the existentialists), merely the dimensions within which natural events deploy themselves. The cosmological inaccuracies of the first chapter of Genesis could be interpreted allegorically without losing their force, and the temporal sequence of events (human events) could be seen as leading up to the central historical event for the Christian, the birth of Christ. The Christian world-view tended to look upon the spatio-temporal order as first and foremost the arena in which was played out the crucial drama of the salvation of man's soul. Subsequent to this came the attempt to found a spatio-temporal order of society which should reflect God's will on earth, and only much later, came active interest in the investigation of nature and the harnessing of its powers in the machine age. The contribution to this last stage made by the Protestant ethic of self-help and by movements like that of Wesleyanism has been described by Weber and Tawney and concerns the historian rather than the philosopher.

The Rationalist account

The science-oriented nature of modern treatments of space and time has more or less completely overshadowed the kind of approach that has been sketched above. It is an approach, however, which needs to be borne in mind when we try to understand what Descartes and his successors had to say on this subject. The most striking feature of the Cartesian treatment is its interest in space to the neglect of time, a feature distinctive of all the philosophies of the seventeenth and eighteenth centuries until a completely different orientation was given to the problem by David Hume. Descartes' preoccupation is not surprising at all if we bear in mind his determination to understand everything mathematically. In the fifty-seventh Principle he writes of time as 'only a mode of thinking', indeed what else can it be, given that the natural world is bifurcated into material substance with its characteristic attribute of extension, and mental substance with its characteristic attribute of thought. 'Mode' language was in fact a very useful one for the rationalists when they came across something which could not otherwise be accommodated within the realm of the substantial. It could explain the awkward presence of parts (individuals) in their 'derivation' from the whole and it could account for space and time. But although, for Descartes, the spatial has primacy over the temporal, it remains to be seen whether what Descartes understands as the 'extended' is reallv synonymous with what we understand by the 'spatial' at all. The primary quality extension is pure three-dimensional space, that is to say, it is an abstraction. It happens that Euclidean geometry can be 'applied' to the actual world although this is not equivalent to saying that the actual world, as Descartes thought, is Euclidean in structure. It remains, therefore, for Descartes to explain wherein lies the difference between extension (space) and extended objects (spatial objects). In his view physical things are to be regarded as modes of matter, these modes being the result of the action of motion; but as matter is not of itself endowed with motion, the originator of motion can be none other than God Himself.

Spinoza avoids this crude reference to a *deus ex machina* since for him nothing can be said to fall 'outside' God. In his view matter is to be discovered in motion and rest. The particularity of things, however, arises mediately through the 'mediate infinite and eternal Mode' of the attribute of extension. In his denial that motion is imparted to things *ab extra* Spinoza may be said to have advanced the scientific viewpoint; but his disregard of time, arising from his adoption of the geometric method, certainly betrays the reverse tendency. From the standpoint of geometry space cannot but have the primacy. Geometry has nothing to say about change and therefore nothing to say about time. Spinoza's starting point, as indeed also his culmination point, is the Eternal, and his problem, as in the case of Plato, is the problem of accounting for particularity, which, in view of his logical method, he can account for only in terms of "derivation". (The cosmological approach on the other hand, exemplified in St. Thomas Aquinas' *Summa Theologica*, proceeds in the reverse direction, from the consideration of finite, i.e., temporal, things, to the consideration of things eternal.) For Spinoza, then, there can be no question of a return to the world of time. Wherever the temporal be found, in causation, in the realm of scientific law, we find its efficacy has been neutralised by the over-all sway of logic. As Alexander pointed out in his Gifford Lectures.... 'causality in the proper sense, which requires time, subsists only in the concatenation of finite things with one another, not in their relation to God'. If Spinoza had admitted time as the other attribute of God, so Alexander thinks, we would be better able to make intelligible the nature of finite existence.

Absolute versus Relative Space and Time

Whether space and time are absolute or relative is really an issue which concerns physics more than philosophy, for the theory propounding the absolute nature of space and time appeared first, not in a philosophical treatise, but in Newton's

Principia and was part and parcel of his contribution to mechanics. The theory holds that space is composed of points and that time is composed of instants, and that both points and instants have an existence independent of the bodies and events that occupy them. Space and time are thus regarded as fixed frames of reference. We can appreciate what this would involve if we realise that, on this view, a single point in space could be spoken of as having a position, and a single instant in time could be spoken of as having a date. Whether this accords with our commonsense assumption that spatiality is to do with side by sideness, i.e. plurality of places, and that temporality is to do with the relation of before and after, i.e. plurality of events, remains to be seen, for there is no *prima facie* reason why scientific theory should have an immediate correspondence with the viewpoint of commonsense. In fact Newton said very definitely that absolute time is something "which is itself and from its own nature flows equally without relation to anything external". Relative time is to be distinguished from absolute time for "the natural days are truly unequal, though they are commonly considered as equal, and used for a measure of time".

Newton was the first thinker clearly to distinguish between the perceptual and the conceptual and to see that the objectivity which science demands is unattainable apart from the use of concepts, or, in modern parlance 'models'. The relation between these models or constructs and uninformed sense was to occupy generations of scientists and philosophers down to Poincaré, Russell and Popper. The second thing to note about Newton's theory in this context is that it was tied up with the physical and mathematical requirements of the rest of Newton's view of mechanics. Newton thought that we did know that there was such a thing as absolute motion and that this required the posits of absolute space and time. A further posit was required, moreover, in the notion of force. Thirdly and finally, Newton spoke of space as the Divine 'sensorium'. 'God, by existing always and everywhere, constitutes Duration and Space'. From this it would seem that, although at first sight the absolute view of space and time would make it easier to regard God as transcendent than on any other view, there is much in Newton's work to encourage a type of immanentism which is only in our own day beginning to attract the sympathetic attention of a certain type of 'liberal' theologian.

It was Leibniz who took up the cudgels in favour of the 'relational' view and the controversy concerning it is to be found in his famous correspondence with Clarke, Newton's pupil. In Leibniz's view time is an order of succession and space is an order of co-existences. Therefore we do not need to posit hypothetical moments or points, and in this respect Leibniz could feel that he was being more faithful to the Newtonian injunction to get rid of superfluous hypotheses than the master himself. 'Instants without the things are nothing at all', and 'space is the place of things, and not the place of God's ideas'. But Leibniz, however pertinent his analysis up to this point, thereafter faced a difficulty. The spatial had already been excluded from the domain of the substantial by him on the ground that substance could have no truck with the divisible. Our spatial and temporal awareness could, therefore, only be accommodated within the fold of our perceptions, not however, the clear and distinct perceptions which belong to the purely conceptual, but what he described as 'confused' perceptions. From this it is evident that Leibniz found the task of relating the perceptual to the conceptual as difficult as did his contemporaries. It was in fact his disagreement with both Newton and Leibniz that was to set Kant on the track of an entirely new approach to the problem.

The modern view has favoured Leibniz rather than Newton although the concept of 'event' and the overcoming of the dichotomy between space and time in the concept of space-time is something that even Leibniz had no idea of. It is Einstein who was responsible for the revolution in our approach to what after all is an old problem. The philosophical, and indeed the scientific, treatment of space and time had hitherto been linked up with the notion of "things", or, in a more sophisticated way, with 'substances'. Einstein substituted this vocabulary by the vocabulary of 'events', each event being related to the other through a relation called an 'interval', and such that any event can be analysed into a time-element and a space-element. An attempt to bring the philosophical treatment of space and time into line with the new theories can be found in the work of

Russell, Alexander, Whitehead and C. D. Broad. The word 'event' would suggest that, according to the new physics, time has a certain primacy. If this be so it would certainly amount to a reversing of the traditional rationalist emphasis on space and geometry and its concomitant spatializing of time, a reversal which might put the experiencing subject in the centre of the picture more than the physicists have ever admitted before, and in a way which the work of men like Heisenberg would seem to encourage.

Subjective and Objective Space and Time

To consider space and time as absolute, as Newton did, amounts to considering them as objective, and it is with objective space and time that scientists are after all concerned. After Newton, however, there came a succession of philosophers who emphasised the opposite side of the picture, the space and time that we are aware of in our own experience. To begin with it was easier to make out a case for the subjectivity of time than for the subjectivity of space, for our spatial experience does, *prima facie*, seem to put us in touch, whether literally or otherwise, with a reality that is non-subjective. The business of analysing just what this involves belongs to epistemology.

It is to Locke that the credit largely goes for realising that there is a subjective aspect to our awareness of time. Our notion of 'duration', he said, comes to us from the flow of ideas in our mind, and not, as philosophers like Hobbes had thought, from our perception of motion. Now the awareness of change certainly presupposes something permanent, and on this Locke spoke with as clear a voice as did Kant years later. However, as Locke followed Descartes in respect of his theory of the self, the required contrast with something permanent was provided by our lasting awareness of ourselves, and it is this which forms the most notable difference between Locke's and Kant's theory of inner sense. It was Locke who pointed out, for the first time, that in the case of space we were dealing with 'lasting distance, all of whose parts exist together', whereas in the case of time we dealt with 'perishing distance, of which no two parts exist together but follow each other in succession'. It is evident from these remarks of Locke that he had given some thought to the problem of the measurement of time, and, for all his interest in the phenomena of inner sense, it was his view that there was such a thing as objective time, and that the objective standard of reference which was necessary if we were to 'measure' time could be found in the movements of the heavenly bodies. It would not be by any means correct, therefore, to speak of Locke as a "subjectivist". For Berkeley, on the other hand, there is no other time than the succession of ideas. How these are to be synchronized in a world consisting of finite spirits Berkeley does not explicitly say. The solution of occasionalism is not open to him as he states very definitely his opposition to this way out in the course of his *Principles*. On the subject of space, however, Berkley has a great deal to say that is of value. It was Berkeley who, for the first time, introduced into philosophy the notion of separate sensible spaces (in his *Essay on Vision*) and he showed that our concept of sensible space as such was built up thanks to the correlation of visual, tactual and kinaesthetic spaces.

Hume's* discovery that the causal relation was a temporal and not a logical one brought time into the forefront of philosophical discussion in a way it had never been before. Hume saw that space and time were not, in the strict sense, perceptual objects at all, but the nearest he could get to offering a solution was to suggest that they were nothing more than the "manner" in which our perceptions came to us. He thus in a way anticipated what Kant was to say later, that although space and time were not themselves "given" they were nevertheless presupposed in whatever was sensibly given.

Kant looked upon space and time as forms of intuition, that is to say, subjective forms without which we would not have experience at all. He set himself against Newton in insisting that space and time were not entities of any kind whatsoever and no less against Leibniz in holding that space and time could not be understood merely in terms of the relation between things. The former alternative was excluded as experience gave us no clue concerning anything 'absolute' at all, and the latter alternative

* For a further treatment of Hume's view of time see p. 161 ff.

was excluded because to speak of "things" and the relations between them already presupposes what we are setting out to establish, that is, the existence of space and time. It follows from the latter consideration that we cannot derive our knowledge of space and time from experience since that experience already presupposes them, and, therefore, we have no other alternative before us but to say that space and time are *a priori*, that is to say, as Kant interpreted this phrase, universal and necessary. The notion of *a priori concepts* was a familiar one in Kant's own day. But Kant saw that it would be improper to speak of 'concepts' of space and time for any particular part of space or time stood to space and time in the relation of part to whole rather than in the relation of instance to genus. Therefore, since our awareness of space and time cannot be spoken of as conceptual we must speak of this awareness as intuitional. In telling us that space and time are *a priori* forms of pure intuition and in denying that they are entities Kant was by no means speaking of them as illusory. His central stress was on the transcendental ideality (their function in making experience possible) and the empirical reality (their being true of experience) of space and time. The forms of intuition are therefore not *merely* subjective, but their subjectivity constitutes the transcendental framework which is the condition of the *objectivity* of experience.

It is not possible within a short compass to do more than comment very briefly on the treatment which Kant gave of space and time both in the Aesthetic and elsewhere in his *Critique of Pure Reason*. In saying that space is one of the forms of pure intuition Kant was not only saying something about the foundation of our perceptual experience, but also, in his view, he was providing an intuitional foundation for geometry. Apart from this, however, it is important to appreciate the newness of Kant's posing of the problem. It is he who asks for the first time not the question 'What are space and time' but 'What is the *function* of space and time in our experience'. Kant has often been criticised for his ignoring of the nature of physical space. But Kant is prevented from dealing with this by reason of his sharp distinction between intuitions and concepts. He regarded sensible space as foundational to all scientific investigation in a way which, at least in the course of verification, it surely is. His analysis of sensible space may show up unfavourably against Berkeley's until we remember that, in Kant's view, one space is the presupposition of all the different spaces. In discerning a formal element in our sensibility Kant was certainly discerning something new and this is a point to remember lest we associate Kant's formalism merely with the intellectual faculties. The problem of the distinction between subjective and objective time is taken up by Kant in his treatment of causality, whether or no we may be convinced by the solution offered by him there. The whole of the Analytic is bound up with time which Kant thought was as foundational to the natural sciences as was space to geometry. It is, finally, Kant's whole treatment of space and time which provides the framework for his definition of what it means for something to 'exist', and which provides him with the vantage-point for denying that we can say anything positive at all concerning what falls outside space and time. It is this which is the ground for his attack on rational theology, and for his refusal to be drawn into any positive characterisation of what noumena may be said to be. The price paid is an inevitable one—the insistence that we can only be said to 'know' what falls within the world of appearances.

It was Bergson rather than any one else who presented the most thoroughly subjective account of time. Indeed in Bergson's case the treatment of time is not an adjunct to the rest of his philosophy but the very heart of his whole metaphysic. Bergson's main grouse is that philosophers have nearly all distorted time (and this goes for Kant too) by making the mistake of spatializing it, and in so doing have ignored what he calls 'duration' or real time, poetically described as the 'continuous progress of the past which gnaws into the future and swells as it advances.' Along with this goes what could be called an inversion of materialism; space and matter, instead of being primary, are offshoots of the time process, what is left behind as a kind of degenerate by-product of the passage of the *élan vital*. What is of interest here is the way in which Bergson rejects the traditional geometric source of the philosophical treatment of space and time, the vocabulary of points and instants, the 'cinematographical' approach, as he dubs it. Not since the days of Heraclitus had there been such an insistence on process, such a rejection of the corpuscular and the minute. To insist that movement and change can only be grasped through intuition was, *ipso facto*, to deny that time can be regarded as having any extensive magnitude at all. For Bergson, as his critics pointed out, there can hardly be any such thing as physical time.* On the contrary, for him, it is "time lived" which is primary and which is erected into a metaphysical principle. The most readable critique of this whole approach is to be found in an article published by Russell in the *Monist* for 1912 in which Bergson's philosophy is shown to merit a large number of unflattering epithets such as 'irrational', 'unscientific', 'mystical' and the like. But, when all is said and done, it was Bergson and none other, who lifted the treatment of space and time out of its traditional scientific background and who provided a treatment which—although unacceptable to the philosopher who believes that philosophy should be as scientific as possible—in intention at least, centred it in an experience intrinsically human, the experience of duration as 'lived'.

The Unreality of Space and Time

The history of philosophy has not been lacking in exponents of the view that, speaking for the moment loosely, space and time compare unfavourably with the rest of reality. To maintain that space is unreal was the lesser temptation, for, at least in the case of space, the various parts are coexistent. Time, however, has a "here, nowhere" character. Neither the past nor the future can be said to 'exist', and the present is a razor's edge extraordinarily difficult to define. There have been various philosophical grounds for holding that space and time are 'unreal', the most famous of which were put forward by Zeno the Eleatic. The so-called paradoxes of Zeno were put forward by their originator with a definite purpose in view, the purpose of showing that the very concept of change was self-contradictory and that Parmenides was therefore right in saying that reality was unchanging. For example, Zeno tells us that at each

* This would need some qualification in a more detailed study of Bergson's treatment of time.

instant an arrow in flight is simply where it is. Therefore, there can be no such thing as a state of motion. Or again, Achilles will never be able to overtake the tortoise because between any two instants he will have to 'traverse' an infinite number of instants which is a sheer impossibility.

A very similar appeal to self-contradiction can be found in Bradley's *Appearance and Reality.* Taking space first, Bradley says that space is not a mere relation, for any particular space must consist of extended parts, and this would mean that space is a relation of spaces, which is self-contradictory. Space would seem to be a relation between terms which can never be found. The dilemma can be put in another way too. Any particular extension must have some quality and so we can legitimately raise the question as to what the relation is between this quality and extension itself. As for time, if time is a relation between units which have no duration, then we cannot speak of the whole as having any duration. Or (the parallel to the second formulation of the dilemma concerning space) how are we to combine the qualitative content of time with the time which it fills? The conclusion, it is to be noted, is not that space and time are 'unreal', but that they are mere appearances, and appearances, although in contrast with reality, are 'adjectival' to reality, that is to say they 'qualify' reality. A searching criticism of the whole method of employing logic for the purpose of establishing conclusions which conflict with commonsense can be found in Russell's book *Our knowledge of the external world.* The appeal to self-contradiction has certainly been one of the chief weapons of the philosopher throughout the history of philosophy, but how useful such an appeal may be raises the issue of how far formal logic can advance philosophical discovery, a matter on which Kant had some valuable things to say.

A vehement protagonist of the view that time is unreal was the Cambridge philosopher McTaggart, who also based his arguments on an appeal to self-contradiction, but in a different way from Bradley. Every event in time is past, present or future, but no event can be all these at the same time, that is to say, they are self-contradictory predicates, and therefore the time-series is unreal. This line of argument is more open to refutation than Bradley's, for no one has ever maintained that one and the same event can be past, present and future at the same time. McTaggart, moreover, could have concluded that events themselves were unreal, but this was evidently not part of his intention. The fact of change in the world cannot be denied. It has been, for the most part, as Russell has tried to show, an inadequate view of logic that has been responsible for philosophers' refusal to recognise it. Above, all, the mathematical treatment of continuity has certainly thrown new light on the paradoxes which troubled Zeno and his successors.

On the other hand, the way of thinking which insists on the unreality of *time* especially calls for a certain appreciation. Behind much of 'idealist' argumentation lies the insight that time is not a 'thing', not a substance. To this even the plain empiricist would agree. The peculiarity of time forces itself upon us in spite of the physicists' teaching that we should no longer operate with the concepts of space *and* time but with the concept of space-time. Time has a certain primacy, as Kant saw, in that not only our data of inner sense, but no less our spatial awareness falls in a time-order. The past does not exist, but *has* existed and we are aware of some of it through the experience of memory, however difficult it may be to analyse exactly what that involves. In the case of the future we have no such undisputed faculty, or at least the data are too scanty for us to generalise with assurance concerning them. The present, which should be the surest of all the temporal dimensions, is the hardest of all to pin down and it slips from our reach. In the face of these peculiarities about time, one approach finds in time the most important aspect of all human experience. This is the mystical approach of Bergson. To the Absolutist, however, time seems inconsistent with the perfection and changelessness with which the Absolute is surely endowed. Logical arguments do but serve as buttresses for what is, after all, a matter of metaphysical conviction. Behind Zeno's paradoxes stands the Parmenidean One. Even a philosopher like Russell, whose contribution to the realist analysis of space and time in this century has been an outstanding one, has felt the fascination of the unchanging world of Pythagorean numbers, and has written that 'to realize the unimportance of time is the gate of wisdom'.

x Causation

Introduction

AMONG the concepts pertinent to man's investigation of nature, there can be no doubt that the concept of causality is of crucial importance. Aristotle's fourfold division of causes into formal, material, efficient and final had been founded on the Greek experience of creativity in the plastic arts. To some extent it covered up the controversy between mechanism and teleology which was to appear later. It was the finalist interpretation of causation which dominated the Middle Ages because the notion of purpose obviously fitted in so well with a metaphysical system centred on the concept of the existence of God. When, in the eighteenth century, Leibniz took pains to offer an 'explanation' of how the mechanical and teleological accounts of nature were reconcilable, he was certainly aware that it was no easy task to provide a rational ground for matters which, in his deep-seated piety, Sir Isaac Newton had taken for granted. The concept of causality had been given a metaphysical use by a succession of philosophers. It had been employed to infer to the existence of God and to infer to the existence of the so-called external world. The causal principle had been regarded as a principle eminently suited to take the inquiring mind beyond the data immediately before it.

Small wonder, then, that it took some time for philosophers to realise that it was a concept which was in use above all in science. The task of the scientist is essentially that of discovering causal lines among phenomena. In so doing the scientist takes it for granted that there is some order among events. If, conceivably, this order were so intricate that we were unable to identify particular causal lines, then nature would be quite opaque to us. In certain spheres, in some branches of medicine for example, we come up against such instances of opacity. It is thanks to the gradualness of change and the repetitive nature of physical events that man's investigation of nature is not without fruit. But what for the scientist is a practical problem, the problem of isolating what is relevant to what in nature, poses itself in a somewhat different way to the philosopher.

The metaphysical problem of causality may be stated in the following way. In saying that C causes E we are affirming that C is different from E for otherwise there would be no ground for our speaking of C as compared with E. And yet in affirming a relation between C and E I affirm that they are in some way continuous. How is this difference and this continuity to be reconciled? It was Hume who first appreciated the difficulty of the problem and felt convinced that all previous philosophical treatments of it had been misguided. It is, therefore, with a brief account of the theories which Hume opposed that it is proper for us to begin.

Causal Necessity as Logical Necessity

The rationalists, among whom Leibniz may be regarded as an example, looked upon the relation of C and E as an analytic one. C implied E. Now if the relation between C and E is regarded in this way, as a completely logical one, then, in denying any particular causal proposition, I am committing a self-contradiction. In saying for example that 'His cold was not caused by getting wet' I am contradicting myself, that is to say I am saying something like what I say when I utter the words 'Mrs. Jones is not a woman.' If C and E are involved in mutual entailment it means to say that E *follows from* C, that C and E are terms in an argument. It should, therefore, be possible for us to have insight into particular causes, for, since C is the ground of E, just by examining C I should be able to infer to E. In reducing the relation of cause and effect to that of ground and consequent it is quite clear that the rationalists expunged all trace of temporality from causal sequences; such sequences were regarded as being purely logical, and instead of the relation of before and after, we were left with the relation of implication. The rationalists, it must be remembered, believed that logic (Aristotelian logic) was the key to reality, and it is this belief which lies at the root of their theory of causality.

But, if the theory were true, it would be possible to 'demonstrate' that C causes E and the scientist's detailed study of nature would be superfluous.

The rationalist account had an initial attractiveness by reason of its provision for the element of 'necessity' which appears to attend our concept of causality. In saying that C causes E the assumption is that E necessarily follows C. In their identifying this necessity with logical necessity, Hume showed, however, that the rationalists were doing something unwarranted. They had failed to recognise the difference between C and E, a difference which, as was said in the beginning, is part and parcel of what we mean by the causal relation. The relation between C and E, Hume showed, is a temporal one and the difference between C and E amounts to the difference between one event in time and the event which succeeds it. Since the contrary of a causal proposition is not self-contradictory this is a clear sign that the relation between C and E is not analytic but synthetic. In saying that it is synthetic we are saying that the predicate of a causal proposition is not contained in the subject. A causal proposition then, as Kant pointed out, is a genuinely ampliative one. It tells us more than what is merely implied in the subject. From this follows the circumstance that the inspection of a single event will not inform us about its cause or its effect (which would have been the case if the causal relation had been analytic). Our causal inferences do not have demonstrative cogency. Or, as the late F. H. Waismann used to put it, E *follows* C but does not *follow from* C. If causal relations concern 'events' and not 'terms' in an argument we have no alternative but to rely on experience for informing us about any particular causal connection. Events do not necessitate. Their relations are *de facto* and not *de logico*. In pointing out that, whatever causal necessity meant, it certainly was not the same thing as logical necessity, Hume made a most important discovery and for the first time stated in so many words that the causal relation was a matter which concerned not the logic of formal argument but the discovery of the actual world.

The 'Production' theory

The second theory of causation which, in Hume's view was incorrect, was the theory that C in some way 'produces' E or 'makes it happen'. Perhaps this is close to the commonsense way of looking at causal connections. The match, or rather, the striking of the match, "produces" the flame. The efficient causality of which Aristotle had spoken in his example of the plastic artist creating a work of art was lodged in the artist's efficacy or agency. This was further taken up by the mediaeval theologians for whom the paradigm of agency was lodged in God Himself. Causal agency, then, was associated with power and with creativity, and the paradigm of creativity was to be found in God who was the source of the entire created universe. In Christian theology two distinct emphases concerning the Divine nature were interwoven. In order to create, the Divine mind must needs have the capacity of thought, for without ideas according to the patterns of which finite things could be 'designed', there could be no such thing as 'creation'. At the same time the executive capacity involved in creating presupposes that God has a will. These two emphases were stressed variously by a succession of theologians. The production theory of causality, it must remembered, was used most convincingly by those who drew on this Divine analogy, as for example, by Bishop Berkeley. The attributing of volition to God at all was, it can be seen, based on a piece of anthropocentric thinking. The ancient Greeks had for the most part confined their "voluntaristic" speculations to the mythical inhabitants of Mount Olympus. It was the "gods" who could be conceived to have wills and to suffer jealousies and indeed almost all the ills which human flesh is heir to. The highest principle of all, the ultimate object of metaphysical endeavour, was, above all, something *intelligible* and not something which possessed a volitional nature. It was the Judaic conception of Yahveh which brought in the voluntaristic element which had been lacking in the Greek tradition. The fact remains, however, that all our thinking about the nature of God's will is based on an analogy with our own human powers of volition. It was claimed that in human volition we have a first-hand experience of bringing something about, of, one might say, "being a cause". The relation between the will and its effect purported to be the one intelligible connection we know, the one case of a 'necessary' relation about which there could be no doubt simply because we could experience the very 'producing' in ourselves. Hume saw that the only way to begin criticising the theory was by examining its presupposition, the presupposition that we have any such direct insight into the relation between our will and its effects at all.

In his *Enquiry* Hume considers whether the will has the power to produce either motion, that is, a physical effect, or whether at will we can raise up a new idea. As to the first, he very properly points out that the union of soul and body is a most mysterious one, and from all the controversy which still abounds concerning the precise difference between men and robots it would seem that we are scarcely nearer a key to the mystery than people were in Hume's time. Hume's point is that, so far from the relation between soul and body, will and physicality, being an intelligible one, it is of all relations the most opaque. As far as the control of the will over the organs of the body is concerned our capacities are most limited. We are not able to move all the organs of the body (and Hume thought it was providential that we could not) and what we can and cannot move we have to learn from experience. As we advance in anatomical knowledge we find that no organ of the body is moved directly but that any movement comes about consequent on a long and complicated series of events in which muscles, nerves etc. come into play. So that, as far as producing motion is concerned, it is plain that we learn the influence of our will from experience alone and what experience discovers is not any subtle source of causal efficacy but only that one event does in fact succeed the other. As to the command of the will over inner experience we find that this too is most limited. This command, for one thing, varies much. In times of sickness or fatigue we have little control over the succession of feelings, images and the like. Over our passions we may have scant control at the best of times.

There remains one last consideration which had appealed to some philosophers, the consideration that the source of our idea of causal efficacy arises from our experience of resistance.

Both Thomas Reid and later, Whitehead, set store by this experience in their defence of a realist theory of knowledge, and Bradley found in the 'effort' of will the most significant thing about its nature. Hume, however, reminds us that we, after all, attribute power to many objects where there is no question of our experiencing any resistance. Most notably we attribute power to God and presumably the fiats of the Divine will are irresistible. We attribute power to the mind in common thinking and motion and here too there is no question of there being any resistance. Hume does, however, admit that although the credentials of our idea of power are untrustworthy and although they afford us no accurate and precise idea of power, yet there is a kind of animal 'nisus' which contributes to the 'vulgar idea, or as we should say today, contributes to the commonsense conception of it.

Hume's analysis of our experience of volition (and Gilbert Ryle has carried the analysis still further in his *Concept of Mind*) left him with the task of accounting for our having the idea of causation at all. We do not phrase the problem in this way today. But for Hume, as a strict empiricist, the idea of causality was a challenge simply because it was an idea untraceable in any obvious way to any source in sense experience. Hume's account, therefore, needs separate treatment, for although much of what he said was subsequently incorporated in what we call the 'regularity' theory, his own interest largely centred in certain psychological considerations concerning how we come to have the idea at all, rather than, as in the case of the modern philosopher reflecting on the philosophy of science, in the status of the concept itself.

Hume's treatment of Causation

Hume's own analysis of the idea of causality divides itself into three parts, his account of what is perceived, what is felt and what is believed. What is perceived, Hume thinks, is merely uniformity of sequence. We perceive events to be 'conjoined' not 'connected'. The feeling is that of being necessitated, a feeling which arises thanks to custom and which shows the wisdom of nature in that the basis of our being able to transcend the immediately given is made dependent not on our feeble powers of 'cogitation' but on something which does not require 'taking thought'. What is believed is that causal happenings occur which we endow with the characteristics of 'necessary connection', 'power', 'force' and 'energy'. In this way the leading example of the mind's tendency to 'spread itself on external objects' reveals itself. Belief is outwardly directed. It is not rational but we can certainly style it "reasonable". In speaking of belief in terms of vivacity of ideas, however, Hume makes belief indistinguishable from feeling. The repetitions, on the basis of which our feeling of being necessitated arises, are not, as Popper has pointed out, *de facto*. Even the perception of a simple repetition can only come about from a point of view. To look upon belief as an occurrence instead of as a disposition is, as the current jargon goes, to make a category mistake. Even so, it would be correct to say that Hume limits reason in order to make room for belief, however inadequate that theory of belief may be.

Hume's treatment of causality had far-reaching consequences. His affirmation that the causal nexus is synthetic and not analytic made it palpable that the causal concept concerned matters temporal, not matters logical. As such the inference could be drawn that the causal principle is something which is valid within and not without experience. It is significant that no one dared to use the causal principle as a creative principle after the work of Hume. It was of course not difficult for Hume's successors to point out the weaknesses in his theory. It can be shown, for example, that the concept of cause involves invariable sequence but that invariable sequence need not involve causality. In explaining 'unique' events, as say in history, we employ the concept of cause even where there is no regularity. Invariable sequence, as Mill showed, sometimes arises from events being the co-effects of some third factor, as in the case of the sequence of day and night being the co-effects of the relation of the earth to the sun.

It was a matter of epistemological importance that Hume should have drawn attention to the presence of elements in experience which were not traceable to any impression. Our ideas of space and time, as also our concept of causality, present a challenge to the strict empiricist. Hume's ingenuity lay in his method of meeting this challenge, the method of looking for the sources of these "ideas" in the observer rather than in the object. But what seemed most paradoxical to any thinker impressed with the objectivity of scientific judgements was that, on Hume's showing, scientific laws appeared to be based on habits of mind. If this were so, surely the objectivity of such judgements would be a mere chimera? Kant's reaction to Hume amounts to two things, his sympathy with the Humean method of tracing back certain elements in experience to the experiencer, a method which his acquaintance with the work of Copernicus had already predisposed him to be in favour of, and his desire to 'save' the objectivity of causal judgements in science. To refute Hume would be to show that the concept of causality is not, in any sense, derived from experience. Kant's attempted refutation consists in showing that so far from our concept of cause being derived from experience it is a concept which makes experience possible. Kant generalises Hume's question about the concept of causality* and seeks to show that the concept is not the only one which cannot be traced back to any particular sense impression. Kant may not have succeeded in showing that irreversible succession amounts to objectivity or that irreversibility indicates a causal nexus, but to criticise him effectively it would be necessary to show the untenability of the whole transcendental standpoint, a task which is not so easy and the onus of which lies on the critic. Later-day empiricists have pointed to the presupposed concept of uniformity of nature which underlies any specific causal investigation, and Bertrand Russell has admitted the postulate of separate causal lines among the postulates included in his later work on human knowledge. Whether such admissions are as far from the sort of thing Kant had in mind when he spoke of synthetic a *priori* concepts, as empiricists in their dread of the synthetic *a priori* imagine, must give us pause.

Recent treatments of Causation

If Hume's discovery that causal inferences are made on the

* Vide *Prolegomena concerning any future metaphysic,* Introduction p. 7. Mahaffy and Bernard Edition.

basis of the perception of uniform sequences is shorn of the psychological accompaniments which Hume thought went along with this perception, we are left with what, in this century, has been called the regularity theory of causation. The theory amounts, not to a thesis as to how we have come to have the conception of one event causing another, but to a thesis concerning the *meaning* of causality. To say that C is the cause of E is to say that C regularly precedes E. One improvement made by subsequent theorists on Hume's treatment of regular sequence was to modify the oversimplification involved in speaking of C and E. These should properly be construed as sets of conditions. So that, when we style the task of the scientist as the search for invariant relations, these relations are to be held to obtain, not between atomically conceived events, but between clusters of conditions the inter-relationships between which may be of very considerable complexity. The apparent exceptions to regularity that certain aspects of quantum theory may seem to involve (that is to say all the range of micro-phenomena which are spoken of as indeterministic) can then be seen as falling within the scope of this complexity, thus amounting, not to an exception to overall uniformity, but to a recognition that the causal lines in nature are sometimes of a degree of intricacy which makes them difficult for us, with our present state of knowledge, to unravel.

Hume was, no doubt, too simple-minded in his assumption that regularities can be perceived *simpliciter*. Ernst Mach was probably the last of a distinguished line of empiricists who believed that the ultimate terminus of scientific verification was to be found in mere perception. The procession of those who saw the guiding role that concepts have in the investigation of nature proceeds from Copernicus, through Kant and Poincaré to philosophers like Karl Popper today. If what such philosophers say is true, then, implied in the very perception of regularity, is a question put by reason to nature, in the answering of which the regularity discloses itself.

Another puzzle to which critics of the regularity theory have drawn our attention is that the theory would seem to deny the applicability of the causal concept to the investigation of 'unique' events. Whether the social and historical sciences require some principle of explanation over and above the 'deterministic' one is a question which apologists of the teleological idea have invariably raised. The regularity theory, however, can always claim that, even though we admit that any particular historical situation represents a unique amalgam of circumstances, in attributing the causes of a war to the ambitions of X, the economic condition of country Y and the 'incident' Z which triggered off the whole affair, we are, after all, invoking causal principles which do, in one way or another, appeal to regularity.

The further objection, that the regularity theory does away with the element of necessity which attends our commonsense conception of a cause, needs more detailed examination, for this opens up the whole problem of induction which, one might say, has taken the place of the old problem of causation as such in recent discussions. What is the "problem" of induction? The mark of deductive inferences is that the conclusions are built up on the basis of premisses and that the conclusion follows from the premisses. Such inferences constitute demonstrations and wherever we have a corpus of such inferences we have what is called a 'system' as, say, the system of Euclidean geometry. The puzzle about induction is precisely that inductive inferences do not have this demonstrative character. One of the main things which give Hume his distinguished place in the history of philosophy is his recognition of the difference between induction and deduction. Hume pointed out that in making inductive inferences we assume that there is an order of events but that this is, after all, an assumption and something that cannot be rationally justified. We transfer our experience of the past to the future,* and this again cannot be justified, for the future is by definition non-existent. "The supposition", he says, "that the future resembles the past, is not founded on arguments of any kind, but is derived entirely from habit". In making an inductive inference there is, therefore, a gap between our premisses and conclusion because our premisses concern the past and present and our conclusion concerns the future. The final puzzle is that the multiplication of instances seems to

* It is also, of course, true that we transfer our experience of the present to the *past*.

strengthen our inference, although why this should be so is again inexplicable. The cogency of deductive arguments is such that the pioneer investigators of the nature of induction were understandably in doubt as to whether inductive arguments deserved the name of 'inference' at all. (Similar qualms are felt in this century by some who write about 'moral reasoning'). Once it is admitted that induction is not on all fours with demonstration the way is open for an independent investigation into its nature.

Modern techniques in mathematics and statistics have thrown considerable light on this whole field of philosophic investigation. The puzzle about continuity which, as we saw earlier, underlies what is meant by saying that C is the cause of E, was insoluble at the empirical level. Russell and others have, on the other hand, stressed that continuity is, after all, a mathematical concept, and the language of series and class which Hume had used and in so doing no doubt put British empiricism on the track it has followed since, has received detailed elucidation in Russell's *Principia Mathematica*. The serious problem of demarcation which arises when we say that C is the cause of E (even expanding this to mean sets of conditions which tend to be co-related) is something which raises serious metaphysical problems. On what grounds can I limit the set of conditions which I call C? Are these grounds merely pragmatic ones? If so, we are hardly entitled to speak of 'grounds'. The traditional metaphysicians throughout the history of philosophy had found the problem so puzzling that they had resort to the hypothesis of a First Cause, which was not only forthright Aristotelianism but also, to their way of thinking, sound theology. Cutting through this welter of metaphysical speculation the contemporary theorist offers us the hypothesis of separate causal lines in nature. If this were not so, he will tell us, it would be quite impossible to set any limit to any particular empirical enquiry.

The certainty which attends deductive inferences is seen to be unobtainable in inductive inferences, and this without regret. About the future, after all, who can say more than that such and such will in all probability happen. Probability is conceived not in the Humean manner in terms of patterns of expectation in the observer's mind, but in terms of statistical averages, the sort of calculation that is especially called for in the field of quantum mechanics. The interesting thing about induction is now found to be its 'mixed' character. If we recognise the leading role which hypotheses play in the investigation of nature we make room legitimately for an element of deduction in induction itself—something which the classical empiricists would have found paradoxical indeed. No less remarkable than the uniformities that we find in nature is the element of diversity, those factors which resist the easy adoption of an over-all theoretic system. If we seem to require the presupposition of uniformity, which is after all closely tied up with the postulate of similarity, we seem no less to need the postulate of dissimilarity. Also the entire technique of formulating hypotheses surely depends on the human capacity for asking questions, something without which the 'descriptions' of the natural scientist could not come into being. The whole discussion of induction, at any rate, it is quite evident, has moved far from the original demand of those philosophers who had grown up within the shadow of the rationalist tradition that induction should be 'justified'. The contemporary stress is on an understanding of the differentiae of inductive procedures and the implications of Kant's teaching in this respect, that the method of experiment is essentially that of putting questions to nature, have perhaps not even yet been fully brought to light.

PART FOUR: GOD, MAN AND VALUE

XI Mind and Body

Introduction

On the commonsense view the relation between the mind and the body presents no problem at all. At one pole we have apparently 'mental' activities like imagining, and, at the other, 'bodily' activities such as the processes of respiration and digestion. The way in which vitamin deficiencies can cause a certain dulling of intellectual power and the way in which prolonged mental depression can result in physical symptoms like sleeplessness and lack of appetite the ordinary man takes in his stride, seeing them not as evidence for a mysterious two-way traffic beteen disparate orders of being, but as matters of everyday knowledge. The corpus of information provided by the sciences of physiology and neurology comes as confirmation of what we believe as a matter of course in our daily life, that is, that the mental and the physical are extremely closely related indeed. A philosophical problem concerning the relation between the mind and the body arises, however, as soon as we begin to reflect on the meaning of three concepts, the mind, matter and causality. It is in fact the complicated history of these three concepts that has given rise to the various theories about the mind/body relation. Moreover, this history belongs peculiarly to modern times, that is to say, from about the seventeenth century up to the present day.

The mainstream of developed Greek thought had given primacy to the immaterial factor, whether this be conceived of as impersonal 'nous' or as the individual soul. Matter, in Plato, is regarded as the principle of intractability, standing for all that is intractable to the Ideas. At the same time its importance as the source of individuation cannot be forgotten. It was Aristotle's conception of form and matter, however, which set the pattern for centuries of theorising about the relation of the mind and the body, for the form/matter distinction lent itself not only to the analysis of things in physical nature but also to the analysis of the concrete nature of man himself. Aristotle had defined the soul as 'the first entelechy of a natural body endowed with the capacity of life'. Given that matter be form in an undeveloped state, as Aristotle had claimed, some of the conclusions of Lucretius in his *Rerum Natura* must inevitably follow :—'Now I assert that the *mind* and the *soul* are kept together in close union and make up a single nature, but that the directing principle which we call mind and understanding is the head so to speak and reigns paramount in the whole body.' But when Lucretius speaks of the nature of the mind and soul as bodily he is by no means anticipating Watson, but speaking quite literally. The body of which the mind is constituted is, he says, 'extremely fine and formed of exceedingly minute bodies.' The influence of Democritus notwithstanding, we are further assured that the nature of the body and the soul must be a 'joint nature'.

Two centuries later it was clear to Plotinus that whether or not the soul were immortal would stand or fall with the status assigned to the body in man. In the *Enneades* he says that 'Hence, if body is a part of us, we are not wholly immortal'. The involvement of the concept of the soul with the concepts of immortality and the existence of God is patent in the writing of men like Plotinus and Tertullian. No less patent is the reliance of mediaeval thinkers on the vocabulary of form and matter in their treating of the relation between the soul and the body. St. Thomas Aquinas says in the *Summa*, 'But since the rational soul is the substantial form of the body, it is impossible that there should be any accidental intermediation between the soul and the body, or between any substantial form and its matter'. The hypothetical pineal gland which Descartes thought it fit to interpose between the mind and the body would, in Aquinas' view, be superfluous.

Interactionism

But in spite of the gamut of Aristotelian concepts which made their way into Cartesian and post-Cartesian philosophy, concepts such as those of essence and accidents, potentiality and actuality, being and becoming, the notion that the soul was in some way the 'form' of the body fell by the wayside except within Catholic theology where it was duly nurtured. It was Descartes who posed the problem of the relation between the mind and the body in its characteristically modern form. The mind was regarded as substantial by Descartes, having as its essence or characteristic activity what he called 'cogitatio' or thought. It is clear from the *Principles of Philosophy*, however, that Descartes did not define 'thought' in any narrow sense, whatever impression he may have left behind elsewhere. He writes, 'By the word thought, I understand all that which so takes place in us that we of ourselves are immediately conscious of it; and, accordingly, not only to understand, to will, to imagine, but even to perceive, are here the same as to think'. Even so the difficulty remained how such a substance could come into relation with a substance whose nature was that of mere 'extension'. The *prima facie* ground of the difficulty which presented itself to Descartes' successors, and which indeed led Descartes himself to his hypothesis about the pineal gland, lay in the very connotation of the term 'substance'. Strictly interpreted, no being could lay claim to the title save God. Furthermore it was of course a mistake, as physiology subsequently showed, to regard consciousness as something *ab initio* independent of physical factors such as the brain and the nervous system.

The interactionist theory in its general form may be stated as follows. If M be taken to stand for the mind and B for the body then the theory holds that M is capable of acting causally on B and B is capable of acting causally on M. It is possible, moreover, for the theory to be stated in a one-sided way so that one sort of interaction is admitted and the other not. An instance of the action of M on B would be the decision to raise my arm followed by the actual doing of the act. All instances of voluntary action are claimed as paradigm cases of such causal transactions. An instance of the action of B on M would be the feeling of malaise following on a rise in body temperature. Perception would also fall within this category. Both classes of examples can be found in abundance and the theory, therefore, has a certain immediate plausibility about it. The exact manner in which the interaction takes place is not only metaphysically puzzling if we are strict substantialists but it is something about which physiologists themselves seem at a loss. We perceive a red patch consequent on the impinging of light-rays on the retina. There seems nonetheless a gap between the series of physical happenings and the occurrence of the experience, or, to put it another way, there seems to be a transition from quantitative change to qualitative change. It is also claimed by critics of interactionism that the theory does not accord with certain principles in physics. If the sequence of physical events B1, B2, B3, B4, suddenly gives rise to M1 are we to assume that the B series therewith comes to an end? If so, this would offend against the continuity of the series of physical events. Not only this, but the law of the Conservation of Energy would also be violated, for energy would presumably be lost when the body affects the mind and *vice versa* when the mind affects the body.

As far as these two objections are concerned one might say, perhaps, first of all, that the series of events B1 etc. could conceivably give rise to M1 without at the same time ceasing to perpetuate itself as a series. The difficulty whether an event of a completely different kind can come about or not, remains. If, however, we say that the mental is nothing more than the physical in another form we are settling for a type of reductionism against which there are grave objections. As for the Law of Conservation of Energy, this is supposed to be applicable only to conservative material systems and thus its relevance here is to be doubted. To deny interaction not only makes it difficult to account for the occurrence of a new sensation (I suddenly feel cold when someone opens the door) but it also makes the presence of artifacts in the world inexplicable. The distinction between artifacts and natural objects will cease to have any meaning. Yet this distinction surely needs to be maintained whether we look upon volition as an independent source of causal efficacy or not. Through action we do have the means of 'interfering' with causal chains in nature even if it be merely to arrest the course of a cold by taking the appropriate medicine. Such studied actions are to be distinguished from reflex actions over which we have no control. It would seem, then, that apart from the prior assumption of dogmatic definitions concerning mind and body as disparate 'substances' we have no foundation for ruling out a *priori* the interaction of the mental and the bodily. Indeed the evidence of everyday experience seems to be all in favour of the hypothesis of interaction, no matter how difficult it may be to lay bare its metaphysical foundations.

The rationalist philosophers who succeeded Descartes, however, thought out a number of ingenious ways of getting round the anomaly which seemed to them to be involved in regarding the self-subsistent, i.e. the substantial, as capable of 'interaction'. All these theories relied, in one way or other, on utilisation of the concept of God as an existent of a unique kind. Occasionalists like Geulincx maintained that when change in one series occurred, whether in the mental series or in the physical series, this was the occasion for God to intervene in order to bring about a corresponding change in the other series. It was God therefore who was the only source of causal efficacy. Such a theory could only appear at all attractive to the theologically-minded, for it amounted to looking upon the world and its happenings as one long series of miracles. It was one thing to call upon God to give a filllip to the entire machinery of nature and another thing to make his constant intervention a matter of necessity. To say the least, such an exigency hardly did credit to the skill of the Creator in the first place. Leibniz agreed that he was "obliged to admit that it is not possible for the soul or any true substance to receive any influence from without, if it be not by the Divine omnipotence." He accordingly hit upon the theoretical device of pre-established harmony according to which "God created the soul, or every other real unity, in the first place in such a way that everything comes into existence from its own substance through perfect spontaneity as regards itself and in perfect harmony with objects outside itself". This amounts to saying that each substance mirrors the entire universe and the harmony between the substances produces "the same effects as if they communicated with each other by a transmission of kinds of qualities, as philosophers generally suppose".

Parallelism

The parallelist doctrine proper is associated largely with the name of Spinoza. It seemed self-evident to Spinoza that the concept of substance could not, without self-contradiction, admit of duality. In his system, therefore, he made room for a duality of attributes instead of a duality of substances in the Cartesian manner. In the corollary to Proposition 21 in his *Ethics* he writes that 'the mind and the body, are one and the same individual, conceived now under the attribute of thought, now under that of extension'. The question of the intervention of God does not arise as the attributes are attributes of God who is the only substance, who is indeed all that is. On Spinoza's metaphysical presuppositions, therefore, there is no difficulty in conceiving how something at the level of mind should be paralleled by something at the level of extension. Subsequent parallelist theories, on the other hand (and there have been other forms of the theory propounded by people like Paulsen, Fechner and others) have not had Spinoza's initial metaphysical advantage.

The central thesis of parallelism can be stated as follows. Although there can be no interaction between the mental series of events and the physical series of events, there can be, and indeed there is, so the theory maintains, a point to point correspondence between the two series of events. For example an act of will is 'paralleled' by an overt action in the physical world, although it would be untrue to say that the act of will had caused the overt action. In this way the theory did justice to the disparateness of the mental and physical series, and gave due deference to the hallowed law of the conservation of energy. The theory also avoided the suspicious break in continuity which seemed inevitable under the hypothesis of interaction. At the same time the theory manifestly rested on certain fallacies. It seemed to assume that cause and effect must always resemble each other, something which we have no ground for believing. Then, if any event in either series could be pointed to which had no parallel in the corresponding series the theory would seem shaky indeed.

The close correlation between brain processes and mental processes which surgical experience in the first Great War brought to light encouraged the hypothesis in the sense that it seemed that, if nothing could actually be found parallel in certain cases the notion of parallelism was correct at least in principle. Even so, it was pertinent to enquire what corresponded in the psychical scheme to the physical 'atoms' or cells and alternately what corresponded in the cerebral scheme to psychical phenomena like desire and attention. A further theorietical blow to parallelism was Lashley's discovery of the equi-potentiality of the cortex, for this showed that apart from certain highly specialised areas, much of the cortex operated according to the principle of mass action and that the association areas were capable of taking over a variety of function if this became necessary owing to damage caused to other parts of the cortex. As far as the 'higher' functioning of the brain was concerned, then, Lashley's work showed that the parallelist hypothesis was incorrect. In any case it would be true to say that, as the twentieth century advanced, both physiology and psychology were increasingly unwilling to look upon the mental and the physical as separate posits at all in the manner in which philosophers had traditionally regarded them.

Epiphenomenalism

Epiphenomenalism represents an attempt on the part of certain philosophers to bring the treatment of the mind/body problem into line with the new 'scientific' approach. If parallelism disallows any causal relation other than within the physical and psychical orders respectively, epiphenomenalism only admits causal relations within the realm of the physical. Part and parcel of the materialist metaphysic, epiphenomenalism regards mental phenomena as mere epiphenomena, that is to say, mere by-products. (On the other hand parallelism had regarded the mental and the physical as being of equal status.) When the body is stimulated by other bodies we experience sensation. When the glands are active we experience emotion. In favour of this theory we have the undoubted fact that there are many automatic processes in the body which do not require the intervention of the mind, processes such as digestion, growth and so on. The close dependence of mental functioning on brain processes too is well known. As against this though, epiphenomenalism, it must be remembered, rests on a general metaphysical hypothesis which itself is questionable, the hypothesis that the laws of physics can account for all the phenomena in the world without exception. The puzzle referred to in connection with the discussion of interactionism remains—how in some cases physical changes give rise to something which is qualititatively distinctive, why, say, the visual perception of news that one has failed in an examination should occasion depression of spirits, or the use of drugs bring about hallucinations. The physical account can carry us a certain way, it can give us the 'conditions' of a particular mental phenomenon, but its qualititative nature, and, when relevant, its feeling tone, remain unaccounted for. Some philosophers claim that we have direct awareness of our own causal activity in voluntary action although the appeal to intuition in philosophy is always most undecisive. It may be that worry is often followed by the onset of organic disorders, but introspection does not yield any clue as to the nature of the relation between the two. The evidence concerning telepathy is not as yet enough to warrant assessment of its relevance to the mind-body problem. Whether we have here a case of genuine communication or a matter of inter-mental causal transaction is still in dispute. Epiphenomenalism, however, does seem to do less than justice to the differentiae of distinctively mental processes, whether these may at the same time always be found to be accompanied by physical correlates or not.

In this connection the older epiphenomenalists may certainly be said to have received fresh ammunition from the ranks of the behaviourists. Although behaviourism is a psychological theory rather than a philosophical one, it has exerted a certain influence on more recent philosophical treatments of the mind-body problem, an influence which may be referred to briefly here. An adjunct of Pavlov's theory of the conditioned response and an extended theoretical development from this theory, behaviourism is essentially a hypothesis about consciousness. It maintains that consciousness is behaviour, thus cutting across the time-honoured distinction between the mind and the body, the inner and the outer. The outer becomes, not the criterion of the inner, but all that there is. Behaviour is public and as such, is conveniently geared to the applicability of experimental techniques. If we take seriously the demand for the unity of the sciences it would follow that, just as in chemistry we observe the behaviour of material particles, so, in a more elaborate way perhaps, we can observe the behaviour of human beings. Just as the laws which govern the behaviour of material particles are essentially laws of reaction, so human behaviour too is to be 'explained' in terms of reaction to stimuli. The thing is, however, that man possesses not only the capacity to react to stimuli but also the capacity to initiate. Many conscious activities have no overt expression in behaviour. The employment of words is, after all, not just the making of sounds but the communication of meanings. Many of the higher level human activities, indeed, seem to have been brought about by man's ability to *inhibit* his reactions, by his ability to use symbolism alternative to the crude symbolism of 'reactive' actions.

Now the desire to bypass dualism has always been a genuine motive among philosophers of often diverse persuasions. Dissatisfaction with the 'transaction' language of the traditional treatment of the mind/body relation stimulated Bertrand Russell's neutral monist phase, represented in his book *Analysis of Mind.* He was, at the same time, significantly, unable to accommodate certain stubbornly 'mental' phenomena like sensations and mnemic material within the collocations of neutral entities which were strictly 'material'. Likewise it was doubtful whether William James' 'pure experience' could be organised into collocacations strictly physical. Discussion of the whole problem, however, even during the early part of this century, tended to be on an ontological footing, the achievements of the behaviourists notwithstanding. It was not until the publication of Ryle's *Concept of Mind* in 1949 that an entirely new approach presented itself.

The 'Concept' of Mind

Ryle's avowed purpose in the work of this title is 'not to increase what we know about minds, but to rectify the logical geography of the knowledge which we already possess'. Many of our everyday expressions tend to be systematically misleading. To attempt to reformulate some of these so as to reveal 'the real form of facts' was a project which was fully in line with the spirit which prompted Russell's theory of descriptions and no less fully in line with Wittgenstein's programme of 'showing the fly the way out of the fly bottle'. Grammar would suggest that minds are something that we all 'have', that they are places of which it can be said that ideas, images and the like are 'in' them. The official doctrine, which Ryle associates with Descartes, regards mind as substantial in a unique sense. Just as the substances spoken of as 'physical' are characterised by an attribute peculiar to themselves, i.e. extension, so mental substances are likewise characterised by a counterpart attribute, thought. Parallel to the characteristic activities of physical substances laid down in Newtonian mechanics there are said to be certain characteristic activities of mind, pure intellectual acts (*acta pura*) which Descartes referred to as 'clear and distinct perceptions'. If physical things were public, as they certainly are, minds were ineluctably private, with the attendant consequence that not only were we called upon to make a hazardous inference to the existence of things in the so-called 'external' world but the existence of other minds also seemed to depend on no less hazardous an inference. The consequences of the unhappy bifurcation of nature brought about by Cartesianism are there for all to see in the series of ingenious attempts made by Descartes' successors to bring the sundered worlds together again.

What Ryle has to offer is, first of all, a diagnosis of the mistake which he believes Descartes to have made and furthermore a suggested therapy, which, carefully avoiding ontological language, should enable us to reallocate our concepts so that future mistakes can be avoided. The diagnosis that Ryle offers is to expound the notion of the 'category-mistake', an occupational disease which not only philosophers but even the commonsense man is prone to. The foreign visitor who insists on being shown 'the university' when he has already seen all the constituent institutions, the child who wishes to see 'the division' when all the soldiers have already passed by, and the spectator who wants to know what the 'team spirit' is, over and above the careful fielding, passing of the ball etc.—all such people are making a category mistake. They are looking for a special sort of extra object whereas they should have found what they were seeking in the relationship between the constituent parts which were presented to them. Applying the analogy of these examples Ryle points out the moral—the mind is not another sort of object. 'To talk of a person's mind is not to talk of a repository which is permitted to house objects that something called the physical world is forbidden to house; it is to talk of the person's abilities, liabilities, and inclinations to do and undergo certain sorts of things and of the doing and undergoing of these things in the ordinary world'. The Cartesian myth of the 'ghost in the machine' is thereby demolished, not, however, that Ryle would have us believe that man is a mere machine. But the elucidation of what being a man involves is something which is progressively shown in the analysis of the concepts of knowing how, feeling, willing, and imagining, given later on in his book.

The question arises, in the first place, whether Ryle is correct in his assumption that the dogma of the ghost in the machine is 'the official theory' of mind and whether, in particular, it is mainly Descartes who is responsible for its theoretical formulation. It is no doubt true to say that the traditional rationalist concept of mind grew out of the earlier metaphysical concept of 'the soul'. The notion that theorising was, *par excellence*, the distinctive activity of souls, was encouraged (at least by implication) by Catholicism, for unless man possessed reason he would not be in a position either to formulate, or to be convinced by the truth of, the Five Ways. At the same time the notion that mind was something inherently private was encouraged by the Protestant view of conscience. Descartes thus, in a sense, is heir to a way of thinking which had already been laid down by his predecessors. To point out that mentality can be, and is, exhibited just as much in the performance of intelligent actions as in the exercise of theoretical symbolic operations is something which needed doing, and it is just this which Ryle sets out to do in his *Concept of Mind*.

The history of philosophy (as we saw) is not a stranger to attempts to bypass the dualism of mind and matter. Among recent attempts sense datum language was a piece of theory which bid fair to eliminate the distinction between the two, but which unfortunately did not fulfil the hopes that had been centred on it. The concept of intelligence, provided by psychology, does seem to cut across the mind/body dichotomy in a rather more plausible way. Scientific method has familiarised us with the procedure of replacing the occult by the overt. The one field which remained for its application was the field referred to in our use of 'mental' epithets. Behaviourism showed how much of human life could be analysed in terms of behaviour. Just as scientific laws predict the probable course of events 'mental' epithets like 'intelligent' and 'good-natured' predict the probable behaviour of individuals. Scientific concepts describe a public world. So do 'mental' concepts. Nothing is in principle unknowable or mysterious. On Ryle's view, instead of the 'two-worlds story', we have a homogeneous world in which thought is no longer cordoned off from action. The psychological concepts of attitude and set become the model for the 'dispositional' theory of knowing. Just as an attitude is evidenced in overt ways so a man's dispositional properties are evidenced in his actual behaviour. 'My mind signifies my ability and proneness to do certain sorts of things'. As for 'episodes', those which cannot be brought in under the umbrella of law-like statements may certainly be of importance to the experient, but they cannot be reckoned to be a very important source of knowledge of other minds.

This is not the place for a full exposition of the contents of *The Concept of Mind* which is most certainly the most significant contribution to the subject in this century, nor is it possible to indicate more than sketchily the lines on which it might be criticised. What follows, then, must be taken only as an indication of further possible critical approaches to this important work. Whether the Cartesian dogma parallels the examples that Ryle has given of various category mistakes immediately gives us pause. We learn that the mind is not a 'thing' (the University example). This is incidently what all idealists from Berkeley to Kant and beyond have always insisted on too. We learn that the mind does not have any one characteristic function (the team spirit example). Descartes, however, to do him justice, included a large variety of activities under the term 'thinking'. We learn that the concept of mind is unpackable (the division example) and that, therefore, it is not mysterious. We learn that things which are not ostensively definable are not necessarily occult (the average taxpayer example). We learn that understanding high level generality words involves understanding sets of relationships between different logical types (the Constitution example). We may still, however, not be quite convinced that the category mistakes that Ryle mentions are on all fours with the alleged mistake we make when we speak about 'the mind'. If ordinary language is any guide, (and Ryle picks and chooses among ordinary usages) it is the most natural thing in the world to speak of 'his mind', 'your mind' and so on, although of course it is by no means incumbent on the philosopher to appeal to commonsense as an oracle.

There *does* seem to be a qualititative difference between the mental and the physical, between the throb of pain and the nervous response, which is done less than justice to by the 'one world' theory. One way of marking the difference would be to say that the physical can exist apart from consciousness whereas it is inconceivable that the mental should do so. Much of our experience is inexplicable without assuming mental processes (as distinct from mere behaviour) other than our own. We regulate our lives in no small part through our ability to distinguish between purposive human behaviour and the 'behaviour' of inanimate things. As for Ryle's unearthing of the obverse vocabulary in which some philosophers talk about minds it could be commented that the philosopher's reliance on analogy and metaphor is part of his stock-in-trade. It was certainly integral to the intention of philosophers like Descartes and the idealists that came after him to point out that minds were *anything but* another class of objects albeit of rare kind. In their view the only way to spotlight the difference was to insist on subjectivity as the central thing about mind. If this is relegated to a sphere of unimportance we are landed with a problem which exercises certain contemporary philosophers—the problem of how we are to distinguish between men and machines. If behaviour be the criterion of intelligence we may have to admit that many machines are more intelligent than men. Conceivably machines could be programmed which were endowed with multitracked dispositions so that they exhibited all the variety of response which we associate with typically human behaviour. Man's subjectivity would then remain the only thing which differentiated him from machines.

Recent discussion about how robots are to be distinguished from men is but one way in which the topic of the relation between mind and body appears in contemporary writings. Man is essentially an 'intentional' being, it has been pointed out, and 'intentions' bridge the artificial gulf which some of the traditional philosophers had fixed between thought and action. Ideas tend to realise themselves in an overt way, Bradley had said, during his analysis of the nature of willing. Intentional activity, it is plain, is very different from automatic activity and it is to be doubted if a machine could ever be credited with having intentions. Furthermore, contemporary interest in man as a language-using creature bears the possibility of a fresh approach to the mind/body problem. Linguistic activity is one activity among others, it is part of life. And yet it is sufficiently different from other activities to warrant separate analysis. Words are not mere sounds. They possess meaning, not, however, that they do so on their own account, but rather that they are endowed with meaning in virtue of customary usage. In spite of this, each use of language takes place in a fresh context. Language springs out of a subjective hinterland, takes shape in a context, issues forth in sounds, that is to say, in something physical, and has its significance in an intersubjective world that is inherently psycho-physical. Intentionality and the use of language would seem to be aspects of experience well-fitted to take us beyond the traditional mind/body dualism. For both of these illustrate something that the existentialists have been reminding us of in recent years—the incarnated nature of human existence.

The findings of physiology and neurology cannot be written off. It is no longer possible to retain the anthropologically primitive notion of a soul or mind 'inhabiting' a somewhat recalcitrant body. The body is the place where I am. That suffering ennobles was only too often appealed to by those who would degrade both the body and the soul. To speak of 'the person' instead of the 'soul' or the 'mind' may have certain advantages. The 'person' is not a ghost in the machine, but a being who can be degraded beyond measure by physical suffering. The life of the person is not confined to cognitive ventures but includes feelings and intentions. His life is not altogether conscious but is fed by unconscious streams inaccessible no less to introspection than to the detached gaze of the spectator. Of such a being as this, of such beings as we ourselves are, one should theorize warily.

XII Evolution

The Problem

THE concept of evolution was by no means always part of the mental furniture of the western mind, familiar though it be to us today and, indeed, ever since the end of the eighteenth century. Pre-Aristotelian philosophers were much concerned with the problem of Being and Becoming. But on the whole they conceived this problem in terms of the definition of identity, the reconciling of metaphysical reality with the phenomenon of change, the relating of the eternal realm, which was not object to change and decay, to the perceptual world of flux. The older connotation of 'becoming' fell short of the concept of development, a concept whose importance, after all, would only strike a philosopher whose main sphere of interest was the world of living things. When Aristotle made the concept of development the keystone of his philosophy, therefore, he was doing something new. Organic things, Aristotle saw, not only change (for inorganic things do that too) but they change in a certain direction. The acorn becomes, not a pine, but an oak; the puppy becomes a dog, and the child becomes a man. Now, as a biologist, Aristotle was as much struck by the characteristic differences between living species as by the way in which each living thing seemed to be directed towards an end. If the first of these insights led him to his theory of natural kinds, the second led him to his doctrine of *nisus*, the view that each individual (whether plant or animal or human being) was inspired by a directive principle which made it become one thing rather than another, an oak rather than a beech, a man rather than an animal. The picture that Aristotle had of the organic world was that of a multiplicity of living individuals each belonging no doubt to a class (or, as he called it, a species) and, as such, having certain common characteristics in virtue of that class-membership, but each also, *qua* individual, moving towards an end which was immanent in each. Each individual proceeded from potentiality to actuality, determined not by any antecedent event, but by the operation of final causality, by a *telos* which, while constituting the common character of the group, also constituted the essence of individuality. In this way, then, in Aristotle's philosophy, was born the concept of development. It is important to note, however, that no matter how dynamic the character of Aristotle's metaphysics is when we compare it with that of his predecessors, the different species according to Aristotle remained quite fixed. There was development within each individual no doubt, but there was no notion of a progressive change from one species to another, no notion, as it were, of a ladder of change.

The Christian account of the origin of the living world was likewise wedded to a view where all species were fixed immutably, "each according to his own kind". The account of special creation, as given in the book of Genesis in the Bible, lends itself to comparison with Aristotle's account. The various species, according to the Bible, came into existence thanks to a direct act of creation on the part of God, hence the name of the theory—that of 'special creation'. This means to say that, unlike in Aristotle's theory, where each creature follows the immanent working of a principle inherent in its own nature, the path of development of the creature is, according to Genesis, determined by design, that is, by an idea in God's mind. In both accounts all species are regarded as being co-present and there is no notion of one species developing into another, no notion, that is, of evolution.

In comparison with the two views that have been under review the concept of evolution appeared as a bombshell, a revolution in theory which required a revision of thinking far more drastic than that which had admitted the distinction between mere change and development. The concept of development had included that of direction of change, movement towards an end, change and yet continuity. The concept of evolution went further in discerning a further pattern in the process of change, the pattern of progression from simple and indeterminate types of life to that of complex forms of life. The organization of the living organism was found to be capable of increasing complexity. Evidence for this came from the science of geology at the end of the eighteenth century. Strata of rock were found to contain exciting evidence in the shape of fossilized remains of the living things of previous ages, evidence which not only showed that the structure of these creatures was much simpler than that of those of our day, but revealed a similarity which pointed to a direct line of development from earlier to later forms of life. The historical way of thinking prevalent in those times provided a fillip to the genetic approach which had, *via* the influence of geology, come into biological studies. Perhaps for the first time biologists felt that they had at their disposal a concept which was more fertile than the mechanical models, drawn from chemistry, to which they were accustomed.

The impulse behind the new way of thinking was the same impulse that had always inspired the working scientist, the desire to uncover the intelligibility of things, the desire to discover a principle which, when applied, would lay bare the pattern of order in nature. The concept of evolution was of immense significance because it showed, perhaps for the first time, that the biological sciences required concepts which were not altogether identical with those of the inorganic sciences. The living world had an intelligibility of a different order, and the new and exciting tool for unlocking the secrets of organic nature was the concept of evolution. It was a concept that set biologists working on very different lines from those they had followed before. The historian may see it as an application of the genetic procedures which belong essentially to his own discipline. To the biologist, however, it meant more than that. It set him hunting for the key to the development of living process in the analysis of organization. It set him hunting for the key to structure in the notion of function. Change in the organic world was not mere change but was mutation. The general concept of evolution suggested the rule according to which the mutations took place. Interest in atomic events gave way to concentration on whole processes in time, processes which could be unpacked into the minutiae of microscopic changes taking place over periods of time which defied the imagination of man.

The impact of the new concept on the Victorians was tremendous. Theologians immediately realised the changed status which would accrue to man. As against the Biblical account, man was related not so much to the angels as to the monkeys. The concept fitted in well with the Victorian faith in progress, for the long process from amoeba to man seemed to amount to strong evidence in favour of that faith. That evolution had come about through a competitive struggle between the various species was readily intelligible to a generation familiar with Adam Smith's theory of perfect competition. The implications of the concept seemed to augur well for the future. When Tennyson wrote of freedom broadening 'slowly down from precedent to precedent' he could look back with satisfaction on the long road whence we had come. There seemed in fact to be no limit to the applicability of the concept of evolution. Herbert Spencer was quick to see its possibilities as a means of refurnishing the ethical theory of hedonism. Metaphysicians of various brands who shared a common interest in the phenomenon of change, as against a static world of eternal entities, were attracted by it. Nietzsche, some years later in the century, saw no reason why the evolutionary process should stop short with the advent of man. Some day there might be a superman. Unfortunately he was under the illusion that the advent of supermen would be confined to the Aryan peoples. Even a liberal like Bernard Shaw was tempted by the thought of a race which should go further than man had been able to go. In our own time, Père Teilhard de Chardin has linked up the concept of evolution with that of theism and foresees a possible 'Omega point', as he calls it, when men will have as real a sense of community as they will have a realisation of their relation to God in Christ. The concept of evolution, it is evident, is by no means played out. But the word 'evolution', after all, states the problem rather than solves it. What does the metaphysical concept of evolution, on analysis, amount to?

The Mechanist theory

The progress of mechanistic explanations of natural phenomena, since the seventeenth century, had been so great that it was not surprising that the same mode of explanation should be extended from the consideration of inorganic things to that of organic life. According to the hypothesis of mechanism any given phenomenon could be accounted for by an examination of the antecedent events which were said to 'determine' it and such an examination constituted 'explanation'. A phenomenon was said to be 'intelligible' just in so far as this prior process of determining could be discovered. The specific hypotheses made by Charles Darwin concerned the manner in which the prior determining came about within the general framework of the mechanistic model. Mutations in the organic world, Darwin said, were governed by the principle of 'natural selection'. This in turn was unpacked into the following hypotheses. Living things were subject to a continuous struggle for existence. (This was the picture of nature which Tennyson described as being 'red in tooth and claw'). As a result of the struggle for existence there came about a survival of the fittest. The fittest survived thanks to the mutations that had come about through chance variations. Lamarck's giraffe example had already familiarised biologists with the latter notion. Instead of the giraffe's long neck being evidence of a divine dispensation the phenomenon had come about through the circumstance that only creatures with long necks could have access to supplies of food beyond the reach of lowlier creatures, and, in times of famine, could outlast their fellows. That this was not something that had come about during the course of a single generation was an integral part of the theory. Sub-microscopic changes took place from generation to generation and the new characteristics were transmitted to succeeding generations by heredity.

Such an account of the evolutionary process is called 'naturalistic' because whatever variations take place are attributed to the pressure of external circumstances. Herbert Spencer put this as follows—the lives of living organisms consist in the 'continuous adjustment of internal relations to external relations'. There is no need to posit any supernatural explanation of the emergence of life from inorganic nature, nor indeed of the emergence of human life from animal life. The new came about through a rearrangement of the old. There was a tendency for the more complex to evolve out of the simple, a process which, after all, was as typical of the order of change in physical nature as of the order of change in the organic world. The Biblical account of special creation seemed to be a redundant hypothesis, and as it was good scientific methodology to apply Occam's razor wherever possible, here was a chance to apply it. Ernst Haeckel's popular book *The Riddle of the Universe* tried to allay the doubts of those who wondered whether the gap between the non-living and the living could be explained by reference to the concept of evolution by saying that the evolutionary process had come about 'gradually'. The notion of quantitative changes passing over inexplicably into qualitative changes was something which Marxist theory was to make increasingly familiar to nineteenth century philosophical theorising.

Many thinkers embraced the evolutionary hypothesis with enthusiasm, although some wondered whether the hypothesis need be inextricably associated with the dogma of mechanism, for a dogma it had certainly become. Mechanism depended essentially on a form of reductionism. Wholes were analysed into their constituent elements and were regarded as a mere sum of their parts. But was the living thing a mere chemical compound? In the case of a living organism was not the whole more than the sum of the parts, a Humpty-Dumpty which, once reduced to its constituent elements, could never be 'put together again'? Sellars in his book *Evolutionary Naturalism* protested 'Are we not laying stress upon the material and disregarding the form? It is the organization which is novel and with which new properties must be correlated.' Was the difference between the inorganic and the organic only a matter of the distribution of particles? Doubts were raised—and these were metaphysical doubts—whether the developed could be completed explained by reference to the undeveloped. If a species were really new then it could not have come about through mere reshuffling of existent elements. Without the invasion of a new principle nothing new could emerge. The question was what this new principle should be called. The mechanistic hypothesis at least had the theoretical advantage of including living things within the fold of the same over-all model. To admit a non-mechanical principle would amount to admitting a radical element of duality in the universe and this was not acceptable to the tidy-minded. Most of all, the mechanist way of regarding the phenomenon of life seemed to make man's appearance on the scene a matter of the merest contingency. Was consciousness a mere development out of the tropisms of plants, and was human thought a mere refinement of the conscious processes which even animals are familar with? Mechanism had provided a hypothesis as to how the mutations of living creatures had come about. But to "evolve" meant to develop in a certain direction and mechanism had no room for the concept of direction. Could the concept of evolution be divorced from that of purpose?

The Teleological theory

While the mechanical approach derives originally from Democritus, the teleological approach derives from Aristotle's concept of final causality. Now a final cause means, literally, determination by 'end' and the 'end' of anything lies in the future. The end of the acorn is the developed oak-tree. Aristotle believed that the ends which inspired the growth of things in nature were unconscious. In man, however, the end is something which man can himself pursue consciously—the end of being a fully rational being. Through his capacity for forming ideas man is, moreover, able to construct artefacts. Both living things and artefacts are determined teleologically, with the difference that artefacts are made by a deliberate act on the part of man. The teleological approach received a new impetus at the hands of the theologians, for the ideas according to the patterns of which things were determined could be looked on as ideas in God's mind. In fact, right up to the time of Lamarck and Darwin, evidence of adaptations in nature suggested one thing and one thing only to the reflective man—such adaptations were evidence of the hand of Providence, confirming men in their belief that God was an intelligent Being, and, as such, had ideas according to the patterns of which all things had been created by Him and "without Him was not anything made that was made".

If the immediate reaction of the religious consciousness was to see in Darwin's theory something that went right against the teachings of the Book of Genesis this was not a reaction that in the nature of things need be such. If God were omnipotent there was no reason why He should not be capable of working through the evolutionary process. If the ways of God were fearful and wonderful the findings of Darwin could be regarded (as in this century men like William Temple regarded it,) as further evidence of this. Outside the context of pure Aristotelianism the natural association of the teleological way of thinking with the concerns of theology has perhaps been made clear. But there are purely metaphysical considerations as well which have led some philosophers to adopt a teleological interpretation of the evolutionary process.

A living being, it may be urged, is a whole which cannot be analysed into a mere summation of parts. The organization which biologists tell us is the distinguishing characteristic of organic phenomena, is a teleological organization, something purposive. Many, if not all, of the organs of the body can be accounted for only teleologically. What are the lungs if they are not designed for breathing, or the stomach if it is not looked on as an organ designed for digestion? The concepts of progress and degeneration are only explicable in relation to an end. The undeveloped can only be explained in relation to the developed. We classify a seed with reference to what it is going to become, and not according to its chemical constitution. An examination of the connotation of the word 'evolve' shows how we speak of things as evolving 'into' something else. That is to say the process has a 'direction'. It is not a mere fortuitous succession of circumstances. Something new comes out of the evolutionary process and this can only be explained if the process is purposive. Certainly in the case of living things low in the evolutionary scale the *nisus* which inspires them is unconscious. But the concepts of life and mind are closely connected and in the case of man the conscious meaning of purpose comes to full flowering.

There is one thing to which the category of development is indisputably appropriate, says H.W.B. Joseph, and that is the human mind. A mind is not an aggregate whose components have been drawn from elsewhere. In mind we have the profoundest diversity and yet the profoundest unity. The evolutionary process becomes, as it were, aware of itself in man. The self-motivation which we associate with purpose is found in its most complex form in man. Self-motivation, moreover, is integral to individuality and man is the most individual of all creatures. Aristotle was right in drawing attention to the presence of a *nisus* in every living thing, but his main interest remained in the *type*, those characteristics which make a creature of one kind rather than another. The idealists, in stressing the importance of the so-called 'accidents' in addition to the 'essence', thought they were correcting a fault in Aristotle's treatment of individuality.

One further way in which some thinkers made room for the notion of a non-mechanical principle was by reference to the concept of 'entelechy' which was, after all, a respectable Aristotelian term. Driesch and his followers, the 'vitalists', maintained that all living processes were regulated by something immaterial which they called 'entelechies', and they said that the entelechy acted as a 'unifying cause', which was really to state the case for teleology in slightly different language. In, conclusion, the modern teleologists thought that not only could the direction of evolutionary processes not be explained without reference to the notion of purpose but that (as in the case of the employment of the concept by the Greek philosophers) their approach had the great advantage of providing us with the concept of a 'cosmos', that is, a universe which, as its root meaning indicates, constitutes a genuine 'whole'.

Critics of the teleological account of evolution began by doubting whether the biologists themselves made use of the concept of purpose. The issue posed by the vitalists certainly shows no sign of dying a natural death. But if the laws of chemistry and physics are not the only ones, we shall have to admit a radical rift in the universe, a rift between those processes which are determined mechanically and those which are determined teleologically. In a Deistic metaphysics like that of Leibniz this was something which did not occasion too many qualms. In Kant's philosophy too we have a dualism between the order of causal necessity and the order which is moral. Some metaphysicians, however, find any form of dualism unsatisfactory, although this is a definitely metaphysical view in itself.

The notion of a '*telos*' or purpose involves that of determination by the future. How can the future determine the present, some may ask. Determination by the future, Bergson said, still remains determination and therefore all sense of novelty is destroyed if we accept the teleologist's hypothesis. What empirical evidence have we in favour of teleology? Nature is in many ways wasteful and there are many discontinuities in natural processes. The whole analysis also, it may be said, smacks too much of anthropocentric ways of thinking. Just because man is a creature who is capable of self-direction we have no ground for generalising this to include nature as a whole. The assumption seems to be that man is the crown of creation and therefore the processes that can be detected in him are to be used as operative concepts for giving an over-all account of the evolutionary movement as a whole. Finally can the teleological account of evolution be divorced from theology? If we maintain that the process of evolution is inspired by a purpose, the natural question to ask is as to whose purpose this is, and the inevitable answer comes that it is God's purpose which is at work within nature. To the theist this may be not merely an illuminating hypothesis but a matter of conviction. The non-theist, however, may find the association of the teleological idea with theism uncomfortable. That the teleological account of evolution gives a special status to man seems undeniable. The mechanist account may not, to some minds, seem very flattering to man. There is, however, another way of employing the teleological idea, and that is the way in which Kant uses it, as a heuristic principle, an 'as if' concept which should not be taken literally so much as applied as an illuminating hypothesis, throwing light on these spheres of nature to which it seems applicable.

Creative Evolution

Bergson's criticisms of the two views which have been under consideration are most pertinent and they form the introduction to the exposition of his own theory. Bergson believes that the scientific procedure of searching for deterministic causal lines really amounts to the search for repetitions. As such the scientist focusses his attention on similarities, and dissimilarities escape his notice. A scientific law is an abstraction from the stream of actual process. That the sphere of science was confined to 'identities' was maintained also by Emile Meyerson, Bergson's countryman. As against Bergson it might be said, however, that it is precisely departures from regularities that stimulate discovery. The very reductionism which is peculiar to chemistry and physics in particular, in Bergson's view, constitutes an argument in their disfavour. He says 'In reality, life is no more made of physico-chemical elements than a curve is composed of straight lines.' The mechanistic model hinges on the assumption that the same cause will probably be followed by the same effect. But in the study of biology we sometimes find that the same effect is produced by different accumulations of causes. For example, the eye of the Pecten mollusc resembles that of a vertebrate and yet crustaceans and vertebrates are on separate lines of evolution. If the mechanistic hypothesis were correct there should be no such phenomenon at all. Above all, mechanism glides over what, to Bergson, is the most significant thing about process—the fact of duration. Now in making the past the lever of the present Bergson thinks that mechanism deprives time of all efficacy. The essence of duration is its unpredictability, whereas the essence of determinism and mechanism is predictability.

Finalism, as mechanism in reverse, is just as deterministic as the latter. Mechanism amounts to the determinism of the past, and teleology amounts to the determinism of the future. 'It substitutes the attraction of the future for the impulsion of the past.' By regarding the future as incapsulated in the present in the form of potentiality, finalism destroys the nature of duration as much as mechanism does. If finalism were true there should be no disharmonies in nature. Everything should be part of one grand design. On the contrary we find that nature is full of discords and full of surprises. The future does not pre-exist. It comes with the shock of something new. It cannot in any way be said to inhere in the present in the form of an idea. If mechanism errs by leaving man and his lived experience out of the picture, finalism errs by extending too far the human experience of planning and acting. Plans are given in advance, but evolution creates as it goes along.

It remained, then, for Bergson to replace the concepts of

mechanism and teleology by one of his own. The key to the process of evolution for him is the 'élan vital' or life force, which is creative, that is to say, it is an impulse which is at work in nature and which, at times one feels, Bergson wishes to say is nature. The progress of the life force is completely unpredictable. But it is not to be regarded in a linear fashion. The evolutionary process is 'open'. It has no goal, and it has many paths. 'There is harmony or identity of impulsion, and not of aspiration'. But three terminal points can be distinguished in this process, and these are torpor, instinct and intelligence, all of which diverge in different directions. Instinct and intelligence are alternative ways of adaptation. There is no *prima facie* case for the alleged superiority of intelligence, as is usually thought. In some ways the instinctive creature is superior to man, and there is a quasi-instinctive faculty called intuition which Bergson thought it was proper for man to cultivate. The diversity of direction of which the creative force of evolution is capable is described by Bergson in a vivid way as follows :— 'We are here dealing with a shell which has immediately burst into fragments, which, being themselves species of shells, have again burst into fragments, destined to burst again, and so on.'

The essence of the life process is time. It is both indeterminate and creative. The physicist wrongly spatializes time. But time can only be lived through. It can only be grasped, or rather entered into, through intuition. Connected with this is the strange status Bergson gives to matter. Bergson inverts materialism. Instead of saying that mind is an epiphenomenon of matter he says (although not in so many words) that matter is an epiphenomenon of the life force. In so saying he pits himself against the entire Renaissance concept of nature as the scene of human activities. Matter is arrested flux and is not a thing. It comes about through a lessening of the tension of the spiritual force which the élan vital is. Intellect has evolved in order to cope with matter, but it is helpless to grasp anything other than the relative fixities which we call matter. The essence of duration passes it by. The position of man is none the less a special one. Human beings are centres of indetermination. They are not units where all is 'given'. "For a conscious being, to exist is to change, to change is to mature, to mature is to go on creating oneself endlessly. Should the same be said of existence in general?" This is a passage which proved suggestive in different ways to neo-Thomists like Maritain and existentialists like Sartre. Also, in so far as man is the only creature who, through intuition, is in principle capable of grasping the inner nature of the creative process through intuition, his uniqueness of status is assured by Bergson.

When Bergson's book *Creative Evolution* first appeared it seemed that Bergson's theory was better able to do justice to the element of novelty in the evolutionary process than were the alternative theories. Not since Hume and Kant had the problem of time been so exhaustively treated. The disharmonies of nature which the absolutists seemed to iron out were given due recognition and there was no facile attempt made to present a schema of an unnaturally tidy universe. The atomism of the Darwinians gave way to stress on the process character of nature, something which perhaps not since Heraclitus had been given due attention. The dynamism of Bergson's approach contrasted favourably with the inevitabilities of the determinists, and the status of man seemed to appear in a more creditable light than on the Darwinian view. Mind was not merely a chance by-product of the evolutionary process but was something capable of rising to even further heights in the faculty of intuition. French philosophy had certainly not come across anything as exciting as the work of Bergson since the time of Descartes who was, no doubt, a philosopher of a very different kind.

Irrationalism was somewhat new in the French philosophical world. There were distinguished precedents for an irrational type of metaphysics in Germany in the work of Schopenhauer and Nietzsche and there have been yet others since. Bergson's metaphysic counts as a form of irrationalism in so far as he maintains that the inner nature of reality is not something which is logical. Its nature can only be grasped by a non-rational faculty. To those who regard the task of investigating the nature of reality as a task for reason this will be looked on as a defect. It is urged by some that the notion of 'creative' evolution is as anthropocentric as that of teleology. Man is a being who knows what it is to create. In his own case creation is always out of a pre-existing material. But whether 'creation' is a word which can be given any connotation outside the human context is something which can be questioned. To speak of 'creative' evolution is to do scarcely more than state the problem. What does 'creative' mean? (The same criticism can be made of the 'emergent' theory of evolution. What does 'emergent' mean?) Furthermore, Bergson's explanation of matter is quixotic. If 'in the beginning' there was only the life force and no medium in which it could work, wherein consisted its 'force'? In annihilating matter *ab initio* it sounds as if there is nothing for the life force to work on.

The notion of a pure flux may likewise give us pause. If Kant is right in pointing out that the concept of change is unintelligible without the contrasting notion of permanence then there can be no meaning in the notion of a flux *simpliciter*. The dynamism of Bergson's metaphysics may be attractive after the static block universes of the logically-minded (there is much to parallel it in the impressionism of Debussy's music and the fluid colours of Manet's paintings). But if we compare it with the metaphysic of Aristotle we find that the dynamism of Aristotle was counterweighted by his concept of matter and that Aristotle's universe was a solid and concrete one. By contrast Bergson's view needs to be linked up with the twentieth century discovery of dynamism in other spheres, say, in that of economic theory. Dynamic models seem to have so much more relevance to a changing world than have static equilibrium models. But it is incumbent on a philosopher to leave as little as possible out of account and in this respect the solid billiard ball world of the older empiricists still stakes its claim to philosophical consideration, fascinating though the Bergsonian world be.

Finally, if we turn to one of the most distinguished of contemporary critics of Bergson, Bertrand Russell, we find that Russell was not only critical of the Bergsonian view of duration (for Russell himself was concerned with the space-time of physics) but he was equally critical of Bergson's denigration of intellect to a place inferior to that of intuition. Not only was it false to imagine that intellect was as cut off from intuition as Bergson had thought, but Russell believed that Bergson had committed the fault of ascending at times into rhapsody, whereas it should be the philosopher's business to keep his own subjective desires as far as possible from his philosophizing. Russell, moreover, criticized the Bergsonian view of intuition from the vantage-point of a very definite view of his own regarding intuition. In Russell's view there could be no other sort of intuition than sensible intuition, and in this he was in substantial agreement with Kant.

XIII Self

Introduction

THERE are few subjects in metaphysics which are more interesting than this. The word 'self' is not a very common one in ordinary language. We are probably more familiar with the reflexive form e.g. myself, yourself, himself and so on. Earlier philosophers wrote much about the 'soul', and if we turn to the writings of this century we find that yet another term has gained considerable currency—that of the 'person'. The word 'self' is perhaps a conveniently neutral word which avoids the religious connotations of the former term and the existentialist aura of the latter.

Selves are very evidently unique phenomena. Even in saying this one is saying something which would give offence to many. Selves are not phenomena at all, some would say. What we mean, however, is something at first sight obvious, something which the man in the street would agree with, and even philosophers too in their day-to-day life—selves are not the same as objects. True enough, selves are incarnated. This is a point that was for the most part overlooked by earlier thinkers although it was something that St. Paul for one was very much aware of. People have a spatio-temporal existence. They have a beginning, live, and then, as far as we can see, come to an end; at least, if they continue, they do not do so in exactly the same way that they did before. Whatever account we give of the self we shall have to remind ourselves constantly of the fact that the self is intimately related to the body. The body is the place of my existence. Objects too have a spatio-temporal existence. How then are we to distinguish between selves and objects?

The most remarkable thing about selves is that they are conscious. Not only this, for animals are after all conscious too, but selves are self-conscious. Is this a circular statement? Perhaps not. On the evolutionary view man has emerged on the scene of things after a long process in which mutation followed mutation. The most amazing thing that emerged during this process was the gradual growth of what one might call 'awareness', something that can be pointed to in an embryonic form in tropisms in plants and which comes to full flowering in the self-consciousness of man. In order to remove the circularity from our earlier statement it could be said that man is a being who has the peculiar faculty of being aware of himself in a manner which, as far as we can see, is denied to other animals. This faculty finds special expression in his capacity for articulate speech. One somewhat demythologised way of putting the same thing is to say, with Gilbert Ryle, that man is a creature who 'knows what he is doing'. We are, of course, for the moment begging the question as to whether this 'knowing what one is doing' can be accounted for without reference to a focus called the 'self'.

Another remarkable characteristic of selves is their capacity for memory. The memory of animals (again, as far as we can make out, for it is dangerous to speculate about creatures with whom we have scant means of communication) is relatively short. Rats have what is called a 'steer' and higher animals can be conditioned to behave in ways which suggest that they have a memory but which might be explicable solely on the basis of conditioning, and we all know that elephants are said never to forget. The time-bound nature of man's existence is something which takes on a special character, for man is able not only to live in the present, which indeed he must, but to recreate the past in memory and to look to the future in expectation or dread. Whether, in memory, we are in direct contact with a datum or whether memory amounts to a rare constructive activity of the mind is an issue which concerns epistemology.

Selves are plural and one of the strongest arguments given in favour of metaphysical pluralism is precisely this fact. Selves, however, are capable of coming into a form of association with each other which seems far removed from the aggregation (or, alternatively, coalescence) that is to be found in the world of physical objects. If there is the 'I', 'You' and 'He' there is also the possibility of 'We' and the recognition of this in others in the word 'They'. But the self is not something simple. Are we to deny selfhood to the split personality, or are we so to define selfhood that it can encompass the diverse phenomena of abnormal psychology? If the self is something which possesses unity, are we, in justice to abnormal cases and to the intermittent consciousness of normal life, to regard such unity as a matter of degree?

The question of the identity of the self is no less fraught with puzzles. In what sense are you the 'same' as you were ten years ago? There are similar puzzles too about the identity of physical things. Hume has given a brilliant analysis in his *Treatise* showing how empirically-based are our criteria for judging one thing to be the same as it was at some earlier date. In the case of physical things, however, the problem is less difficult, for we have at least continuity of physical structure to guide us. (To have said 'similarity' would have been to beg the question). In judging of the identity of persons general structural resemblance may or may not be there. The criteria of identity for the agent and the spectator are bound to be different. To the agent organic sensations are probably an important source of the sense of identity. In addition the agent has his memory as immediate evidence of who he is. To the spectator the criteria will be continuity of physical structure and behaviour and perhaps (and here we are on dangerous ground) personal factors like *rapport* with himself. When we say 'so and so has changed' we often say this on the basis of a change in the other's attitude to ourselves.

Perhaps the characteristic of the self that has most impressed the philosopher is that the self is that which knows. Now this brings up the whole question of what it means to 'know'. Consciousness has always been considered to be the presupposition of knowing. But philosophers have been by no means in agreement as to what sort of self knowing demands. Knowing in the case of man (and once more we are not clear as to the exact sense in which animals may be said to know) is bound up with his ability to speak, with his capacity to put his knowledge into propositional form. Man has a dual capacity, both to do and to think, and some philosophers would object to this way of putting it, saying that both reflect what might be called his 'intelligence'. On such a view man's knowledge would not be something to be exhibited merely in propositional skills. It is not difficult, at any rate, to see that whatever view we take of the self is closely linked up with the view we take as to the meaning of 'know'. No less important is the insight, shared alike by scholastics and contemporary philosophers, that the self is not merely a contemplative being but a being who acts, however wide the disagreement as to what 'being' may be or as to the appropriateness of using the word 'being' at all.

So far we have been concerned with some of the many complex facets of selfhood and it is good to bear these in mind when looking at the theories which philosophers have advanced on the subject of the self, for, for the most part, we shall find that perhaps no philosopher has been able to do justice to them all.

Is the Self a Substance?

The view that the self is a substance was held by the rationalist philosophers of the seventeenth and eighteenth centuries. But the origin of the theory is to be found earlier than this, in the writings of Plato and Aristotle, and in the scholastic philosophy of the Middle Ages. The elaborate theoretical system built up by the Schoolmen embodied a most ingenious fusion of Greek and Christian ideas, some of which, at first sight, seem irreconcilable and some of which seem more congruent than others. One example of the latter is the kinship of opinion in the Platonic and the Pauline treatments of the passional side of man's nature. From Plato's famous myth of the chariot and the wild horses which need to be kept on a tight rein by the charioteer it is quite plain that Plato believes that, apart from the control of reason, there will be no order in man's life, no *sophrosyne* or moderation. St. Paul, on rather different grounds, believes that unregenerate man (and this, of course, is not the same thing as emotional man) is likewise a creature who has fallen short of his high calling. If anything the Schoolmen returned to a view of the soul which was far closer to Greek than to Judaic roots. This at any rate seems to be the case if we think of the dogmatic stress they all made on rationality as the differentia of the soul. At the same time Christian teaching insisted that the human soul was a thing of immense value, something for whose sake Christ died. It would be therefore inappropriate to deny the status of the highest category of all, that is, the category of substantiality, to such a being. The doctrine of the Fall, however, showed that man had to some extent fallen from grace since the time of Adam, and therefore, in comparison with God, man's substantiality must be regarded as finite. In this way the Aristotelian theory of hierarchy of substances became fused with the Christian insight that man was, after all, an imperfect being. Recognition of man's imperfection, that is his finitude, was particularly marked in St. Augustine for whom imperfection was conceived not just as deficiency but as sin. Man's inadequacy, even in respect of his faculty of reason, was done justice to also by St. Thomas Aquinas in that it was precisely on account of man's imperfect reason that the ontological argument was regarded by him to be an impossibility. Man does not have the capacity of adequately framing an idea of God, the reason being that he is unable to intuit the Divine nature.

When the Cartesians spoke of the soul, then, it should be by now evident that they were drawing on a long tradition, a tradition whose contents were woven into the warp and woof of Catholic thought. The conception of the soul as 'substance' carried with it a very definite connotation comprising ultimate particularity, causal independence and persistence, that is, continuity. Ultimate particularity meant the unanalysability of substance into elements, or what we may call indivisibility (a differentia which convinced Leibniz that extension could not be spoken of as substantial). Causal independence was no less essential to substance, for that which is capable of being causally acted upon is capable of being changed, that is of having its essence altered, and that is, not being a substance. To say that substance is causally independent, it can be seen, is tantamount to saying that substance is changeless, that is, eternal. Small wonder, then, that the traditional doctrine held the soul to be immortal. Persistence amounts to the same thing—a continuity of existence which has no end. It is understandable then, that Descartes should have maintained that the soul always thinks, otherwise wherein could lie its continuity? It is strange to reflect on the elevated status such attributes would give to man, if indeed it could be shown that man's soul is substantial. In a sense thinkers like David Hume and Jean Jacques Rousseau gave a picture of human nature that was far closer to the teachings of Christianity than was the picture given by the rationalists.

Now the rationalists thought that the prime business of the soul was to *know* (such being their Platonic bias) and the presupposition of knowing is consciousness. Knowledge, so they held, presupposes self-identity. For instance in the case of inferential knowledge, when we follow through a connected argument (and the paradigm for Descartes, we should remember, is the linear type of inferential argument to be found in Euclidean geometry) the same self which recognises the premisses must recognise the conclusion. Locke, the empiricist, seems to have taken over this piece of doctrine unexamined, for one of his main criticisms of 'demonstrative knowledge' is the dependence of such knowledge on memory and the involvement of the latter with a unitary self. The time had not yet come for disentangling the notions of a unitary self and a substantial self. Knowledge was thought to demand both a unitary self, that is unity at a time, and an identical self, that is unity over time. Memory seems to give us direct evidence that the 'I' which exists now existed in the past, and even Hume is unclear on the question whether it is memory which *discovers* unity or whether it is memory which *brings* about unity.

The rationalists further held that we have immediate awareness of a substantial self, or what C. D. Broad calls a Pure Ego, in introspection. Descartes thought he was making a great discovery when he propounded his 'Cogito ergo sum' because this was, in his view, the one statement which possessed intuitive certainty and at the same time existential import. To him, therefore, it was the one clear and distinct perception which concerned the realm of existence. There are other philosophers outside the rationalist camp who have also (very differently of course) based their theories of the self on an appeal to intuition, Bergson for one.

The final trump card produced by the Cartesians is the view that above all in *willing* the self exercises its substantiality.

This is, once more, a piece of pure scholasticism, something which in the history of modern philosophy, finds its clearest expression in Berkeley. According to this view, volition is regarded as a first-hand and self-conscious activity of 'production', of making something happen. Theologians seem to have had the knack of arguing analogically both ways, from the efficacy of the human will to the greater efficacy of God, and from the creativity of God to the small-scale creativity of man. Hume, at any rate, thought both were pieces of mistaken psychological theory and debunked the whole account of volition on which it was based. In our own day, however, the traditionalist position has been extraordinarily ably argued afresh by Austin Farrer in his book *Finite and Infinite.*

The rationalist theory of the self does not stand up very well against a battery of arguments from both epistemology and psychology. Kant showed that whereas knowledge does require a cognitive subject this is by no means the same thing as to say that knowledge requires a substantial self. The detailed way he argues this is to be found in the Paralogisms of his *Critique of Pure Reason.* There is little in the fragmented story which psycho-analysis brings to light which could deserve the title of 'ultimate particularity'. The self, the empiricist will say, is reducible to its experiences, although whether presupposed in the notion of 'experience' is something which is itself not an experience is something to give us pause. Causal independence is a characteristic far removed indeed from selfhood. Not only is the self acted upon by the world and by God (if these simplifications can be pardoned) but selves act upon and modify each other*. If this were not so how could the phenomenon of human 'influence' be accounted for? The self, moreover, is most dependent on the body. This is so even if we use the words 'self' and 'mind' interchangeably (Descartes spoke of *mens* rather than of *anima*). As for the attribute of persistence we have, against this, the undoubted intermittence of conscious life to reckon with, and it is only of God that it has been said that He neither slumbers nor sleeps. In fairness, though, it is proper to mention in this context that Leibniz made room for

* Vide my *"Our knowledge of other Selves"*—Asia Publishing House, 1963.

something very like a theory of the unconscious in his recognition of minute perceptions of the soul, something which was implied in his view of consciousness as being capable of degrees.

The evidence of memory, is, as was hinted above, unclear. If memory could give direct acquaintance with the self as an entity this would be the strongest plank in the rationalist platform. But memory, after all, acquaints us with something historical, something which is of the essence of time. It acquaints us with the sense of pastness, something, therefore, to which entity language is hardly appropriate. The appeal to intuition is always a dangerous one in philosophy. Intuition may be fallible, and in any case the deliverances of intuition are unverifiable by the spectator. The evidence of intuition, some philosophers have said, is more in favour of the existence of a core of organic sensations which underlies conscious and even unconscious life, and this again is far from the discovery of anything resembling an entity. Other philosophers have pointed out that the verdict of intuition is in 'favour of the existence of something relational and not substantival at all. Finally, the nature of volition is no longer analysed in terms of efficient causality by modern psychologists. Whether after the new analysis is made much remains of man's freedom of the will is a matter which can be dealt with elsewhere.

The Empiricist theory of the Self

On a strict empiricist view the concept of substantiality is a redundant one. It is necessary to say 'strict empiricist view' because Locke, although he was certainly an empiricist, retained the concept in a watered-down version. Berkeley also (being many other things in addition to being an empiricist) retained the concept, insisting that the self or spirit was substantial *par excellence.* It was David Hume who denied the applicability of the concept of substance in its last stronghold—the self. The empiricist account of the self is also known as the 'serialist' or 'phenomenalist' theory, but the main lines of the theory even in this more recent terminology had already been laid down by Hume and it is safe to turn to him for an authoritative version of the empiricist account.

Hume's starting point is something which he had maintained

prior to his dealing with this specific problem—that is—that all ideas are traceable to, or 'cashable' in, as William James would say, preceding impressions. His procedure, therefore, in dealing with any putative "idea" is to examine its credentials by trying to trace the preceding impression from which it was derived. This procedure he had already tried in examining the idea of causality, finding that in this case no simple impression reveals itself and he carries out a similar examination in the case of the idea of the self. What remains of permanent importance about Hume's theories both of causality and of the self is not so much the particular answers he gives to the problem but his diagnosis that our 'ideas' in these two cases are of a special kind, not being traceable to any simple impression. His first assumption, then, is that ideas are to be investigated by hunting for the impressions which give rise to them. His second assumption is that all our perceptions are distinct. He writes . . . . . ". . . since all our perceptions are different from each other, and from everything else in the universe, they are also distinct and separable, and may be considered as separately existent, and may exist separately and have no need of anything else to support their existence." In this way Hume makes use of his atomic view of the contents of the mind to counter the view (which Locke had supported) that perceptions must inhere in something, to counter the rationalist theory that thoughts are modifications of the soul.

As far as tracing our idea of the self to an impression is concerned Hume confesses that in his own case he can find no such impression. "For my part, when I enter most intimately into what I call myself, I always stumble on some particular perception or other, of heat or cold, light or shade, love or hatred, pain or pleasure." He "ventures" to say of people in general "that they are nothing but a bundle or collection of different perceptions, which succeed each other with an inconceivable rapidity, and are in a perpetual flux and movement." In this manner Hume puts his finger on the most striking characteristic of the self—a characteristic which had been completely ignored by rationalist philosophers—its temporality. Now the traditional concept of substance had involved both simplicity, i.e. the absence of complexity, and identity, i.e. the absence of change. It is clear, Hume thought, that whatever the self may be, and that we have still to determine, the characteristics of simplicity and identity are foreign to it.

Now the manner in which in practice we judge objects to be identical can give us a clue. In effect we judge the identity of objects in terms of relation. What we actually perceive is a "succession of parts, connected together by resemblance, contiguity or causation." In ascribing identity to variable objects, as we certainly do, we are really ascribing it to a fiction. We do not, in our actual experience, come up against anything of the nature of absolute identity. But if this is so we realise the inapplicability of the word 'substance' to what we find in experience, and this even more so when we examine the subjective flow of perceptions in us as distinct from the succession of perceptions which purports to be informative of the external world. Hume finds himself unable to perceive any 'real bond among our perceptions' and traces the connections that we feel to a customary associations' of ideas. The principle of union therefore, is not a common relation to a core but an inter-relation among the perceptions themselves. In talking about these relations Hume recognises the importance of the part played by memory and says 'The memory not only discovers the identity but also contributes to its production, by producing the relation of resemblance among the perceptions.' Two metaphors enable Hume to expound further the way in which he conceives our various experiences to be related. The mind is a stage across the floor of which the various perceptions pass (we must be careful not to take the floor of the stage literally, otherwise we should be introducing the concept of substance again), and the mind is like a republic or commonwealth in which no citizen is king.

The technique that Hume uses, it can be seen, is much the same as the one he uses in analysing the idea of cause*. He reduces the idea into three parts; what is perceived, what is felt, and what is believed. Selves (and objects too) possess a relative existence. There is nothing in them to justify the use of entity language. Man's existence is time-bound (as Heidegger

* Vide Ch. X.

would say). Nothing can overshadow the inherently successive nature of our subjective life. The various experiences which make up the succession affect each other internally, and this is surely an insight which is borne out by the findings of modern psychology. The self is a 'bundle', and a bundle, it may be noted, is not a mere aggregate. Self-identity is more a matter of degree, a matter of more or less. Our awareness of ourselves is a 'function' of the various experiences we have, i.e. it is not an awareness of anything ontological. It is not surprising that introspection does not discover a centre or core in these experiences for there is no such core there.

The biggest problem that the serialist faces in substituting the concept of relation for that of substance is that of making clear exactly in what that relation consists. A merely temporal succession would seem to be a purely *de facto* succession, and memory, on such a view, would be something of a miracle. William James was just as convinced as Hume was of the temporal character of the 'stream of consciousness' but he offered the supplementary hypothesis that a certain qualitative modification was handed on from one event to the next, that one experience was incapsulated into the next, that is to say, James refused to segment subjective life in the way in which Hume had done. The serialist use of relational language in discussing the self is based on a form of atomism which must give us serious pause. There can only be relations between discrete terms in a series, and it remains a matter of serious question whether there be in fact any such discrete terms in the case of mental life. The language of series belongs properly to mathematics, or more specifically, to arithmetic, for the operations of addition, subtraction and the rest presuppose separate terms between which the operations can be effected. The question is whether a mental 'event' possesses any such discreteness. The work of the whole 'stream of consciousness' school of writers was designed as a protest against such a view and can be found in a literary form in the novels of Virginia Woolf and others of the Bloomsbury Group. It was their achievement to substitute the notion of 'stream' for that of 'event', a Heraclitean substitution which in itself was laden with many problems. The whole history of epistemology is shot through with the inherent difficulty of specifying exactly what constitutes the 'unit' of mental life. The substantialists did not have to face this problem because they could fall back on the language of modification, qualities and inherence. But just as (to take perhaps a rather shaky analogy) if "Hamlet" is to be played without the Prince of Denmark the small-part actors must be really good, so if we are to do without the soul there must be no ambiguity about our remaining mental furniture. To conclude on this particular point of discussion, it is misleading to speak of the self as a series because mental events are abstractions from a continuous process (not of course completely continuous, but 'gappy' in parts). The atomistic 'chemical' background which lies behind much of empiricist thinking on epistemology is even less acceptable today, with the findings of psychology as they are, than it was in Hume's day.

It was against Hume's atomism that Kant was protesting when he insisted that a purely serial notion of the self, i.e. a mechanical notion, would make nonsense of knowledge. However diversely constituted the empirical self may be (and this Kant did not deny), the self, that is the transcendental self, does function as a unity in knowing objects, and this is a vital part of the story of how objective knowledge is possible, a story upon the telling of which Hume did not embark. Subject is co-relative to object, or even more simply, knowing demands a knower, otherwise we would be merely the arena of a buzzing blooming confusion. Why Kant thought this was so is linked up with his 'synthetic' view of the nature of knowledge, a view the need for which is partly inspired by the very same atomistic view of Hume which he was so concerned to criticise. But, at the same time, Kant was sure that the various synthetic operations of the understanding were grounded in a principle which itself possessed unity, and this principle he called the synthetic unity of apperception. But to take the view which Kant took involves admitting that there is something more to the self than what can be found on simple introspection, and this was a step which Hume as a consistent empiricist—and there is none more consistent than he—could not take.

Hume appears to have thought (and evidently so does Gilbert Ryle in his *Concept of Mind*) that the failure of introspection to reveal anything in the nature of a 'self' in the traditional sense is a knock-down argument against the view that there is in fact anything such thing. The weakness of the empiricist account is its assumption that the self should be the sort of thing that can be yielded up to introspection. The simple-mindedness of the Cartesian view that the 'I' is accessible to consciousness is responsible for this. It is the greatness of Kant's approach to the whole treatment of the self that he sees that in the very nature of things the self cannot possibly be accessible to any kind of inspection. The hunter cannot hunt himself. That which is the subject of knowledge cannot at the same time be the object of knowledge.

One other criticism which is sometimes levelled against the Humean view is that it destroys the connotation of 'existence' which, as we have seen, certainly did attach itself to the substantialist account. Substance was that which exists *par excellence.* At times empiricists speak as if the perceptions themselves were existents of a special order. In losing their derivative character, that is, in losing their dependence on a core or substance, it may indeed seem that mental events themselves constitute, in however Pickwickian a way, a peculiar class of 'existent'*. However this may be, to the empiricist the self as such may be said to *subsist* rather than exist. In extenuation it may also be said that even Kant does not get as far as affirming the 'existence' of the self. But those who are emancipated from the vocabulary of being wisely use the word 'exist' advisedly. It is only by bringing in an expanded form of empiricism, such as is found in twentieth century phenomenology, that the existential nature of the self has once more come in for consideration.

The empiricist or phenomenalist theory of the self has received fresh interpretation in recent years, especially in the works of A. J. Ayer. Ayer's phenomenalism draws on three sources, the Humean reduction of selves to sense-contents, behaviourism, and Russell's theory of logical constructions. In Ayer's view Hume's account is faulty in that Hume admits that he is unable to discover the principle of connection between perceptions in virtue of which they constitute a single self. Ayer

* Hume does, after all, speak of perceptions as "distinct existences".

thinks he has solved Hume's problem by defining personal identity in terms of bodily identity and he says that "bodily identity is to be defined in terms of the resemblance and continuity of sense-contents." That organic sensations do form an important element in our awareness of ourselves cannot be denied, but whether personal identity can be 'defined' in this way is to be doubted. Reductionism in terms of bodily behaviour is as objectionable as reductionism in terms of sense-contents, because although it may apparently have the advantage of avoiding the solipsistic tendencies of the latter it falls open to the serious objection that much of human life is not "manifested" in overt behaviour at all. In this respect the account given by Gilbert Ryle is an improvement on Ayer's for Ryle does recognise the part played by speech as well as behaviour in informing us what selves are like. The phenomenalist, however, in his account both of our knowledge of things and persons, is bound to refer questions of 'existence' to the occurrence of actual and possible sense-contents, a procedure which, if not denying the occult altogether, of necessity reduces the 'occult' to a position of insignificance.

The other contemporary theory of the self which must be mentioned is that of existentialism. The most noteworthy feature of the existentialist treatment of the self is the way in which it lifts the discussion out of its usual context of cognition. That man is a being who acts rather than contemplates had been emphasised by philosophers before. But such accounts had either, with the scholastics, centred man's activity in his essence as a substance of a unique kind (as a centre of volition) or, with the pragmatists, interpreted action in terms of the mere production of changes in an external environment. Existentialism discovers man's selfhood in his freedom, his power to shape his own destiny through his own decisions. In employing the word 'person' rather than 'self', the existentialist reminds us (as Dilthey had done a century earlier) that man is not only a being who tries to know but a being who feels and acts. In saying this he draws attention to something else that had been neglected by other philosophers, the fact that man's most significant relation is not his relation with the external world (which gives rise to all the time-honoured problems of epistemology) but his relation to his fellows, and the different existentialists undertake with varying degrees of success the analysis of just what this involves.

An adequate theory of the self has to include a treatment of the cognitive subject which knowledge demands, a treatment which Kant has given authoritatively in his Critique of *Pure Reason*. At the same time recognition has to be made of the empirical self, the successive nature of which had so impressed Hume. But man is also a being who can act morally and the capacity he has to rise above the empirically determined sequence of things which happen to him and to make a free decision has to be done justice to. Finally, one has the impression that philosophers have often been misled by phrasing our problem as the problem of *the* self. The problem needs to be re-phrased in pluralistic terms—the problem of how selves encounter, communicate, get to know, and ultimately live with each other—a matter which, when we examine it, we find to be less a problem than a task.

XIV Freedom and Necessity

Introduction

In the foregoing chapters an attempt has been made to bring out the nature of some of those problems which deal with man's relation to the physical world. Is man a mere part of the physical universe or does he in some sense stand apart from it? In our anthropocentric way of looking at things it is natural for us to regard man as the crowning product of the evolutionary process. But does the advent of man, Darwin notwithstanding, constitute in some sense a radical break with what went before, and can the differentiae of the human world be done justice to if we see in man merely the result of the operation of mechanical forces? The desire to see in reality a 'cosmos', a universe which, from the very definition of the word, connotes a unified whole, has been a leading theme in the history of philosophy. And yet, at the same time, the Greek discovery that in man the power of reason comes to self-consciousness in a way denied to anything else in the cosmos forms the starting point for a whole stream of thought which sees in the nature of man something unique and which seeks to define this uniqueness in diverse fashions. Those who speak of the freedom of the will are among those concerned with this uniqueness.

A table or a chair cannot be said to be free, for it cannot be other than what it is. It is inexorably determined by the laws of physics and chemistry. Even a tree or an animal is determined by its inner constitution, although in the case of living things we recognise that this constitution is of far greater complexity than that of inanimate objects. Man's physical being is likewise governed by certain laws which physiology and its cognate branches of science tell us about. It does seem, however, that man does possess a peculiar capacity for (at least at times) ordering his life according to his own choosing, a capacity reflected in his choosing, say, to go by bus instead of by taxi, and, less trivially, in his choosing to be a doctor instead of a teacher. When we say that a man is free we are recognising the capacity for choice which he seems to have. Philosophically speaking what we are saying is that man has within himself the power to "act", a power reflected no less in the taking of medicine to curb the course of a disease than in the choice to embark on bridge-building in Uganda. And here the difficulty begins. In what way are such courses of action to be explained? Events in nature reveal their pattern to the disciplined scrutiny of antecedent events undertaken by the scientist. Are we to adopt the same method in our attempt to explain the action of a human being? The *determinist's* answer is in the affirmative. A full investigation of a man's antecedent life, including physiological, psychological and social data will, it is claimed, provide a complete 'explanation' of how he came to do what he did. The *libertarian,* on the other hand, maintains that it is wrong to confuse an action with a mere event. Human actions (or at least some human actions) are free in the sense that no amount of information concerning a man's antecedent experiences, predispositions and the like, can ever be strictly relevant to the determining of his choice simply because choice itself constitutes a unique sort of causation. But this is to anticipate. Historically the problem of freedom did not first emerge in the context of the attempt to reconcile two diverse patterns of intelligibility, the intelligibility of the strictly human and the intelligibility of the causal order of nature. The problem first became pertinent in the context of theology, in the doctrinal exigency of reconciling human freedom with the omnipotence of God.

The Christian view of life was singularly unaffected by a concept which had been a dominant one to the Greek mind and which had inspired the writing of tragedies of a degree of greatness in many ways unparalleled since—the concept of fate. In place of this concept Christian theology had to hand the notion of destiny, which, by reason of the assumption that God was none other than Providence, i.e. a Being who was loving and good, was completely shorn of the catastrophic implications of the earlier concept. Man was, however, endowed with freedom of choice, for otherwise his opting for the fruit of the forbidden tree could not have come about. The fall of man, represented allegorically by Adam's eating of the apple given by Eve, initiated what theologians call 'original sin', a concept which is, in a sense, a misnomer since, according to the Book of Genesis, man was 'originally' in Paradise*. The problem was to reconcile this freedom of man (without which he could not be regarded as a fitting object of praise or blame) with the omnipotence of God, for this was no less important a part of staple Christian belief. As a creation of God I might have been expected to be perfect which very evidently I am not. If, since the fall, I am 'bound', through my descent from Adam, to sin, it would seem that no other lot can befall me than that of damnation. The cry of St. Augustine in his *Confessions* is a poignant one : 'Who made me?' Did not my God, who is not only good but goodness itself? Whence then came I to will evil and nill good, so that I am justly punished?' The project of attaining salvation was obviously doomed from the start unless there be active intervention on the part of God and the exercise of His Divine grace to pull me out of the pit into which I have fallen. A less gloomy view was taken by Pelagius who was sceptical about the doctrine of original sin and who thought that moral virtue was attainable through man's own efforts. While the doctrine of predestination seemed to many to be a corollary to the belief in Divine omnipotence, many did not go the whole way with St. Augustine and later, with Calvin. The classical Catholic position, as put foward by St. Thomas Aquinas, was that man has a conditioned or limited freedom. Divine grace is certainly in demand, but to refuse man a certain modicum of freedom would be to deny him his proper status in the hierarchy of created beings. Only God can be spoken of as perfectly free, a freedom about which we have tangible and visible evidence in the whole created order. When later philosophers came to speak of man's freedom as essentially creative they were in fact arguing on the analogy of what the scholastic thinkers had said about the activity of God Himself.

There is a world of difference, it can be seen, between the controversy with which religious thinkers concerned themselves and the modern dialogue between the determinist and the libertarian. It was inevitable that a clash should eventually

* Theologians who subscribe to the doctrine of original sin do so on the ground of our common descent from Adam.

come about between theological exigency and scientific practice and indeed it came to a head for the first time in the works of Descartes. Descartes was very aware that there was a gulf between the absolute freedom of God and the relative freedom of man. If man had no freedom, however, the demands of morality would be nullified, for in that case man could do no other than what he in fact does. Man as an incarnated creature, however, is in the unfortunate position of being betwixt two worlds. Cartesian dualism made it no less difficult to account for volitional action than to account for perception. Descartes seems to have thought that the power of the will was greater than that of the understanding and 'that it is chiefly my will which leads me to discern that I bear a certain image and similitude of Deity'. This did not prevent him from holding that it was the will which was responsible not only for sin (which had, after all, been said before) but also for error. The will is freest when associated with clearness of the understanding. The free will is 'capable of giving or withholding its assent'. It is therefore exhibited not in choice but in judgement and it is the capacity for judgement which distinguishes us from automata. In seeing freedom as concerned (although at the level of judgement) with knowledge, Descartes reveals an unexpected affinity with Spinoza.

The dichotomies which exercised his predecessors could not in the nature of things present any problem to Spinoza. The contrast between freedom and Divine omnipotence disappears since the whole of reality proceeds through determination out of the Divine ground or Substance. The distinction between freedom and determinism gives way in Spinoza to the distinction between freedom and ignorance. The intuition of freedom, on which libertarians lay so much stress, stems from the driving power of man's self-assertive impulses according to Spinoza. But this is only a semblance of freedom. The free man is he who acts according to 'adequate ideas', that is to say, according to reason. Such acts 'follow from' our nature as rational beings. But since to conceive adequately is to conceive all things in God the only free man, properly speaking, is he who knows God.

Determinism

The case for determinism rests on a specific thesis as to the nature of the scientific explanation of the physical world and on the assumption that this thesis is no less applicable to the explanation of human actions. The determinist sees the world as an interconnected system of events such that what occurs in the present has been determined by something occurring in the past. Given what happened in the past, the present could not be other than it is. Complete knowledge, as Laplace had envisaged it, would be knowledge of all the interconnecting links in the system, even extending into the future, and would be of the order which theologians of an earlier generation had attributed to the Supreme Intelligence, that is to say, to God. In the natural sciences the determinist viewpoint was typified in Newton's system of mechanics. Applied to the investigation of human actions it resulted in a statement like that of Schopenhauer to the effect that 'Every man, being what he is and placed in the circumstances which for the moment obtain, but which on their part also arise by strict necessity, can absolutely never do anything else than just what at that moment he does do. The notion of 'necessity' in this context, as Mill pointed out, had unfortunate connotations. We may on the one hand confuse it with logical necessity, or, what is more sinister, imagine that our own motives and desires constrain or compel us in some way. 'Power' language is used by another determinist, Holbach, in the following quotation : 'Man, who thinks himself free, is a fly who imagines he has power to move the universe, while he is himself unknowingly carried along by it'. The determinist cause, it would seem, was fortified not only by scientific considerations but by a certain amount of confusion of philosophical terminology.

Much remained to be clarified. What for example were the causal determinants of a particular action? The sociologically-minded could refer to environmental factors. Or, alternatively, I could refer back to the concept of 'character', saying that my character was the cause of my actions. But here came the rub. Was my character the ultimate cause or only the proximate cause? The hardest of determinists would maintain that my character too was strictly determined. The most convincing of those in recent times who have taken this view was the famous American advocate Clarence Darrow who succeeded in persuading juries that the prisoner in the dock could have done none other that he did in the circumstances and so could not be held responsible for his act. This brings out another aspect of the free-will/determinism controversy which we have not mentioned hitherto.

The issue was not merely an academic metaphysical one, but had ethical importance too. If a man's actions were strictly determined in the manner that events in physical nature are determined no one could be held 'responsible for' his actions and therefore no one could be the fitting object of praise or blame (moralists always seem to have been more concerned with the latter rather than the former, probably because while the law awards punishments for those who transgress, the reward for doing good has been traditionally assigned by the religious-minded to a future state of being). Thus, although the possibility that we have in fact no right to judge others received support from the Biblical injunction that we judge not lest we ourselves be judged, moralists followed the legalism of those concerned with the maintenance of order in society, and so the view that judging others is out of court, which seemed to go along with determinism, struck most moralists as very shocking. The determinist case was strengthened, among other factors, by the over-statement of the opposite thesis by libertarians. In its extreme form indeterminism seemed to be holding that the free act was one in which there was no element of determination at all, and in that case it was difficult to see how a man's act could even be said to be 'his' at all.

The most fashionable kind of determinism in this century has been the Marxist variety, where the ultimate causal factors are located in the economic forces at work in society. On such a view human action has an almost maieutic function, and in spite of the injunction that we are to change reality, the real purpose of human intervention, we are told, is to bring to birth something already inherent in the course of events. The final strand relevant to the case for hard determinism today is to be found in the works of scientists like Einstein, Eddington and Planck.

Some thinkers regard the principle of indeterminacy in physics as evidence of an inherent surd element in nature, which amounts to saying that, on this view, the theory of determinism has been proved wrong within its very citadel, the explanation of events in physical nature. The alternative approach does not look upon the new principle as constituting any threat to the general dominion of causal law. To speak of indeterminacy, it will be said, is to refer to the boundary between what is known and what is unknown. Susan Stebbing, for example, has pointed out that the glee with which Heisenberg's principle was greeted by some libertarians has been misplaced. To speak of a loose-jointed universe tells us no more than that we still have not found out about the joints. But it is time to turn to the other side of the picture and to see what the advocate of free-will has to say.

Free-will

The case for free-will has been stated by Sidgwick as follows:—". . . . no amount of experience of the sway of motives even tends to make me distrust my intuitive consciousness that in resolving after deliberation I exercise free choice as to which of the motives acting on me shall prevail." This appeal to intuition has indeed been one of the strongest planks in the libertarian platform, in spite of the warning of history to the effect that appeals to intuition are very often shaky. As to what exactly the evidence of intuition is in this particular case is unclear for not all intuitions speak with a single voice. Some agree with Bradley in finding the differentia of willing in the sense of causal efficacy, an awareness of 'bringing about'. This kind of approach has emerged more or less unscathed even in spite of Hume's very damaging analysis of the experience of willing in his *Enquiry*. Libertarianism has been based on diverse metaphysical assumptions. William James' famous essay on 'The Dilemma of Determinism' was clearly founded on his general pluralistic metaphysic. His form of indeterminism, he says, 'gives us a pluralistic, restless universe, in which no single point of view can ever take in the whole scene; and to a mind possessed of the love of unity at any cost, it will, no doubt, remain forever inacceptable'. The theistic interpretation, on the other hand, is reared on a corpus of views concerning the relation between the mind and the body and the mind and nature. In recent years this whole interpretation has been thought through in a new and refreshing way by Austin Farrer.

The idiom of decision cannot be the same as the idiom of explanation, for whereas the latter reflects an essentially third person viewpoint the former is exclusively grounded in the first person. Free-will cannot be done justice to, as it were, from the outside. Only too often the determinist speaks as if the admitting of free-will would amount to denying all uniformity in the field of human conduct. But this is a distortion of what the libertarian wants to draw our attention to. The libertarian wishes to say that it is just possible, if not indeed likely, that the relative regularities of human life may not be of the same type as those of the physical universe. An earlier generation of metaphysicians used to introduce the concept of teleology at this point in order to explicate just what the difference was. The free-will advocate refers us to what Campbell has called a contra-causal type of freedom, of which we not only have direct evidence in experience but which, at the same time, makes intelligible the moral demand and provides the differentia of the sort of existence which is specifically human. To ignore man's endowment of freedom, is, therefore, to miss the secret of *what he is*.

To the libertarian a lot turns on the analysis of choice, for it is here that we are to find the locus of man's exercise of freedom. Recent discussion of this particular problem tends to beg the question. To say that a man is free has been identified with saying that 'he could have acted otherwise' if certain other conditions had been fulfilled (Nowell-Smith), with saying that 'he could have acted otherwise . . . . . . if he had willed otherwise' (Moore), or with saying that 'he could have chosen otherwise' (Campbell). None of these formulations advance us much as the problem of what choice itself is is left conspicuously untackled. Campbell comes the nearest to getting to grips with this problem. He points to the creative character of free actions, and choice is presumably the spring of such creativity. Now the word 'creative', from Bergson down to Berdyaev, has been a tantalising one for a certain type of philosopher. But before we can employ it in the present context we do surely need to explore what we mean by the 'self' or the 'person'. We would do wrong if we were to imagine that the act of choice (perhaps better, the complex choice-situation) can be analysed in abstraction from the total being which expresses itself in many and diverse activities. Just as the dichotomy of man into actor and spectator is a false one so also are the dichotomies of motives and acts over against the self, and that of myself versus my character. In what sense does what I do proceed from what I am? We certainly have a problem here. Catholic thinkers have an advantage at this point in their taking over of the scholastic doctrine of the substantial unity of the mind and the body. Adequate treatment of this problem (and many allied problems concerning the nature of man), as Dilthey remarked in another context, needs a more developed psychology and a more developed phenomenology of experience than we have at our disposal at present. Until this need is met, the libertarian succeeds in leaving us with the conviction that an action is, in some very important, although hitherto not completely discovered, sense, to be distinguished from a mere event. That this should be so, that a man's actions should, in his short span of life, mark themselves off from the general cavalcade of natural happenings, is what moral philosophers have been getting at in their insistence on the nature of man as a moral being.

The free-will advocate has been open to criticism at every turn, and some of these criticisms are rooted in the unfortunate overtones attached to the word 'indeterminism'. The case was often spoilt, as was suggested earlier, by being overstated. There was no need for the libertarian to erect a wall between act and character, or to deny that a great many of our actions can be predicted by an observer (although not by ourselves). I am perfectly 'free' when I play chess even though an intelligent observer can predict that when I move the castle I 'cannot do other than' move it straight up or across. The context of discussion moreover has been, for the most part, unduly narrow, framing the issue as that between a crude natural necessity on the one hand and personal freedom on the other. But, as the existentialists have pointed out, my most stubbornly 'determined' experiences are brought about not through my conflict with anything physical but through my encounters with other persons, and Hegel had said much the same thing long before. A more serious, because more fundamental, objection run into by the libertarian has been provided by the debunking of the concept of the will by philosophers like Gilbert Ryle, a debunking foreshadowed, in intention at least, in Hume's famous chapter on "Liberty and Necessity" in his *Enquiry.* Just as, if it is improper to speak of the *soul*, the issue of whether the soul be immortal or not will not arise, so, if the concept of the will be itself in question, the issue of whether the will be free or not will amount to a pseudo-issue. Some comments will be offered on this new and somewhat drastic approach in due course.

Free-will and Determinism

There are some philosophers who adopt a half-way position between that of the libertarian and the determinist, and the text-books usually class Kant among their number although, as will be seen, Kant's treatment of the problem falls apart from all other treatments in that Kant offers a solution peculiarly his own. Kant's understanding of what the problem in fact is, is stated most clearly by him in his work *Religion within the Bounds of Mere Reason* where he says that the difficulty is "how predeterminism, according to which voluntary actions as events have their determining grounds in the preceding time (which with whatever it contains is no longer in our power) can be consistent with freedom, according to which the action as well as its contradictory must be at the moment it happens in the power of the subject; this is what we want to understand and never shall." Kant, with Hume, is convinced that the causal relation is essentially a temporal relation, that is to say, it concerns the relation of before and after. The crucial question is whether the causal relation, understood in this way, is to be regarded as universal or not. Kant manages to extricate himself from the inexorable implication of his own argument by drawing the consequences of his distinction between phenomena and noumena, a distinction which he had already applied in his analysis of our knowledge of objects of sense. Applying this distinction to ourselves we arrive at the concepts of the phenomenal self and the noumenal self.

The phenomenal self, in common with all phenomena, is subject to the universal law of causation, and it is the regularities of our 'phenomenal' life which the psychologist studies. Of the noumenal self, however, this cannot be said, for the noumenal is, by definition, that to which the categories can have no application. It is the noumenal self, Kant believed, which is the source of a sort of causal agency different in kind from the causal necessity that we find in nature. Kant's solution, it can be appreciated, is a frankly dualistic one. Man is envisaged as a citizen of two realms, the natural one (and his citizenship of this realm is governed by the fact that his physicality makes him, from one point of view, a part of nature) and the moral realm, his participation in which is brought about by the fact that he possesses a moral consciousness, that is to say, a consciousness which makes him aware of the categorical nature of the 'ought'. These are the terms, then, in which Kant's theory of 'self-determinism' is to be understood. The criticism can always be made of any dualistic theory that it leaves unanswered the question as to how the terms of the duality are to be related. Kant's own metaphysic provides him with a neat answer to this particular puzzle. If freedom is to do with the noumenal self it is only to be expected that we should not understand it fully, for the very concept of the noumenal is that of a 'limiting' concept about which nothing positive can be said. Kant had already said something on similar lines about the relation of sense and understanding in that these 'perhaps spring from a common, but to us unknown, root.' It is in the Antinomies that Kant gets to grips with the theoretical problem of 'reconciling' the moral order with the empirical.

What is of special interest for us in this context of discussion is the clarity with which Kant sees the involvement of the basis of morality with the notion of the supersensible. Sensible experience by itself can give us no hint of what freedom might mean. Without an appeal to something beyond experience, the concept of freedom is a 'scandal', a paradox, something which is unintelligible. Now the outcome of the whole critical approach has been the showing up of the inherent impossibility of going beyond experience in a theoretical manner. Kant's treatment of freedom provides him with the starting point for an approach to the supersensible by another route, the route of the verdict of moral experience. Just as in the Analytic he is concerned with plotting the transcendental conditions without which sensible experience, i.e. knowledge, would be impossible, so in the Antinomies and in the *Critique of Practical Reason* he is concerned with the ground of the moral life, the freedom without which man could not be regarded as an ethical creature. The spontaneous cause which, in Kant's view, the free will is, is 'original', that is to say, unlike causes in the realm of nature, it is undetermined by antecedents. It can be understood, against the background of Kant's work as a whole (and this *is* how it should be understood) as a parallel treatment to his discussion of the spontaneity of the synthetic unity of apperception which stands in contrast to the mechanical associations in the mind of which Hume had spoken. So understood we can see Kant's treatment of freedom as a kind of extension of the transcendental approach, that is to say, the approach which, speaking simply, hunts for the conditions without which things (in the case of the first Critique, knowledge and in the case of the second Critique, moral experience) would not be as they are.

An entirely different way of 'reconciling' free will and determinism, conspicuous by its lack of concern with metaphysics, is to be found in the works of Hume, Mill, and, in recent days, Schlick and A. J. Ayer. These philosophers are often said to adhere to 'soft determinism' (*pace* William James) or to the 'pseudo-problem' theory. Hard determinists, they say, have been under a number of mis-apprehensions. They have confused (or some of them have) causal necessitation with logical necessity, they have peopled the world with mysterious 'forces' and they have looked upon causes as 'compelling' and 'constraining' in the way in which one person may sometimes compel another. Causal laws, on the other hand, are not be to be looked on as 'prescriptive' at all. Causal laws are only shorthand descriptions of perceived uniformities. They enable us to predict, it is true ; but that does not mean to say that the future is thereby 'predetermined'. Our motives can, without risk to the cause of morality, be looked on as a species of cause. Responsibility indeed rests on this, for otherwise how would I be able to say that this is 'my' act ? The influence of Wittgenstein can be discerned in the number of 'game' analogies usually introduced at this point. If I am playing a certain game there are certain rules to be followed, but this does not mean that I 'must' make any particular move.

The most challenging piece of analysis relevant to this whole approach is Ryle's discussion of the concept of will. He follows Hume in debunking the will as a model of efficacy, and his starting point, like that of Hume, is the verdict of introspection. His main insistence is that volitions are not a species of effect, and within the framework of his rejection of the dualistic theory of the mind/body relation, he attempts to bring in willings, along with feelings, knowings how etc. within the fold of propensities. Whether in debunking substance language we need go as far as Ryle does, however, may occasion reflection. He maintains that 'Most voluntary actions do not issue out of conditions of indecision'. But what about those which do ? If 'knowing how' is made analogous to, 'being able', willing is surely analogous to 'trying' or 'intending'. The fact that we cannot enumerate, introspect or describe volitional units, does not necessarily indicate that there are not in fact any. It is just possible (as Kant said of the transcendental subject) that willings are just the sort of thing that cannot be enumerated, introspected or described.

The question can always be raised whether any third person treatment can ever do justice to what volition is Ryle's entire treatment can ever do justice to what volition is. Ryle's entire it is, is throughout a third person treatment. The existentialists on the other hand offer an analysis which is first person to a degree. While there is much in their work which is perhaps not strictly 'philosophical', there can be no doubt that no other group of thinkers in our own time, or perhaps even before, has given such deeply felt consideration to the experience of 'decision' as they have. One inadequacy which we have detected in most of the theories which have been under review has been the only too often glib reference to the concept of choice. An adequate analysis of choice, it was suggested, cannot but be bound up with a fuller understanding of what it means to be a 'person'. Sartre goes as far as to say 'The free project is fundamental, for it is my being'. If freedom exists in a situation this means that my freedom works itself out in a context of conditions, that is to say, in the context of the determined. A criticism like that of René le Senne, that Sartre replaces the idolatry of determinism by 'idolatry of the arbitrary' is perhaps not altogether warranted. Kant's linking of freedom with the supersensible reappears in the work of philosophers like Marcel who has said that 'A man cannot be free or remain free, except in the degree to which he remains linked with what transcends him, whatever the particular form of that link may be'. Finally, existentialist discussions of freedom show, *inter alia*, that here at least is one problem which cannot, without trivialising it, be reduced to the level of analysis of language.

XV The Proofs of the Existence of God

THE proofs of the existence of God form the core of rational theology or classical theism. The scholastic philosophers propounded these proofs with great skill, believing as they did that there were rational grounds for belief in God's existence and that before a man can be expected to accept what God reveals there is a reasonable demand that he should first be convinced that there is a God. Thus St. Thomas Aquinas writes ". . . .the existence of God and other like truths about God, which can be known by natural reason, are not articles of faith, but are preambles to the articles, for faith presupposes natural knowledge, even as grace presupposes nature." The idea of a 'natural theology' lays stress on the capacity of man's reason, unaided either by revelation or by any extra-ordinary religious experience, to know that God exists. The natural theologian utilises what he has been given, his God-given faculty of reason and his awareness of a natural order, that is to say, a cosmos, which, being made by God, bears the stamp of God's Divine reason on it and which therefore (both man and the world having been created by God) yields itself up to man's enquiry. The background of the proofs is an undoubtedly ontological view of the world in which the intelligibility of the created order is guaranteed not, as Descartes put it, by the thought that anything else would amount to deception on the part of God, but which is guaranteed through the rationality of the Divine nature (as shown in His possessing ideas according to the patterns of which things were created), the rationality of the universe (since it had been made according to the Divine pattern), and the rationality of man (a being who not only had reason as his essence, for even Aristotle had said this, but who had been created "a little lower than the angels").

Given such an impressive cosmology, the programme of the natural theologian did not seem so grandiose a project as it may strike the sceptic today. The scholastic philosophers, moreover, did not envisage sense and understanding as the separate faculties that we tend to regard them in modern times. Intellect was not merely a discursive faculty, something that groped among mere concepts. Intellect possessed a penetrative power, a capacity for cognising the essences in the hierarchical order of being. On such a view of our cognising powers the cosmological way of theological thinking was the obvious way. In arguing from features of the created order to the nature of their Creator we were, one could almost say, hardly inferring, but rather reading off the signs vouchsafed to us by the Divine language. There is a world of difference between cosmological thinking so viewed and the later attempts of philosophers to make use of the traditional arguments along with an epistemology which bifurcated perception and intellection. It is important, in assessing the weight of the proofs, to bear in mind a climate of thought where the term 'scholastic' had not yet fallen into disrepute, and also where the model for rational operations was not yet the kind of procedures found in Euclidean geometry.

The main aim of the rational theologian is to establish *that* God exists. As to *what* He is, this is a matter on which revelation will give us authoritative information. In the Book of Exodus God is spoken of as 'He who is', for the pronouncement made by God Himself—'I am that I am'—affirms in no uncertain terms the nature of God as self-existent being. God is not merely the *ens maximum* (i.e. the greatest being that exists) but the *maxime ens* (that which completely is). At this point Catholic theology draws on the Aristotelian conception of 'being', that is to say, the notion of efficacy. The 'Being' of God is shown in His efficacy, i.e. creativity on the greatest scale of all, His creativity of the whole universe. And this is why it is possible for the human intellect, finite though it be, to proceed as it were in reverse, by regarding the whole choir of heaven and furniture of earth as 'evidence' of the existence of God. Not that it is necessary to do so, or that without so doing man would be in doubt, but that there is abundant evidence which any rational man will see to be such and which puts on a reasoned foundation those truths which, through faith, he is already in possession of. The proofs, then, as St. Thomas stresses, are to be regarded as 'preambles'. He further says "This proposition

'God exists' of itself is self-evident", but "because we do not know the essence of God, the proposition is not self-evident to us, but needs to be demonstrated by things that are more known to us, though less known in their nature—namely, by effects." Now each and every particular existing thing depends for its existence upon a pure act of existence. But the mystery of existence is not to be yielded up at the level of contingent existence, but only in Him of whom, and of whom alone, it can be said that it is His essence to exist. The major certainty is possessed by faith, but the major evidence is possessed by reason. The service the proofs render is to lead us *via* the knowledge of essences to the mystery of existence itself, and this is possible because there is one Being in whom essence and existence are identified.

The Ontological Proof

Of the various proofs the ontological proof is the only one which is purely a *priori*, that is to say, the only proof which does not draw on any evidence from experience. This proof is the creation of St. Anselm and is to be found in his work the *Proslogion*, the complete title of which in the Latin contains the famous phrase 'Fides quaerens intellectum' (literally 'faith seeking knowledge') and which may be said to sum up the whole programme of the natural theologian. What answer, St. Anselm asks, is to be given to the fool who 'hath said in his heart, there is no God' (Psalm xiv. 1)? What content is to be given to the word "God" when it is so uttered? Does the 'fool' realise what he is saying? Is he contradicting himself? God can be defined as "a being than which nothing greater can be conceived". To conceive of such a being and to conceive of it as lacking existence would be self-contradictory, for an existent being is 'greater' than a non-existent being. "There is, then, so truly a being than which nothing greater can be conceived to exist, that it cannot even be conceived not to exist". It is interesting to note that, unlike in certain other forms of the argument, St. Anselm does not (at this stage) make use of the word 'perfection'. All turns on the question of the *conceivability* of the idea of God. Does the idea of a being 'quod non major cogitari potest' contain any positive content, or is it what we would call today a sort of limiting concept? It is necessary to remind ourselves that St. Anselm was not only an Augustinian (the first chapter of his *Proslogion* is very reminiscent of the *Confessions*) but a Platonist, that is to say, a philosopher for whom essences are at the same time existents. To a Platonist there would be no gulf between thought and Being. But it still remains to be shown what exactly we are conceiving when we conceive a being "than which nothing greater can be conceived." The most sympathetic interpretation of the argument is not that it is trying to make out that the fool is perpetrating a formal contradiction when he says "There is no God" (although St. Anselm would maintain this also) but that St. Anselm is attempting to point out what exactly is involved in the concept of God. There is an implicit reference to the Biblical affirmation that God is 'He who is'. The difficulty arises, however, in deciding whether this statement is analytic or synthetic. On the modern view all existential statements are synthetic and, therefore, this one too will be synthetic, but spuriously so, as we have no intuition of God on the basis of which such a synthetic statement could be made. On the other hand if we regard "God is He who Is" as a tautology the fool's statement becomes a mere self-contradiction. Behind St. Anselm's argument there seems to be not only optimism concerning the possibility of conceiving the concept of God (an optimism that does not square with man's finitude) but also the assumption of the Christian doctrine that only of God can it be said that it is His essence to exist.

The whole point of the argument is to show that the idea of God is a unique idea, and there is none other like it. If it were possible to conceive the idea of God, some would say we would 'see' that it was the essence of God to exist. But to succeed in this project would mean that one was God, for existence is not concept but act. St. Anselm's use of the words "greater than" seems to lay him open to the charge of treating existence as a predicate. Existing in reality is spoken of as being greater than existing only in the understanding, so that to deny the character of existing in reality to God is to make our idea fall short of the requirement 'than which nothing greater can be conceived'. St. Anselm's dilemma is a serious one. Either we insist on the uniqueness of the idea and 'point out' what is involved in it (i.e. that it is God's nature to exist) and if we do this we are open to the Thomist objection that as our understandings are finite we are not able to frame such an idea at all; or we become open to the Kantian objection that it is not possible to make the transition from possibility to actuality merely on the basis of an idea. The most sympathetic view that can be taken of St. Anselm's argument (and it is quite evident that his form of the proof is infinitely superior to that of Descartes) is that he is not intending to diagnose the 'fool's' mistake as a formal self-contradiction, nor is he making the mistake of regarding existence as a simple predicate, but he wishes to stress the uniqueness of the concept of God, the uniqueness of God's essence. In doing so he is probably speaking more as a man of religion than as a philosopher.

Anselm's argument first came in for criticism from his own contemporary, Gaunilo. Among others, Gaunilo has two special points to make. He attacks, as St. Thomas was to do after him, the view that it is possible to frame an adequate idea of God. The relevant passage is as follows :—"I, so far as actual knowledge of the object, either from its specific or general character, is concerned, am as little able to conceive of this being when I hear of it. or to have it in my understanding, as I am able to conceive or understand God himself; whom, indeed, for this very reason I can conceive not to exist. For I do not know that reality itself which God is, nor can I form a conjecture of that reality from some other like reality. For you yourself assert that reality is such that there can be nothing else like it." His second point anticipates one of Kant's main criticisms in the Dialectic. Gaunilo asks whether we would imagine that if we were to conceive the idea of a perfect island this would prove that such an island did in fact exist. "For he ought to show first that the hypothetical excellence of this island exists as a real and indubitable fact, and in no wise as any unreal object, or one whose existence is uncertain, in my understanding".

Thanks to Gaunilo's criticism, and also the preference which St. Thomas had for cosmological thinking, the argument was dropped during subsequent centuries, and the theological thinking of the Middle Ages concentrated on the way of analogy. The argument, however, was resurrected by the rationalist philosophers of the seventeenth and eighteenth centuries, and refurbished in the first place by Descartes. Descartes' starting point is our alleged ability to frame 'clear and distinct' ideas and he claims that we are able to frame a clear and distinct idea of God. Now the model of clear and distinct ideas for him is our mathematical ideas and so it follows that on his view the perception of the existence of God is as certain as any of the truths concerning figure or number. The idea of God is defined by Descartes as 'the idea of a being supremely perfect' and existence is regarded by him as 'an absolute perfection'. Therefore 'it is not in my power to conceive a God without existence, that is, a being supremely perfect, and yet devoid of an absolute perfection.' This inconceivability is stressed by Descartes by reference to other parallel impossibilities, first the impossibility of separating the idea of a mountain from that of a valley, and secondly the impossibility of separating the equality of the three angles of a triangle to two right angles from the essence of a triangle. He admits, however, that the first example is not quite on all fours with the case of the idea of God, for in the case of the mountain we are not claiming that any mountain actually exists, only claiming the mutual involvement of the concepts of mountain and valley. In the case of God, though, it is a question of 'the necessity which lies in the thing itself'. The necessity which obtains in our perception of the truths of mathematics seems to him to be on fours with the idea of God and its necessity because in each case if we only attend to the meaning of our terms we will perceive clearly and distinctly what is involved in them. 'For is there any truth more clear than the existence of a Supreme Being, or of God, seeing it is to his essence alone that (necessary and eternal) existence pertains?'

Descartes' form of the argument lays itself open to all the charges levelled against it by Kant. As a preface we must note that the connotation of the word "idea" is very different in Descartes' writings from what it was in the *Proslogion*. Ideas for Descartes are segments of consciousness, particular subjective contents. On such a view any question concerning existence poses problems, for the claim that something exists is a claim that something is not merely subjective but objective. Kant, like Gaunilo, begins by admitting that there is no difficulty in giving a merely 'verbal' definition of a concept, but points out that 'this yields no insight into the conditions which make it necessary to regard the non-existence of a thing as absolutely unthinkable.' The unsuitability of Descartes' geometrical example is singled out. In geometry we are not dealing with the existence of anything at all, and so this analogy shows us nothing, ". . . . the unconditioned necessity of judgements is not the same as an absolute necessity of things". If we reject both the predicate and the subject of a judgement no contradiction results. Now the claim of the rational theologian is that there is one concept, and one concept only, in the case of which to say that its object does not exist is to say something contradictory. But on Kant's view it is illegitimate to introduce the notion of existence into the mere concept of a thing. Concepts deal with the possible, and from a mere concept we cannot tell whether the object is actual or not. In order to see whether a concept has reference to anything real we need to go outside the concept. Possible experience is the only way we have of determining whether anything exists or not. In Kant's view all existential propositions are synthetic and therefore it is not possible to show that in one putative special case the predicate of existence cannot be rejected without contradiction. The word 'is' stands merely for the copula of a judgement. It only "serves to posit the predicate in its relation to the subject". Existence is not a predicate. "A hundred real thalers do not contain the least coin more than a hundred possible thalers." We may frame a concept as we will, but, when the question arises as to whether the concept refers to anything real, possible experience is our only criterion.

Kant's whole aim is to stress that the concept of existence can only be used univocally. The test of referring to actual and possible experience is something that cannot be avoided whenever we wish to make use of the word 'exist'. Now the difficulty is that in the case of the existence of God this a reference which is *ipso facto* excluded, for God cannot be an object of possible sense experience. The stress on the univocal character of existence is something which philosophers other than Kant have made as well. In Berkeley and Ryle for example we find a similar unwillingness to grant that the word 'exist' may have different meanings in different contexts. The philosopher who claims that there are uses of the word 'exist' other than the customary use in referring to the sensible has to explain exactly what he means. There is no doubt that within the context of actual and possible experience we have a clear criterion for distinguishing between the meaningless and the meaningful. But it is very necessary to bear in mind the gulf which obtains between the epistemological and the ontological ways of thinking. It was the ontological way of thinking which dominated mediaeval theology and its fertility was intimately associated with the use which the mediaeval theologians made of the method of analogical argument. It was a method, however, which, as St. Thomas Aquinas saw, was more fruitful if employed cosmologically, for the ontological way of procedure founders on the initial impossibility of a finite understanding ever framing the notion of a God whose essence it is 'to exist'.

The last part of Kant's criticism of the ontological argument is directed specifically against the Leibnizian form of it. Leibniz had said that Descartes' proof had missed out one essential stage. It was necessary first to show that the concept of God does not attempt to unite incompatible attributes. The most perfect being 'means the being of whom no simple positive predicate can be denied.' Now all positive simple predicates are compossible just because they are all positive. Leibniz then goes on to adopt the Cartesian view that existence is a perfection, and that if the most real being is possible it is also actual, for otherwise we would be withholding a simple positive predicate from the nature of God. In Kant's view, as we have already seen, it is a mistake to confuse conceivability—that is, after all, the merely analytic criterion of possibility—with actuality. Kant concludes by saying "And thus the celebrated Leibniz is far from having succeeded in what he plumed himself on achieving—the comprehension *a priori* of the possibility of this sublime ideal being."

As far as other philosophers are concerned it remains to review in brief what each had to say. The ontological argument, qua argument, is superfluous for Spinoza for in Prop. XI of his *Ethics* he says "God, or substance, consisting of infinite attributes, of which each expresses eternal and infinite essentiality, necessarily exists." In any case for Spinoza there would be no question of making a transition from thought to Being since thought is one of the attributes of Being. Locke treats the proof in his usual commonsensical way. He thinks it is a poor way of establishing the existence of God, for although some men may have an idea of God, some have 'worse than none'. As an empiricist he was well aware of the difficulty of making existential propositions on the basis of a theory of ideas, especially after knowledge had been defined as a matter of seeing the agreement and disagreement between ideas. The very uniqueness of the idea of God constitutes a difficulty, if, as Locke and Kant both agree, the central thing about human knowledge is its relational character. Our minds are equipped for subsuming particulars under a law, but when we have a unique particular before us, this method is *ipso facto* denied to us. Locke, therefore, concluded that the sensible thing to do was to rely on those proofs "which our own existence and the sensible parts of the universe offer so clearly and cogently to our thoughts."

Hegel and his followers staged a big comeback for the proof but to them the ontological proof presented no problem, for to the Hegelian there is no opposition between thought and reality. If thought be immanent in reality and reality be the Absolute, the Absolute or God necessarily exists. Caird rephrases the proof as follows :— ".... as spiritual beings our whole conscious life is based on a universal self-consciousness, an Absolute Spiritual Life, which is not a mere subjective notion or conception, but which carries with it the proof of its necessary existence or reality." In recent years there have been attempts to revive the ontological proof, but, in view of the searching criticisms which Kant has directed against it, it seems unlikely that any of these attempts will meet with success.

The Cosmological Proof

The cosmological proof counts as an *a posteriori* proof because it begins with something that is derived from experience, namely, the concept that something exists. It would thus appear to have an initial advantage, but we shall see that, in depending on the ontological argument as it does, it is not as firmly rooted in empirical data as the other a *posteriori* proof, the teleological proof. The cosmological proof has two forms. The first is known as the argument from contingency and it was the third of St. Thomas Aquinas' famous 'Five Ways'. The original proof in the *Summa Theologica* runs as follows :—

> "We find in nature things that are possible to be and not to be, since they are found to be generated, and to corrupt, and consequently, they are possible to be and not to be. But it is impossible for these always to exist, for that which is possible not to be at some time is not. Therefore, if everything is possible not to be, then at one time there could have been nothing in existence. Now if this were true, even now there could be nothing in existence, because that which does not exist only begins to exist by something already existing. Therefore if at one time nothing was in existence, it would have been impossible for anything to have begun to exist; and thus even now nothing would be in existence—which is absurd. Therefore, not all beings are merely possible, but there must exist something the existence of which is necessary. But every necessary thing either has its necessity caused by another or not. Now it is impossible to go on to infinity in necessary things which have their necessity caused by another, as has already been proved in regard to efficient causes. Therefore we cannot but postulate the existence of some being having of itself its own necessity, and not receiving it from another, but rather causing in others their necessity. This all men speak of as God."

A "contingent" being means one which, in the nature of things, need not have existed. If I look at any particular object in the world it is true to say that it might just as well have not been there. We can conceive everything else being there even though that particular thing be not there. If we push back the demand for an explanation, therefore, we see that there must be a necessary being which is the ground of everything contingent. Now much difficulty attends this concept of a necessary being. Kant has pointed out that in so far as the argument culminates with this concept it stands or falls with the ontological argument, for it was this latter argument which purported to show that there is a being whose existence is necessary in the sense that His non-existence is 'inconceivable'.

In order to appreciate the argument in its original context it is wise to remember the ontological character of Thomistic philosophy. We are accustomed to thinking in terms of 'contingent' and 'necessary' propositions, but Aquinas is speaking of contingent and necessary 'being'. On the ontological view of things if there is relative existence there must be absolute existence too. What exactly is the nature of this 'must'? The ontologist has a special theory as to what is meant by 'intelligibility'. The modern scientific view is that a thing has been 'explained' when you have succeeded in showing its relation to other things. There is very obviously no end to such a method of procedure, at least theoretically. You might, for example, succeed in showing how the common cold was linked up with some form of virus infection and this may in a sense be a sufficient explanation for your immediate purpose. But if you are concerned with preventive medicine you will be likely to have to go further than this and you may need to investigate a whole network of qualifying conditions like the relation of the symptoms to the amount of haemoglobin in the blood and so on. Such 'explanations', we all recognise, are never 'complete'. Now it is precisely a 'complete' explanation that the ontologist is after. He is not satisfied with a relational explanation of things, but he wants to see all things as grounded in something absolute. This ground is not to be conceived as a merely logical ground (although ontologists usually thought it was a logical ground as well) but as an ontological ground. It is not easy for the modern mind to grasp the sort of ideal of complete intelligibility which inspired the ontologist. It is, as has been suggested, close to the notion of 'being grounded' and this in turn suggests "being derived from".

In view of the above, the criticisms of the argument from contingency, although they are certainly inevitable ones, do in a sense miss much of the weight of what the ontologist has to say. However the criticisms are serious ones. It is objected that the argument makes the mistake of regarding existence as a predicate, whereas the truth is that no existential proposition is logically necessary. This is a Kantian objection. The Kantian can admit only two sorts of necessity, logical necessity and causal necessity. To him there is no third kind. The concept of absolute necessity remains, on this view, a mere programme, a concept without content. Further, it will be maintained, there can be no such thing as complete intelligibility. This again is a mere project of pure reason and a project that must always remain unfulfilled. Nothing can be intelligible in itself. Its intelligibility consists in its relation to other things. Things are dependent on each other, and there is no point in introducing a spurious logical flavour into the discussion by bringing in the words 'contingent' and 'necessary'. Since so much turns on the idea of 'conceivability' it is only fair to realise, says the critic, that we are quite unable to 'conceive' what perfect intelligibility would be like, and therefore Kant said no truer word than when he insisted that the whole project amounted to the 'ideal' of pure reason.

The second form of the cosmological proof is known as the causal proof. It forms the second of Aquinas's arguments and in the *Summa* runs as follows :—

> "In the world of sense we find there is an order of efficient causes. There is no case known (neither is it, indeed possible) in which a thing is found to be the efficient cause of itself; for so it would be prior to itself, which is impossible. Now in efficient causes it is not possible to go on to infinity, because in all efficient causes following in order, the first is the cause of the intermediate cause, and the intermediate is the cause of the ultimate cause, whether the intermediate cause be several or one only. Now to take away the cause is to take away the effect. Therefore, if there be no first cause among efficient causes, there will be no ultimate, nor any intermediate cause. But if in efficient causes it is possible to go on to infinity, there will be no first efficient cause, neither will there be an ultimate effect, nor any intermediate efficient cause; all of which is plainly false. Therefore it is necessary to admit a first efficient cause, to which every one gives the name of God".

The main thing that the proof maintains is that a causal series cannot 'go back to infinity'. Now in order to explain this the defender of the proof makes a distinction between causes 'in fieri' and causes 'in esse'. The former (literally a cause 'in becoming') is a cause which helps to make something happen.

A cause 'in being', however, is a cause which sustains an effect 'in being'. An example of something which is a cause in both senses is a fire which both begins to make the room warm and which continues to keep it warm. Now the Thomist is saying that there cannot be an infinite series of causes 'in esse'. The reasoning follows closely the theologian's reasoning in interpreting the Biblical phrase 'In the beginning'. As far as creation is concerned the point is not that God's act is an act which is temporally prior to any form of existence whatsoever, for this would be to make Him part of the temporal series, but that all *depends* on God. God is not only He who initiates but He who sustains. The Thomist here leans to some extent on the Aristotelian theory of the Unmoved Mover. God is not a mere first term in a causal series, not primary in that simple sense, but is the ultimate ground in which things live and move and have their being. The core of the ontologists' meaning is a concept of cause which, in the last analysis, is not serial but hierarchical. Such was Aristotle's view, and such also is Aquinas's view. The linear view of time and of the causal series is no doubt part and parcel of the investigating of causal connections within nature, but the rationalist theologian has something very different from this in mind. God is ontologically first in the sense that He is the one on whom all depends. This interpretation of the 'first cause' also has the advantage, it will be claimed, of affirming the presence of God here and now. To think of a 'first cause' in any other way than this would be to reduce God to a *Deus ex machina* who merely gives a fillip to the universe.

The causal form of the cosmological proof is open to a whole barrage of criticisms, most of which stem from the modern insistence on the temporal nature of causal transactions. Causality is concerned with happening and not with being. It only operates when we are investigating the order of happenings in nature. Of the four connotations given to the term 'cause' by Aristotle the scientific view singles out the connotation of efficient causality, that is to say, an antecedent event responsible for the "production" of an effect. The very essence of the concept of cause, to the scientist, is its linear character. To ask for a 'first' cause, therefore, is to ask for the impossible, for either the so-called first cause X will be part of a series in which case it is pertinent to push our questioning further back and ask what caused X, or the putative cause is separate from the series in which case its efficacy is lost. We cannot at one and the same time preserve the unique status of the 'first' cause and uphold its efficacy. So far from there being a demand for a cessation of the series, any such cessation would destroy the notion of cause altogether. The notion of the conformity of events to law is something which, in the very nature of the case, is only applicable to regularities, that is, to patterns of events which repeat themselves. It cannot tell us anything about the status of what claims to be a unique particular. Causality is relative not absolute.

If the serial nature of the causal concept be fully understood then it is evident that it is wholly unwarranted to ask for the cause of the series 'as a whole'. Causal questions can only be raised *within* that whole. Further it can be objected that the causal proof does not establish the existence of a God as such. Nor need one infer to a *single* cause from which everything is derived. There might just as soon be a plurality of 'primary' causes. The Kantian line of criticism which has been outlined above is incontrovertible if the essential involvement of the concept of time with that of causality is taken seriously. At another level, however, the philosopher who is interested in religious language will see the whole discussion as yet another example of a problem which we came up against earlier, the problem of analysing the use which the religious thinker makes of terms which, in other contexts, have a very clear-cut usage. It seems the case that the philosopher of religion *does* use words like 'cause' and 'exist' in very special ways. Religious language cannot help being analogical. Either we admit that this is so, and try, as some of the thinkers in the field of philosophical theology are attempting to do today, to plot carefully the devious paths of some of these analogies, or we resort to neologisms. The latter is probably the more desperate alternative.

The Teleological Proof

The teleological proof is the second of the a *posteriori* proofs under consideration. It is also known as the argument from design. Whereas the cosmological proof argues from existence in general, this proof argues from determinate experiences, namely those which suggest an element of design. In a sense it is a species of causal proof because it argues that the presence of certain phenomena in nature could only have come about through the agency of a special cause, this is, intelligence. The proof was especially influential in the eighteenth century thanks to the influence of Leibniz' writings and the belief of philosophers like Wolff that the order of things in the universe seems to be for the special advantage of man. The biological sciences were as yet in their infancy, but they were sufficiently advanced for men to have been struck by the amazing adaptiveness of creatures in the organic world, and this, it should be remembered, at a time when men had come to take the Newtonian hypothesis of a more or less mechanical universe as literally true.

Three things need especially to be borne in mind if we are to see the teleological proof in its proper context. The first is that the philosophers who made use of this proof were for the most part Deists. This means to say that they thought that reason was the only tool required by the theologian. The work of the Cartesians and their followers on the Continent had given the method of demonstration tremendous prestige and there seemed no reason why this method should not be equally successful in theology. The second thing is a general hedonistic temper which extends from perhaps the third quarter of the eighteenth century up to the time of the so-called Philosophical Radicals. This is something which may certainly strike the social historian as odd if he thinks of the troubled days of the French Revolution, the aftermath of the Napoleonic Wars and the many evils which, *inter alia*, accompanied the progress of the Industrial Revolution. And yet the majority of philosophers seemed to have been convinced that the order of mundane things was expressly ordered to man's advantage and that the Divine pattern, which was visible in the cosmos of created things, was especially transparent in man himself, the lord of reason, the crown of the universe, whose intellectual powers were seen at their height in Sir Isaac Newton. Man had happiness as part of his birthright, and, indeed, if he used his reason wisely he *could* be in fact happy. Those who suffer do so through some defect in themselves—this, one might hazard—was the motto behind much of French aristocratic thought in the seventeen eighties. This, says Leibniz, and he speaks for the times, is the best of all possible worlds. Admittedly this kind of facile philosophy was brilliantly satirised by Voltaire in *Candide* and by Hume through the mouth of Philo. But the impetus of the Enlightenment did carry along with it a hedonistic undercurrent which may to us, looking back on the ferment of those days, seem difficult to understand.

The third factor to be borne in mind is that the teleological proof belongs to the pre-evolutionary stage of the biological sciences. The Biblical account of creation in Genesis, if interpreted literally (and fundamentalism was for the most part, the order of the day until well on into the nineteenth century) assumed that individual species had been brought into existence through separate fiats on the part of God. Combine this, as Christian theology did combine it, with the view that Ideas do not, as Plato thought, exist in an eternal intellectual realm, but are lodged in the Divine Mind, and you get the teleological view—the view that all things have been created according to *paradigma* (patterns or archetypes) in God's mind. All that the teleological 'argument' does, in fact, is to present this view in reverse—if we look around us we see that the world is full of 'contrivances' that are not due to man's agency. Arguing analogically there is every reason to believe that they are the effects of some intelligence or other. Now the beneficent disposition of these contrivances gives us every evidence for believing that the design that we see in nature must be due to the agency of a Divine Mind which is none other than God.

The word 'contrivance' was used by Paley in his famous *Evidences of the existence and attributes of the Deity* which created a stir when it appeared in 1802. A watch cannot cause itself. The eye cannot have come about by chance. "Arrangement, disposition of parts, subserviency of means to an end, relation of instruments to a use, imply the presence of intelligence and mind". Hume puts the proof as follows :—

"The curious adapting of means to ends, throughout all nature, resembles exactly, though it much exceeds, the productions of human contrivance....... Since therefore the effects resemble each other, we are led to infer, by all the rules of analogy, that the causes also resemble; and that the Author of nature is somewhat similar to the mind of man; though possessed of much larger faculties, proportioned to the grandeur of the work which he has executed." In Shaftesbury the argument reappears with a shift to stress on the beauty of the universe. Beauty is the informative power which works through the Divine design.

Now the adaptations which impress the teleologist seem to be threefold. There is, first, the adaptiveness of things to thought. The categories of thought are in some way geared to the nature of things. This is, of course, a highly metaphysical statement. But two examples will suffice to show what it might mean. Our relative notions of permanence and change are intimately connected with the fact that it so happens that, at the perceptual level, changes happen slowly, or at any rate slowly enough for us to take account of them. Those changes which happen fast escape our limited capacities of perception. A more shaky example is the following. It so happens that we have always, up to now, found that the sun rises tomorrow. In cases like this, therefore, we have found that the future resembles the past and our inductive procedures are founded on this supposition—not that we do not sometimes come in for rude shocks. The second uncanny adaptation is that of living organisms. The various organs of living things are to be understood in terms of function and the structures of beaks, claws, lungs and heart are fearfully and wonderfully 'made' for the functions which they perform. Evolutionary ways of thinking have admittedly changed our reaction to phenomena like these, but there is no doubt good reason for Kant to say that "We are brought face to face with so many marvels immeasureably great that all speech loses its force, all numbers their power to measure. our thoughts themselves all definiteness. . . . ." The third adaptation is that of the inorganic to the organic. There is air to breathe, water to drink and so forth. From the evolutionary standpoint, again, we may wish to restate this, e.g. not that there is, beneficently, air to breathe, but that the lungs have evolved as the most efficient organ for absorbing oxygen into the blood-stream.

Now, as in the case of the other proofs, it is not hard to find ways of undermining the teleological one. But Kant has warned us that 'it always deserves to be mentioned with respect' and that it is the 'most accordant with the common reason of mankind'. To begin with, Kant is surely right in diagnosing that the physico-theological proof, as he calls is, is based on the cosmological (it after all discerns a special type of cause) and therefore on the ontological. Further it makes the assumption that there is a close analogy between the universe on the one hand and artifacts on the other. Mill produces an interesting point against Paley in this connection. He says that in the case of the watch I reason from watch to watch-maker because I know by direct experience that watches are made by men. In the case of the universe and God I have no such direct experience.

As a proof, moreover, it establishes a lot less than is apparent at first sight. It leads to the inference of the existence of an architect, not a creator, if we follow the analogy strictly. If we chose our data suitably we can even argue to the existence of a devil and not to that of a divine being at all. One could as easily also argue to the existence of a plurality of celestial beings (whether benevolent or malicious) as to monotheism. Many have pointed out that in certain of its aspects nature is capable of inspiring us with horror. Hume informs us "...... inspect a little more narrowly these living existences, the only beings worth regarding. How hostile and destructive to each other! How insufficient all of them for their own happiness! The whole presents nothing but the idea of a blind Nature, impregnated by a great vivifying principle, and pouring forth from her lap, without discernment or parental care, her maimed and abortive children!" An even more gloomy picture is painted by Clarence Darrow in Chapter 44 of his autobiography *The story of my life* (this chapter, however, does contain passages very reminiscent of Russell's 'A free man's worship' and has a hint of the almost stoical conclusion which Russell draws). Darrow says 'Even had this planet been meant for life, it plainly was not meant for human life. Three-fourths of the surface is covered with water, which would show that if it was ever designed for life it was designed for fishes and not for men'. The Tennysonian view of nature as "red in tooth and claw" is one perhaps for which there is even more evidence in our own day. The shallow optimism of Doctor Pangloss can hardly appeal to many today. Further the proof is, we should not forget, an empirical proof, and, it may well be argued, if we are good Humeans, that from empirical premisses only an empirical conclusion can follow. Whitehead takes this line when he says 'Any proof which commences with the character of the actual world cannot rise above the actuality of this world.'

To the modern mind the teleological way of thinking is hard to defend in view of the theory of evolution. If all forms of life can be shown to have evolved from earlier forms, the account given in the Book of Genesis seems to be out of date, and the hypothesis of divine patterns according to which the whole is designed seems to be a redundant hypothesis. Certainly Darwin's *Origin of Species* came as a bombshell when it appeared. But, on reflection, it can be seen that the theologian can reinterpret his doctrine to take in the findings of Darwin. The word 'evolve', in a sense, does not explain anything. Rather it states the problem in a different form. The phenomena of evolving species are fresh grist to the mill of the theologian who wishes to refer us to the marvels of nature. The theist's God, as William Temple has shown, is the God who is at work through process. The theory of evolution is able to further our attempt to understand the ways of God to man.

But what of the proof as a proof? The conclusive assessments come from Hume and Kant. Hume says "A purpose, an intention, a design, strikes everywhere the most careless, the most stupid thinker; and no man can be so hardened in absurd systems as at all times to reject it.... all the sciences almost lead us insensibly to acknowledge a first Author.." He further comments that the cause of order in the universe 'probably bears some remote analogy to the human mind.' Although Kant showed that, as an argument, the physico-theological proof was impossible, yet he pronounced that 'It would therefore not only be uncomforting but utterly vain to attempt to diminish in any way the authority of this argument.' He believed that it 'enlivens the study of nature' and 'extends our knowledge of nature by means of the guiding-concept of a special unity, the principle of which is outside nature'. That Kant himself was increasingly impressed by the fertility of the teleological approach is clearly borne out by his third Critique. It is for the biologist to say whether he is, in practice, guided by the notion of mere complexity of organisation, or whether, implied in the concept of 'function', is something that closely resembles 'purpose'. Even if we can argue on the basis of teleology to the existence of an efficient, intelligent, ethical being, this will still be less than the God of traditional theism. And yet, to the man who already on other grounds does believe, nature does offer ample grounds for that belief.

The Moral argument

Kant's critique of rational theology, as has been seen, amounts to a demonstration of the unsuccess of pure reason in its speculative employment. Kant's own view, however, was that it is possible to argue convincingly from the facts of moral experience to the existence of a Divine Being. He offers what are, in effect, two different lines of thinking on the subject of 'moral theology'. His starting point in both cases is expressed in the *Critique of Pure Reason* as follows :—

> "I assume that there really are pure moral laws which determine completely *a priori* (without regard to empirical motives, that is, to happiness) what is and is not to be done, that is, which determine the employment of the freedom of a rational being in general ; and that these laws command in an absolute manner (not merely hypothetically, on the supposition of other empirical ends), and are therefore in every respect necessary. I am justified in making this assumption, in that I can appeal not only to the proofs employed by the most enlightened moralists but to the moral judgement of every man, in so far as he makes the effort to think such a law clearly."

Kant takes for granted, it is plain, the unconditionality of obligation. From the argument of the Antinomies, moreover, we already know that he believes man to be a citizen of both the natural and the intelligible world, and that man is a citizen of the latter in virtue of his status as a moral being. The question, then, is whether anything can be inferred from man's sense of obligation, or, to put it another way, whether a moral world is necessarily a Divine world.

Kant's first line of thinking begins with an examination of the concepts of happiness and morality, and is an interesting refutation (among other things) of the utilitarian charge that Kant paid scant attention to man's natural desire for happiness. In the world of fact, as Kant is realistic enough to see, virtue and happiness by no means always go together. The man who is worthy to be happy may, like Job, be called upon to suffer the slings and arrows of misfortune. In Kantian terminology, virtue and happiness are not analytically related. It is not self-contradictory to say that any particular man is virtuous but not happy, or that another is happy but not virtuous. Virtue and happiness are synthetically related. A ground is therefore required to show how the relation may be brought about. This ground can be neither empirical (as we have seen that empirically virtue and happiness are often far apart) nor can it be logical. It can be, it follows, none other than a transcendent ground, that is, a Divine Being, an intelligence 'in which the most perfect moral will, united with supreme blessedness, is the cause of all happiness in the world.' The same reasoning leads us to the necessity of postulating a future life. "Thus without a God and without a world invisible to us now but hoped for, the glorious ideas of morality are indeed objects of approval and admiration, but not springs of purpose and action". Kant goes on to say that moral theology has the advantage of leading to the concept of a sole, all-perfect and rational primordial being who is at the same time omnipotent, omniscient, omnipresent and eternal. Such a view also connects up the order of nature as a system of ends with the Divine purpose. Even so, it is to be noted, moral theology establishes not a dogma, not a proof, but 'a postulate which is absolutely necessary in view of what are reason's own most essential ends'. In this way Kant employs the moral argument to connect the two worlds whose existence he had established in the Antinomies. Linking this further with Kant's concept of a Kingdom of Ends, this Kingdom can be at the same time regarded, at least heuristically, as the Kingdom of God. God is not merely a necessary being, but the one and only holy will, the only will that is supremely good. This first line of thinking, then, is closely related to the Antinomies, the *Groundwork of the Metaphysic of Morals* and to the *Critique of Judgement.*

Kant's second line of thinking, unfortunately not so fully stated as the first, develops the implications of the third formulation of the categorical imperative. If we examine the notion of the moral 'law' we are led to inquire into the source of this law. This source can be none other than the Divine Legislator. In the Kingdom of Ends finite beings are subject to the sovereignty of God. It is God who is the sovereign of the society of rational beings. In saying this, however, Kant was not modifying whatsoever his profound conviction that the moral law carries unconditional authority on its own account. He says ". . . . . . we shall not look upon actions as obligatory because they are the commands of God, but shall regard them as divine commands because we have an inward obligation to them." To obey the moral law out of fear of God was, on his view, thoroughly unmoral. But the man who already is convinced of the authority of the moral law will be led, through his moral experience, to the concept of a Being, whose existence is 'necessary', not on theoretical grounds, but from the demands of the moral consciousness. Thus we conclude, *via* both these lines of thinking, not with the demonstrative cogency of a 'proof', but with moral certitude.

Two fundamental questions remain for consideration. Is it in fact the case that moral experience necessitates belief in the existence of God? A comparison with Kierkegaard is suggestive here. Kierkegaard shows the independence of the aesthetic, the moral and the religious stages of existence. It is possible for a man to remain at the moral stage of life, the "universal" stage (compare the first formulation of the categorical imperative). And yet it is only the man who has lived at the moral level who can ever be capable of rising to the final religious stage. Whether religion does in any sense 'complete' morality is a subject which would take us further afield. As far as his stress on the absolute and unconditioned nature of the moral demand is concerned Kant is surely right. The stoic temperament will stop here, whereas those who interpret the moral order as being spiritual in nature will be led, through their moral experience, into the religious dimension. The second question is to do with the general propriety of speaking of the 'goodness' of God. Kant's theological thinking is not, in general, conspicuous for its use of analogy*, except in the very important exceptions of his employment of the teleological idea in the third *Critique* and his treatment of goodness in his moral argument for the existence of God. The only form of goodness with which we are acquainted is the goodness of the good will and this on Kant's own showing. Whether from this we have a sufficient base for arguing analogically to the idea of a 'supreme good' is something which might give the theologian pause.

As to Kant's general intention, however, there is little ambiguity. Reason has to make room for faith. But the findings of faith are by no means unreasonable. There are rational grounds for belief in the existence of God although these are not theoretical grounds. The power which is denied to pure reason is given, in the last analysis, to practical reason. The moral 'proof' serves Kant's purpose of effecting the transition from the *Critique of Pure Reason* to the *Critique of Practical Reason*. It was part of the traditional programme of the metaphysician to establish the existence of God and the immortality of the soul, that is, it was part of his traditional task to pronounce "What we may hope for". Inspite of the devastating criticisms of rational theology given by Kant, it is perhaps evident from his moral argument that he was not completely emancipated from the belief that it was incumbent on a metaphysician to have something reassuring to say about these traditional problems.

*For Kant, of course, there can never be any such thing as an *analogia entis* (analogy of being). It is important to note, however, that Kant is prepared to admit analogical "conception" but not analogical inference. The reason is this. An analogical conception is based on similitude. But between two things which we discern to be analogous there is at the same time an element of dissimilitude, and this is why we do wrong if we base *inferences* on analogy.

His theological thinking always attempted to retain a link with rational methods, as is shown in the title of the work of his old age *Religion within the bounds of mere Reason*, and in this respect Kant's contribution to theology makes an interesting link, and also an interesting contrast, with that of his contemporary Hamann and with that of succeeding generations of German Protestant theologians who stressed the path of faith rather than that of reason.

XVI The Problem of Evil

The nature of Evil

To look upon evil as a problem probably requires a considerable amount of sophistication and capacity for abstraction. Primitive man, dangerous though it be to generalise about him, seems to have a strong causal sense. When anything interferes with the customary order of nature he attributes this to some causal agency or other. Events to his advantage are attributed to the agency of benign powers stimulated to action perhaps because of some propitiatory action on his own part; and events to his disadvantage are attributed to the agency of malignant powers. Some natural agencies, like the thunderbolt or death or pain, he is less liable to regard as evil than his more hedonistically-inclined counterpart in 'civilised' societies. Such phenomena are part of nature's daily workings and are in themselves neither good nor bad. At any rate, in so far as primitive man frames the concept of evil at all, his experience leads him to view it in a particularistic manner—that is, he has a conception of evils in the plural rather than in the singular.

There are periods in history when man's awareness of evil has been stronger than at other times. Job's overwhelming experience of evil came about through a succession of disasters which seemed in excess of the normal lot of men. In times of flood, plague, prolonged warfare or prolonged injustice, man almost comes to personify evil as an operative force in the universe. But the question remains why the presence of evil should call for any explanation as such. There are long periods in geological time, periods whose length defies imagination, when, before the advent of man, the animal kingdom was one big arena of warfare and carnage, and yet one would not regard such periods in pre-history as evil. The presence of evil seems, in some way, to be linked up with human life and with man's capacity for suffering. Death is regarded as evil when it strikes a man in the fulness of his years. Killing in some circumstances is punishable by death, and in other circumstances is rewarded by national applause and investiture. Pain is evil if maliciously inflicted, and yet can be a blessing if thereby diagnosis of disease is effected. There seems good reason, therefore, for raising the question 'What is evil'? and the further question 'Why should there be evil'?

In the first place evils are usually classified into the two categories natural and moral. Natural evils comprise what Mill calls 'nature's everyday performances'. Pain, disease and death are part and parcel of man's day to day life. Every year thousands die of flood, famine and earthquakes. Crops are destroyed by pests and by drought. One half of the many millions of different species of animal life on the globe are constituted of insects which are a constant threat not only to man but to other forms of animal life. Now whereas the incidence of these natural evils seems to be inevitably bound up with the processes of nature, men may justifiably raise the question why they should be so unevenly distributed.

There is no doubt, however, that many evils which were considered inevitable are no longer considered such. The growth of science has considerably reduced the number of evils which are considered 'natural'. Floods and drought are controllable to some extent by irrigation. Pain can be controlled through anaesthesia. Medicine succeeds in prolonging life and the ancient projects of alchemists to find the elixir of life are to some extent being rethought in the modern battle against senescence. Among the stubbornest of natural evils we still have death and such things as earthquakes and it is unlikely that such phenomena can be altered by any effort on the part of man.

The second category of evil is moral evil—evil, that is to say, which stems from man's own will. Hume puts in the mouth of Philo in his *Dialogues concerning natural religion*—an impassioned description of the evils which are due to man himself :—

"This very society by which we surmount those wild beasts, our natural enemies, what new enemies does it not rise to us? What woe and misery does it not occasion? Man is the greatest enemy of man. Oppression, injustice, contempt, contumely, violence, sedition, war, calumny, treachery, fraud—by these they mutually torment each other, and they would soon dissolve that society which they had formed were it not for the dread of still greater ills which must attend their separation.

Some theories about Evils

The simplest 'solution' of the problem of evil is the dualistic one. Zoroastrianism attributes the presence of good to Ahura Mazda, the god of light, and evil to Ahriman, the god of darkness. In this way the universe is portioned out between two rival principles. A considerable influence was evidently exerted by the Persian theory in the Middle Eastern world for the Old Testament speaks of Satan, the prince of darkness who is constantly tempting man, although in Judaism it is very clear that Satan is a subordinate power, not in any sense equal with God. The Manichaean heresy which represents the only example of dualism within Christian theology has been criticised as follows by Hume :—

> "Here the Manichaean system occurs as a proper hypothesis to solve the difficulty; and no doubt, in some respects it is very specious and has more probability than the common hypothesis, by giving a plausible account of the strange mixture of good and ill which appears in life. But if we consider, on the other hand, the perfect uniformity and agreement of the parts of the universe, we shall not discover in it any marks of the combat of a malevolent with a benevolent being. There is indeed an opposition of pains and pleasures in the feelings of sensible creatures ; but are not all the operations of nature carried on by an opposition of principles, of hot and cold, moist and dry, light and heavy? The true conclusion is that the original Source of all things is entirely indifferent to all these principles, and has no more regard to good above ill than to heat above cold, or to drought above moisture, or to light above heavy."

The dualistic hypothesis assumes a god who is less than omnipotent, and who is therefore finite. Now there are various forms of theology which put forward the concept of a finite god, but in each case there is serious doubt whether the concept offered can satisfy the requirements of a 'god' at all. The notion of a finite god, at all events, is far from the theistic view of a God possessing infinite attributes like omniscience and omnipotence as well as the moral attributes of goodness, kindness and the like.

Some rationalist systems of metaphysics deny that evil is really evil. In Spinoza, for example, evil is accounted for in terms of deprivation. Such rationalist systems owe much to the Platonic identification of the good with the rational. In Plato's cosmology evil is "located" in the material factor which is not tractable to the Idea. The Socratic view of knowledge looks on ignorance as a lack, that is, something which is in principle remediable through the maieutic technique of question and answer. Hegel treats evil as the ground of good, a factor which is inevitably bound up with development. Evil thus becomes something transitional, something which is 'good in the making'. But that which is imperfectly rational, on this view, is always capable of becoming rational 'in the long run'. Much of this stems from Hegel's historical perspective. In the perspective of history, injustice, tyranny and war have their proper place. The march of the Zeitgeist is indifferent to the minutiae of historical processes, is indifferent to their 'real' cost in terms of blood, toil, tears and sweat. The liberal historian weighs such minutiae rather differently. Hegel's type of monism was transplanted somewhat uneasily on Anglo-Saxon soil. Bosanquet writes 'Evil, one might say, is good in the wrong place' and Bradley says that although sin is a discord "the discord as such disappears, if the harmony is made wide enough." It is impossible for the consistent monist to give an independent and positive status to sin and evil. But this is, after all, part of the general problem which besets the monist, that of recognising the status of fact within the framework of system.

The theist finds it most difficult of all to account for the presence of evil in the universe though, at the same time, his account is perhaps the most plausible. The problem is posed by Philo* as follows:—

* Vide Hume's *Dialogues concerning natural religion.*

"Is he willing to prevent evil, but not able? then is he impotent. Is he able, but not willing? then is he malevolent. Is he both able and willing? whence then is evil?". Now the theist's account is concerned mainly with moral evil and this the theist attributes to human sin. The Christian view of sin derives from the account given of the Fall in the Book of Genesis in the Bible. The fall of Adam, typified by his act of disobedience against God in eating the fruit of the forbidden tree, is something which happened after a period of time when Adam must be presupposed to have been in a state of natural grace. Michaelangelo portrayed, on the vault of the Sistine Chapel, an Adam newly created, glorious in his pristine innocence. The doctrine of the Fall provides Christian theology with a way of 'explaining' the presence of moral evil. Canon Quick writes in his *The Gospel of the New World*, 'the ultimate source of evil in the world is the free act of the finite and created will which uses its freedom to do wrong and to disobey the will of God.' If we raise the question why God should have chosen to create a being endowed with the capacity of rejecting Him the answer is that there has been "a mysterious self-limitation of the Creator" in order that man may 'of his own free will surrender himself. If man then chooses to do evil, this is not to be attributed to God for, as Leibniz puts it, "created beings derive their perfections from the influence of God, but their imperfections come from their own nature which is incapable of being without limits". Moral evil, then, comes from man's finitude and man has been created by God as a finite creature.

How does man's sinfulness show itself? In his Gifford lectures William Temple explains how the possibility of sin is bound up with consciousness. Man seeks after apparent goods and his apparent good is not always the same as his real good. Evil is a product of exaggerated or misdirected desire. Our self-assertiveness leads us to follow after illusory goods, and only by centering himself in God can man be led away from evil. Now theologians differ in the extent to which they regard man to be prone to evil. The extreme position, represented today by Karl Barth, is that man is thoroughly sinful and without divine grace has no hope of salvation. This view, although it has in modern times, for the most part, been associated with

Protestantism, can be found in as forthright a form in St. Augustine's *Confessions*. If, as Niebuhr says, man 'stands at the juncture of nature and spirit' it is to be expected that he should at times act in accordance with the lower side of his nature. According to the doctrine of 'original sin' (to which some theologians do not subscribe) man has a definite bias to the lower. In the Biblical narrative, however, man's 'original' state, that is, his state before the Fall, was one of simple innocence. It is sufficient for our purpose just to note that on the degree of sinfulness reckoned to be natural to man will depend the view taken as to the amount of grace needed for his salvation. The more sinful he is thought to be the more will his salvation depend on initiative on the part of God. The theist, however, it is to be remembered, is in the unique position of having very definite things to say about the attributes of God. The theist conceives God to be loving, kind and good. Some may feel that the extreme doctrine of original sin would hardly square with such a conception.

There are, it has been seen, evils which seem to have little to do with man's agency. If the theist is able to offer a consistent account of moral evils, he does not seem to be able to account for the presence, and especially the maldistribution, of natural evils. There seems to be no answer to the eternal 'Why', the cry wrung from Job in the midst of his undeserved sufferings. The theist can say that sin enters an order where natural evil already exists. The more pertinent comment, however, that the theist is in a position to make, is that a certain amount of suffering is part of man's lot. Without going to the Schopenhauerean extreme of regarding this world as a vale of tears, the theist is not simple-minded enough to regard the world as having been made for the purpose of man's delectation. Many of the virtues, like temperance and courage, can only be exhibited in the face of evil. The theist will always insist, though, that evil is something positive. It is not merely a surd element in the universe, an element which reason finds it difficult to encompass. Evil is a positive force, calling forth, at times, the valour of Bunyan's Christian, and, at times, the wrestling acceptance of a Prince Myshkin. For the theist, it is plain, the problem of evil is not simply a metaphysical problem. It is to be understood as part of a drama, the drama which concerns man's redemption and salvation. The metaphysician, in the last analysis, may have to admit that there is no reason to deny that there is an element of opacity in the universe. The theist puts this in slightly different language. There is no reason to suppose that the ways of God are all known to man.

The nineteenth and twentieth centuries brought with them a number of modern 'explanations' of evil. The nineteenth century evolutionists had infinite faith in the perfectibility of man. Herbert Spencer wrote '.... progress is not an accident but a necessity. What we call evil and immorality must disappear.' The march of history has certainly seen the gradual elimination of evils like witchcraft, gladiatorial games, slavery and dread diseases like the plague. The effects of science and enlightened opinion would lead us to the conclusion not that evil has a mere transitional status, but that modern man regards evil as a challenge, a phenomenon that can be brought under control. Nuclear energy, for example, is neither good nor evil, but it can be put to both good and evil uses.

The Marxist point of view is that evil is due to bad external conditions and that these can be altered by economic changes. If poverty is an evil, as it certainly is, then it is no doubt true that poverty can be eliminated by so organising the means of production and distribution that the national product is large enough to go round. This at least is so in theory. But in practice there are serious inelasticities, and the most serious ones are in people's minds. Even if everyone were given the same income, within a few years there would again be the spectacle of rich and poor and this was something that many of the Fabians realised, if reluctantly. If evil is the product of circumstances, it is man, after all, who is responsible for the existence of those circumstances. Marxism does at least have the virtue of making us look on evil not as an inalienably given element in the universe, but as a factor which man has it in his power to conquer.

The psychologist's viewpoint is that evils are due to maladjustment. Words like 'Wicked' and 'evil' need to be dropped from our vocabulary. The psychologist has, understandably, nothing to say about natural evil; but as far as human nature is concerned he will stress that whatever a man has become is to be understood by reference to the causal chain of events open for enquiry through the use of specialist techniques. Man is neither 'originally' good nor bad. Such a view has its outcome in the stand taken by Clarence Darrow in the court-room. Whatever a man has become is ultimately the responsibility of society.

Possible attitudes to Evil

As philosophical theories, optimism and pessimism represent alterative attitudes to evil. Both are extremes. The eighteenth and nineteenth centuries were noted for their optimism. Eighteenth century optimism is typified in Leibniz's view that this is 'the best of all possible worlds' and is satirised in Voltaire's portrait of Doctor Pangloss.* Behind this is the whole theoretic structure of rationalistic metaphysics and the pre-evolutionist assumption of the general benevolence of nature. The voice of Hume proclaiming that the world was "a riddle, an enigma, an inexplicable mystery" was not to be echoed until the time of the Tractarians and for very different reasons. If eighteenth century optimism was founded on the myth of omnipotent reason, nineteenth century optimism was founded on the idea of progress. Behind Bury's work lies** not only Darwin, but the expanding economy of Victorian England. Economically there was good reason for believing that "the best is yet to be". It was a matter of personal temperament whether one found a theological reason for it and exclaimed with Browning that "God's in his heaven, all's right with the world", or whether one cast science as the hero of the drama and exclaimed as Swinburne did in his "Hymn to Man" :—

"Glory to man in the highest
For man is the master of things".

Even if Darwin had shown that man was not so much a little lower than the angels as a little higher than the monkeys, the

* Vide Voltaire's *Candide.*
** *The Idea of Progress.*

fact remained that man was the end term in the evolutionary series and there was no reason for disbelieving that the series was capable of continuation. If there could be Utopias there could also be supermen and what could be more optimistic than that? To summarise, then, the theory of evolution, faith in science and an expanding industrial economy were responsible for Victorian optimism. The twentieth century saw two world wars, an eruption of nationalism not always with happy results, and growth in scientific knowledge such as to make a live possibility the greatest scale of destruction conceivable. All things considered, this century has good reason for not being as optimistic as the last.

The pessimist takes his starting point from the admitted disorders and irrationalities of the external world. Not less than these are the irrationalities within man himself. Existence itself seems evil, and non-existence becomes preferable to existence. Schopenhauer seems to have been already convinced of the reality of human suffering even before he came to know anything of Buddhist philosophy. Recognition of the place of suffering in human life has always been an integral part of Christian thought as indeed is to be expected in a religion founded on the Cross. In Schopenhauer this insight is coupled with a complete disillusionment with the Hegelian stress on reason and the conviction that in will, not reason, is to be found the operative principle of the universe. Now will as a blind, unconscious principle is a force which bears man along with it in its inexorable flow. As long as reason was regarded as the central metaphysical principle this was at least something in which man could literally have 'a part'. The dialectical path of reason was at least something which logic could follow. But man cannot be other than a helpless witness to the working of the 'World as Will and Idea'. Even the doctrine of 'karma' was more optimistic than this, for at least man had some control over his unfulfilled 'potencies'.

Von Hartmann, following Schopenhauer, redresses the Utilitarian obsession with pleasure and insists that pain is in excess of pleasure. The very qualities which are human in the highest degree, that is, intelligence and sympathy, only serve to sharpen man's awareness of pain. However we must admit that, among other things, philosophers like Schopenhauer and Von Hartmann did succeed in pointing out how small a part of man's conscious life is occupied with cognitive operations and this needed saying in a country where Hegel's influence was still supreme. But one assumption behind philosophical pessimism, an assumption not usually recognised, however, tends to be that happiness is the ideal form of human existence. Indeed even to raise a query on this point may seem to savour of pessimism. As with all forms of monism, the pessimist disregards all those factors which do not fit in with his theory. In addition to suffering there are experiences which do not deserve this title and in addition to the forces of blind unreason there is, for example, such a thing as simple perception. On the Schopenhauerean view, moreover, there is no room for the free acts of the ethical personality.

On purely philosophical grounds whether one is a pessimist or optimist depends on various factors. First of all a very relevant factor is what attitude is taken to the concept of God. In a theologically-minded age, as the Middle Ages surely was, no amount of natural disasters can occasion a sense of pessimism in men's minds. The theist is neither an optimist nor a pessimist. Those forms of theology which lay extra emphasis on the Fall are still far from being pessimistic, thanks to the doctrine of divine grace. The theist believes that 'All things work together for good to them that love God'. The second factor is what view we take of man's powers. Confidence in man's rationality, as we saw, goes along with optimism. The greater the sense of strength of the powers of unreason the greater the tendency towards pessimism. Next, the number of natural disasters occurring in a particular period of history has an influence on man's attitude to the place of evil in the universe. In times of misfortune reference is made to the 'forces of evil' and to superhuman powers conceived to be working against man and evil acquires an almost cosmic status. Most important of all, however, is the view taken of suffering in human life. The Stoic tradition is a very distinguished one in western thought. If suffering is accepted as part of finite existence this inspires neither optimism nor pessimism but the not exclusively Roman virtue—fortitude.

XVII The Nature of Value

Introduction

MANY philosophical problems, as we have seen, are tied up with concepts employed by the sciences, problems, say, like those of the nature of matter, space and time and evolution. The two-way traffic between philosophy and science has certainly been there whether or no we may think this has been in the true interests of philosophy or not. There can be little doubt, however, that the problem of the nature of value is one which falls outside the purview of the sciences. The concern of science is with facts, with the realm of what "is" and not with the realm of what "ought to be", if indeed there be such a realm. The distinction between fact and value can be understood if we compare the following two sentences, 'The apple is red' and 'The apple is good'. The first of these two sentences is descriptive and the second is evaluative. To say, however, that facts are to be contrasted with values will only do as a starting point. The statement 'The apple is good' is obviously based on certain facts such as the fact that I have tasted it and found it sweet rather than tart, free of maggots and so forth. Even to speak of the apple as red does, some would say, carry a suggestion that the apple is good, for most people prefer red apples to green ones. Or again if I say 'He is a liar' I am making both a factual judgement and a value judgement. Recent linguistic analysis has brought to light the mixed nature of many of the judgements that we make and which the above examples illustrate.

But then someone may object that, although factual judgements and value judgements may sometimes be difficult to disentangle, this does not iron out the distinction which surely obtains between 'facts' and 'values'. This objection is an interesting one because it suggests that a certain complexity of language may not necessarily reflect a parallel complexity in the nature of things. But if we examine it a little closer we find that the concept of 'fact' itself requires analysis. Logicians have scarcely got further with this particular problem than to tell us that a fact is that with reference to which the truth or falsity of a proposition is determined, which does not, after all, tell us much. Parallel to this one might say that value is that by reference to which (for example) the beauty or ugliness of a work of art and the rightness or wrongness of an action are determined. In either case we seem to have an oblique reference to something which is not in itself specifiable. Inspite of what we usually imagine to be the case, it is not easy to give content to the view that values are best defined in contrast to facts, although, as we saw, there is some point in drawing a contrast between description and appreciation as modes of judgement, and even though many of the sentences we use seem to involve a mixture of the two.

Most philosophical problems arise as the result of a process of abstraction from a multiplicity of particulars. We perceive a number of material objects and we formulate the question 'What is matter?'. We perceive things in spatial and temporal relations and we ask 'What are space and time?' We are aware of the presence of evils like famine, pain and cruelty and we ask 'What is evil?'. In Berkeley's view many philosophial problems are of our own making. We coin abstractions at the back of which we have no 'idea' at all. We raise a dust and then complain that we cannot see. The desire to discern a common essence among various particulars is illustrated no less in the way in which many philosophers have discussed values than in their treatment of some of the problems we have just mentioned. However, in actual life, to speak loosely, we encounter 'values' rather than 'value'. Whereas, say, in treating of 'matter', the philosopher has found it irrelevant to his purpose to consider the particularity of various things, one of the main insights that some axiologists have had relates to the diversity of values.

This insight has given rise to the problem of the classification of values. The first big classification made is that between intrinsic and extrinsic (or instrumental) values. Intrinsic values like truth, beauty and goodness are 'worthy' (in the sense of possessing worth) on their own account and not for the sake of any goal that may be attainable through them. Instrumental values, like money and leisure, are worthy in virtue of the goals they enable us to attain. For example, I may spend money in the pursuit of beauty when I go on holiday in Italy, or I may utilise my leisure in the undertaking of research, i.e. in the pursuit of truth. There are borderline cases like that of health which may give us pause. Health may be regarded by some as a good in itself, or by others as the means to the pursuit of recreational values in the shape of sports etc.

The higher values are often spoken of as permanent and the lower ones as transient. That the permanent has a value over and above the transient seems to have come down to us as a relic of Pythagoreanism, and lovers of the natural beauty of the sunset, beauty that must die and all that hastes away too soon, may feel that there is something wrong with this classification. Truth may not be a value under all circumstances, however shocking this may sound at a first hearing. There are times when it is our duty not to tell the truth e.g. to avoid giving an unbearable shock to a patient, or to refuse to betray a comrade in time of war. The distinction of values into higher and lower is itself one which occasions serious reflection. The way of thinking which would place the intellectual values at the top of the scale is witness to a premium set on the contemplative way of life and which has come down to us from Plato. The Platonic and Christian world-views both lodge value in the supersensensible and the eternal. It was not until the latter part of the eighteenth century that the affective life was recognised to have value of its own. In any case it is necessary to recognise that the classification of values into higher and lower is itself the result of a process of valuation.

It still remains for the philosopher to say something about the relation of the various values to each other, since the desire to see a unity among diversity is one of the most stubborn of philosophical desires. The Platonic account of value was especially fertile in this respect, and all values (and indeed all manner of beings) were said to 'participate' in the ultimate value, i.e. the Form of the Good. The theme of 'ground' and that of 'participation' was taken up by Christian theology in so far as all values were to be found in the Divine nature. It was not until much later that the fount and origin of value was found in something much nearer home, human personality itself*. This last way of approaching the problem was followed both by German philosophers like Scheler and Hartmann, and, albeit in a much more down-to-earth manner, by the pragmatists. All these views we shall consider shortly under the heading of 'value and existence'.

The Subjectivity and Objectivity of Values

Must values be regarded as subjective or objective? Is it necessary to 'locate' values, either 'in the mind' or 'out there'? Hare has suggested that the posing of the dichotomy in this way amounts to a wrong use of the Law of Excluded Middle and that there is no *prima facie* reason why values should be classified either as properties or as subjective relations. It is worth examining, however, why certain philosophers should have regarded values as being subjective at all. The main ground for this view seems to have been a consideration of the nature of the process of valuation. It is men who evaluate and who do so from certain points of view. It is by no means only the utilitarians who have found the mainspring of men's actions in their desire to attain pleasure and to shun pain. Epicurus, for example, in the ancient world, seems to have held this view too, although his formulation of it was by no means as crude as it is usually thought to be. Even if we do not take the hedonistic standpoint, some would still maintain that values have no meaning apart from human desires. That this is so can be seen, it would be claimed, if we take the example of a good meal. This has no value for us if we do not have the desire to eat; if, say, we have already dined elsewhere.

Another consideration which supports the subjectivist thesis is the notorious diversity which dogs our value judgements. In certain societies cunning may be regarded as the greatest of virtues and aesthetic standards may be wildly different from our own. An anthropological approach, such as that of Westermarck, is based on data like these. The epistemologist may look upon

* This approach owes a lot to the Christian tradition, for Christian theology holds that in so far as man is made in the image of God he is a being of intrinsic worth.

the problem from a slightly different angle. He may say that there is no evidence for the existence of values in the world of sense experience and that therefore we must look to the subject if we are to find the source of values. But probably the most plausible appeal that the subjectivist can make is to aesthetic experience. There is undeniably an intimate connection between beauty and delight, and everyone has heard of the adage 'Beauty is in the eye of the beholder'. If we analyse delight or aesthetic enjoyment we find that, inextricably bound up with it, is a corpus of associated personal meanings, that is to say, meanings which are peculiar to our own private lives. Then again, the amount and quality of aesthetic enjoyment aroused by any particular aesthetic object varies greatly from man to man and this would encourage the view that the value "beauty" is at least partly subjective.

The above arguments may be examined one by one. Even if valuation be shown to be an inevitably subjective process, this would not necessarily indicate that values themselves were subjective. It is to be doubted, in any case, whether valuation itself can be accounted for merely in terms of feeling. Meinong, a philosopher who has given a very considerable role to feeling in his analysis of valuation, points out that value judgements assume the existence of the values in question. If this were not so we could not speak of 'judgement' at all. When we judge, we judge about something, whether or no our judgement be at the same time influenced by certain subjective factors in ourselves. If there be no value 'judgement' as such then the question of truth and falsity will not arise, and this, in fact, is the view held by certain contemporary philosophers. If we take this view, however, we shall be in fact saying that the man who maintains that Michaelangelo's David is a great work of art is saying something which cannot be spoken of as either true or false, and we shall not be able to tell the man who says that cruelty is good that he is mistaken.

The appeal to relativism is not these days considered as damaging as it once was. Anthropologists tell us that if all cultures were completely different from each other then any comparative study of man would, *eo ipso*, be impossible. Kroeber and Kluckhohn write that 'there is a generalized framework that underlies the more apparent and striking facts of cultural relativity.' As far as aesthetic experience is concerned the subjectivist's analysis is all too simple. Aesthetic experience has its fount and origin in the perception of a sensible object which is endowed with a certain form, a "significant" form if we like to call it such. Beauty is judged and not merely felt. We speak of disagreements on aesthetic matters as differences in taste and we recognise that one man's taste may, whether through initial sensitivity or training, be better than another's. The fact that we make valuations among valuations is perhaps the most telling point that can be made against the subjectivists. To conclude, we can admit that valuation is subjective in that it is a human activity and an activity, moreover, in which feelings, (perhaps in the case of aesthetic experience, feelings of a special kind) have a special part. But valuation is none the less a response made by the subject to certain qualities in the object evaluated. As Alexander puts it in his book *Space, Time, and Deity*, "We have values or tertiary qualities in respect of the whole situation consisting of knower and known in their compresence. Strictly speaking, it is this totality of knower and known, of subject and object, which is true or good or beautiful . . . . . ."

The objectivist, since the time of Plato, has been governed by metaphysical considerations, that is to say, he believes that only by the recognition of the ontological status of value can the nature of value be done justice to. The objectivist, moreover, has shown a special concern for *moral* values for it is these which seem to suffer most on the subjectivist interpretation. Objectivists include many diverse metaphysical standpoints within their fold. The rationalist insists that our value judgements claim objectivity, and that the objectivity of values is the objectivity of excellence. Norms are such that all reasonable beings should acknowledge them. The idealist McTaggart writes that 'Goodness is a quality of the thing judged good, and a thing can no more be good for one man and bad for another than twice four can be eight for one man and nine for another.' The most interesting development of the objectivist thesis from the realist standpoint is to be found in the works of G. E. Moore. Moore's main concern, no doubt, was with ethical value, but, in his view, it was necessary to determine the meaning of good in general before one could properly proceed to the determination of what is good in conduct.* Moore's refusal to allow that good can be defined is to be understood both as a rejection of naturalism in any form and as a parallel to his refusal to allow that 'knowing' (which he treats of in his epistemological works) can be defined either. Both 'good' and 'knowing' are *sui generis*. Of intrinsic value we can say that it ought to exist for its own sake, and that intrinsically good things should be sought for their own sakes. Friendship, justice, courage and generosity are good in themselves.

It is in connection with the explication of the notion of intrinsic value that Moore introduces his conception of 'organic wholes'. There are things which have intrinsic value, things which are positively bad and a third class of things which appear to be indifferent as between good and bad. But, as Moore says ". . . . . . a thing belonging to any of these three classes may occur as part of a whole, which includes among its other parts other things belonging both to the same and to the other two classes; and these wholes, as such, may also have intrinsic value." What Moore has in mind here is a concept of wholes based on the axiom of external relations as against the absolutist conception of organic whole based on the axiom of internal relations and where there is a relation of necessitation between the parts.** Moore's view, therefore, is clearly pluralistic. What is of special interest, in view of the theories we looked at earlier, is that Moore should speak of intrinsic goods as complex wholes involving consciousness of an object and an emotional attitude towards this object. He thereby gives to feeling a 'conditioning' role no less important than was given by Meinong. In highlighting the values of personal life, such as personal affection and aesthetic enjoyment, he has, at the same time, much in common with a philosopher like Hartmann. His focussing on the general problem of the nature of good points forward to Urmson's work on grading and to Hare's investigation of commendation. In a way, too, one can see Moore's work as a wise

* One is here reminded of the way in which Aristotle relates his treatment of moral excellence in particular to the treatment of excellence in general.

** In Moore's understanding of an organic whole "The value of such a whole bears no regular proportion to the sum of the values of its parts."

straddling of the uncomfortable distinction between the 'subjectivity' and 'objectivity' of values with which we began.

Values and Existence

The task of relating values and existence is, *ab initio*, fraught with difficulty. If by value we understand that which is ideal, that which 'ought to exist', we seem debarred from saying that values exist. To say that values do *not* exist, on the other hand, would seem to reduce them to the level of nonentity. There seems to be a close connection between values and 'ought', especially in the case of moral values. But to say that we ought to bring values into existence would seem to make their existence in some way dependent on us. Another way of relating values and existence may be to say that the ideal makes a claim on us and that this is what is meant by the connection between excellence i.e. value, and "ought to be". The concept of value and the concept of existence are very evidently not co-extensive, as there are things which are neither good nor bad. If we maintain that values exist, then we shall also have to admit that disvalues such as suffering, ugliness and sin exist too. Moreover, sometimes we attribute value to the non-existent, for example, we ascribe value to the non-existence of pain. A further difficulty is that, in modern times especially, that is to say, with the growth of the empiricist outlook, we have come to associate the existent with the perceivable, or at least, with what can be shown to be related to the perceivable. The existence of the supersensible, the transcendent, (and if values are ideal they must be presumably transcendent) is something which we admit with difficulty. There can be no doubt, it is clear from the above, about the difficuty of the problem.

The Platonic answer to the problem has exerted a great influence over the centuries. If the permanence of values is to be done justice to, they cannot in any way be housed in the world of particulars, the world of change. Values are objects of contemplation existing in an eternal sphere. They are intelligible essences which are at the same time existent. Absolute existence is to be distinguished from relative existence, that is to say, the concept of existence is not univocal. There is a radical rift in the nature of things. It follows that the Forms (among which are to be found not only values but all universals) are only accessible to reason and that a method must be prescribed in order for them to become luminous to the enquiring mind. This method Plato provides in his account of the 'dialectic'. Plato sets the pattern for many subsequent treatments of value in his insistence that the crowning value has ethical import. The Form of the Good is both the highest metaphysical concept and the apex of ethical endeavour. The theory of participation provides him with the means of accounting for the relation of the plurality of values to the concept of value itself. The difficulty which attends his theory is the same difficulty which attends the theory of Ideas in general, that is, how two disparate orders, the absolute and the relative, are to be related and this is a problem which does not immediately concern us here.

The Platonic account, no doubt, relates values to the notion of existence in general. To Plato values exist *par excellence*. It seemed to thinkers who came after, however (and this in spite of the work of the Sophists and the work of Socrates), that the task of relating values to human existence had not yet received the attention it demanded. It was left to Christian theology to find in the human person something of intrinsic value. Man made in the image of God could not but be so regarded. This belief in the worth of man, fused with the pre-Christian discovery of man's rationality (a progressive discovery which was the gift of Greek thought to the mediaeval and the modern world) is what lies behind Kant's special concern with moral value. This concern amounts to no less than a fully thought-out answer to the crucial problem of defining the place of man in a world of fact. The *Critique of Pure Reason* proclaims in no uncertain terms the barrenness of the concept of 'existence' when it has been shorn of its space-time connotation. When the rationalist theologian speaks of a Being who exists 'necessarily' he deprives the word 'exist' of its original meaning. Throughout the first Critique Kant insists on the univocality of the concept of existence. If we are to speak of the *existence* of God, as indeed we must if we are religious men, we do so from the standpoint of faith and not from the standpoint of theoretic reason. But what of the existence of man? In so far as man is a physical being man is part of the world of fact, part of the order of causal necessity. Man's empirical existence, that is to say, is conditioned. In so far as he is a moral being, however, man belongs to a supersensible order of dignity and excellence, a moral realm, a Kingdom of ends of which all rational beings are members. It is at this point that we discover the core of Kant's teaching on the problem of value and existence and not in his notion of a Summum Bonum conceived to satisfy traditional philosophical prejudices. Kant affirms a dualism no doubt, the dualism between the physical order of causal necessity with which science deals and the moral order in which man participates as a being endowed with practical reason. But it is man who spans these two orders. It is no wonder, then, that many subsequent German philosophers should have spoken of man as the 'bearer' of values —a way of putting it (barring the interpretation favoured by Nietzsche) for which there are many supporting indications in Kant's own work.

If Kant's philosophy of value centres on the concept of goodness the work of the idealists may be said to centre on the concept of truth. Coherence is the central value principle and it is coherence which provides both the definition and the criterion of truth. Only that which is completely individual exists and has value. Only the Absolute is completely individual in the sense of being a harmonious whole, and so the object of highest value can be none other than the Absolute. Parts have only a relative existence and therefore a lesser value. Behind this metaphysic stands the shadow of the axiom of internal relations, the logical principle the application of which leads to what William James called a 'block universe'. If the ideal is actual then the gulf between value and existence disappears.

The idealist viewpoint as presented in a work like that of Bosanquet's *The Principle of Individuality and Value* brought down a shower of criticism upon itself. On the absolutist showing, it was said, evil will be regarded as partly good; the atrocities committed in this century, for example, will be part of a 'harmonious whole'. Disvalue, instead of being something positive, will be conceived in terms of privation, a falling short of the Absolute. Worse even than this, persons will be but adjectival to the whole. To many this sounded all too reminiscent of the

Hegelian Zeitgeist and was all too closely connected with the anti-liberal Prussian dogma that the state was the embodiment of the Absolute on earth. Personal idealists like Howison and Rashdall tried to redress the balance by rehabilitating the person as the locus of value, a Kantian insight which had been lost sight of in a wave of idealist theorizings.

It remains to sketch briefly the fortunes of this last way of thinking, the treating of value and existence with special reference to the human person and the refusal to divorce the metaphysical problem of value from the concrete being which is man. Two very diverse types of philosophy took up this theme. One is to be found in the work of Max Scheler and Nicolai Hartmann in Germany and the other across the Atlantic in the work of the pragmatists. On Scheler's view values are real objective entities which are totally different from all states of feeling. They are ideal objects but they are given to us in and through feeling. (To understand this it is necessary to bear in mind the main thesis of phenomenology in general—that every conscious state has an 'intention' or objective content.) There is an objective realm of values and among the various values there is a hierarchy at the apex of which are the 'sacred values' or "the values of holiness" encountered in the religious life. Another feature of his theory is the role given to love. Scheler speaks of love as bringing new and superior values into existence. Love opens our eyes to values higher than those which mere 'interest' can discover. Characterising his treatment of value as a whole it could be said that Scheler is opposed both to the utilitarian ethic of interest and to Kantian 'formalism'.

In turning to Hartmann's monumental *Ethics* we find a unique amalgam of two very diverse approaches, Platonic objectivism and the Kantian stress on the person. As in Scheler, here too we have a hierarchical view of values; the higher values are dependent on the lower and yet the latter are autonomous in their own field. It is for this reason that no theistic conclusion can be derived from our moral experience. Hartmann's opposition to Kant comes in with his critique of formalism, again something which he shares with Scheler. Values are 'concrete, material and objective'. 'Material' here, of course, must be understood in contradiction to 'formal'. 'Man's sensing of values is the annunciation of their Being in the discerning person'. Values are 'self-existent', but they announce themselves as 'enlistments of emotion'. The cognitive role given to feeling by Hartmann is explored even more fully by Scheler in his book *The Nature of Sympathy*. What is of interest for our purpose is the way in which both Scheler and Hartmann grant feeling a key role in the experience of value without falling into the trap of relativism, something which philosophers of the utilitarian tradition at least, were never able to do.

The pragmatists bring man into the picture in a very different way. Schiller defines value as 'a personal attitude of welcome or the reverse, towards an object of interest'. Such a definition has an affinity with an 'interest theory' like that of the realist Perry. To Perry value is not an attribute of any object; rather it is a *relation* holding between an interest and an object. In the analysis of what 'interest' may mean we are driven back upon desires. The behaviourist influence on value theory reveals itself in Schiller's statement that values 'arise out of the mind's practical attitude when it reacts upon stimulation'. The so-called "tertiary qualities" are but qualities which we project into objects. In a sense the opposition between fact and value breaks down for what is an *object* for us is also determined by our practical interest in it. All objects are pervaded by values, for to the pragmatist there is no separation of the practical and the theoretical. All valuation, as Dewey has it, is really revaluation, although presumably there is an original core of fact which we must presuppose as providing the initial stimulation. Now the value about which the pragmatists have the most to say is truth. To William James truths 'are everlastingly in process of mutation'. About this we have said more elsewhere*. Suffice it to say that the pragmatist and instrumentalist approach does try to 'humanise' the philosophical treatment of value, and does, from one point of view, iron out the distinction between value and existence, but in a manner, one must remember, diametrically opposed to that of absolutism.

To the theist the question of relating values and existence presents no problem, for God is the home of values and God

* Vide Ch. VII, p. 128 ff.

is the only Being whose essence it is to exist. It is claimed by many philosophers of religion that consideration of the concept of God throws light on the main problems of axiology, that is to say, the problems of determining the hierarchy of values, whether values are personal or impersonal, and the issue of the subjectivity and objectivity of values. God is regarded as being at the apex of the hierarchy of beings and as containing all values within Himself. Personality is the bearer of value, and if God is the Divine Person it follows that He is the supreme bearer of value. It was Hoeffding's view that the essential element in religion was faith in the conservation of value. The demand that there be something in the cosmic order which is favourable to value can only be satisfied if we postulate the existence of a transcendent Being. If all values are found in God this at the same time proclaims the actuality of God, for only of God can it be said that He is both ideal and actual. What theism does, (one could put it this way) is to identify two concepts which in Plato were kept distinct, the Form of the Good and God. The unity of all values is thereby affirmed because God is at once the supreme object of knowledge and admiration and the supreme Good. The interpenetration of values which leads the poet to say "Beauty is Truth, Truth Beauty" is further illuminated in religion by the 'beauty of holiness' of which Newman spoke. The "eternal" nature of values can be done justice to only in one of two ways, by positing a Platonic realm, or by the theistic interpretation. God is the ground of all values. They, no less than ourselves, live and move and have their being in Him.

Most writers on value have given special consideration to moral value, for here is a value which carries with it a demand for certain courses of action by ourselves. There is a connection, that is to say, between excellence and what we ought to do. Moral philosophers have been at pains to examine the springs of moral action and also to consider the weight of the 'can' which seems to be presupposed by the 'ought'. The theist can say that God's love for us provides the motive and His grace the power. It is interesting to note in this connection that Kant seems to have re-thought in later life the more or less Pelagian approach of his ethical works and that in his book *Reason within the bounds of mere Reason* he examines afresh the nature of the human 'can'.

The Linguistic approach

The logical positivist treatment of value in this century has been remarkable first and foremost for its complete elimination of reference to ontology. This is what we would expect in view of the positivist guillotining of inference to transcendent entities. If reference to substances is to be done away with in our material object discourse, such reference cannot be allowed to remain in our discourse about values either. The shift in the terms of the discussion is a most important one. We have ceased to treat of "values" and have turned to "talk about values", that is to say, to value judgements. This is why the present section is entitled the linguistic approach. The contemporary approach is not without its forerunners however. Hume had already insisted that value judgements are not descriptive. Schlick's identification of value with feeling is witness to a general position not very dissimilar to that of the Utilitarians. I. A. Richards' distinction between emotive statements and statements of fact left no more room for a third category than Hume's famous "great divide" passage in his *Enquiry* had done. Moore's warning against the naturalistic fallacy was heeded all too well. Ayer wrote 'A valuation is not a description of something very peculiar; it is not a description at all'. This was the same as saying that talk about value does not belong to the 'totality of facts'. Wittgenstein had said that 'The sense of the world must lie outside the world. In the world everything is as it is and happens as it does happen.' As it stands this is a pronouncement which would have met with Bishop Butler's approval. But Wittgenstein was not interested in developing any implication that the first of these two sentences may have for the tender-minded. The lesson drawn by his followers was that it was not proper to think of value-talk as being 'about' something. Rather it should be analysed for what it was, i.e. a species of talk.

The central thesis of the positivists concerning value sentences is that they are expressions of emotion. Being non-judgemental the question of their truth and falsity does not arise.

The thesis is carefully distinguished from subjectivism in that the subjectivist thinks that value judgement are 'about' the speaker's feelings and that on the subjectivist view, therefore, the question of their truth or falsity *does arise*. Since when I express certain moral sentiments I am merely evincing my "moral disapproval" I cannot be contradicted. Apparent disputes are found to be disputes about facts. There is no question of achieving "agreement" with my adversary, but what I can do is to try to win him over by appealing to the facts or to 'persuade' him by the use of emotive language. The persuasive function of value language is developed far more thoroughly by Stevenson than by Ayer. The full-fledged emotive theory speaks both of the expresive function of value language and also of its persuasive function. The persuasive definition analysis is interesting not the least because it draws attention to the fact that much of our 'value-talk' makes other people do things. A simple example may make this clear. If I tell you that the apples at X's shop are good you may quite well decide to go and buy some from him too. Whether the logic of commendation by itself is adequate to account for strictly *ethical* discourse is, however, but one of the problems that beset the theory.

A few other problems may somewhat summarily be referred to here. Most of these concern the sub-class of value judgements which we call ethical judgements. The elimination of any concern with ontology carries with it, in the case of the positivist analysis of ethical sentences, the elimination of the concept of 'ought'. It cannot be obligatory to feel. Along with this the distinction between the subjectively right and the objectively right disappears. The appeal to 'approval' especially, requires further analysis. We approve in virtue of something. That is, the judgemental element cannot be left out. Moreover, having deprived the word 'moral' of its meaning, Ayer cannot reintroduce it by speaking of 'moral sentiments' and 'moral disapproval'. We may well ask wherein, on his view, 'moral disapproval' differs from non-moral disapproval. The reduction of the ethical problem to the analysis of a certain sort of language may even be said to amount to a new kind of naturalism, in spite of the avowed desire of the positivists to avoid falling into the naturalistic fallacy.

It is only fair to say, however, that the discussion of ethical language and value judgements in general has already developed beyond the stage detailed so far. There has been a growing recognition of the mixed character of such discourse and an attempt made to disentangle its various empirical, imperative and expressive strands. Discussion has shifted from the earlier stress on 'feelings', to the analysis of moral 'reasoning'. Thus, although there is no overt move away from the homogeneity principle with which the positivists began, that is, no bifurcation of the natural and the moral at the ontological level, diversity is being given adequate recognition at the linguistic level, and there may some day be a reaction against the cultivation of meta-ethics and a return to the tilling of the original soil out of which our valuational experience springs.

Epilogue

There can be no single answer to the question "What is philosophy?" for philosophy is a subject which itself has a history, and this is relevant in a manner which is not paralleled in the case of any other subject such as science or art which of course have their own histories. Philosophers like Hegel, and, in our own day, Collingwood, have made us increasingly aware of this fact. At one time, for example in Greece six centuries before the birth of Christ, cosmological guesses seemed to be the prerogative of the phiolosopher, and, if one were to ask Thales or Empedocles what the task of philosophy was they would have replied 'To find out what things are made of'. This particular task has by now been completely taken over by the scientist and therefore for a philosopher to encroach upon this sphere is rightly regarded today as unwarranted. There are, however, two ways of philosophizing which have gradually distinguished themselves and it is possible to discern to what extent a philosopher aligns himself with the one rather than the other. One way consists in an attempt to *supplement* the sciences by reference to an order of being with which the sciences do not themselves deal at all, and the other in an attempt to *criticise* the sciences, or rather, criticise their conceptual foundations.

The attempt to supplement the sciences is equivalent to the programme of traditional metaphysics. The metaphysician wants to *know more*, more of a different kind. The scientist also wants to know more, but for him the extension of knowledge proceeds, as it were, laterally. His investigation into nature leads him to discover more of the same order as that which he already knows. The attempt to know more of a different kind can, it is evident, be carried out only through speculation, for speculation is nothing but a guess as to the nature of what is not actually known. Now the natural disposition which leads philosophers to metaphysics is, in great part, the desire to discover some underlying unity which is beyond or behind phenomena. In order that such a unity may be discovered it is necessary to attain a point of view from which the elements of plurality, discord and relativity fall into their proper perspective. In an analogous way it is not possible to gain a synoptic view of a whole city unless the spectator is situated at a high vantage-point like a tower or a hill. To gain such a vantage-point was the goal of the traditional metaphysician. Each metaphysical system offers a theory of the nature of the goal and an indication of the way in which it can be reached.

In respect both of the nature of the goal and of the method for attaining it many philosophers derived considerable inspiration from mathematics. Numbers seemed to possess just those qualities of permanence and perfection which must surely likewise qualify an ideal supersensible object of knowledge. The important place given by Plato to mathematics in the process of dialectical thought, the Cartesian absorption with geometric thinking and Bertrand Russell's employment of the techniques of mathematical logic are all witness, albeit in different ways, to the spirit of Pythagoreanism. If the conviction that demonstration was the proper method for the philosopher to pursue was inspired by Greek geometricians, this conviction certainly received reinforcement from Aristotle's systematisation of syllogistic logic. The mystical tendency, no doubt present in no small measure in philosophers like Plato and Spinoza, tended to be submerged in those of lesser stature by a concern with mere proof. Above all, traditional metaphysics was continually dogged by the inherent difficulty of its programme—the difficulty of specifying what its supersensible goal exactly was, a goal which, by definition, the senses could not inform us of, and with relation to which reason seemed equally helpless, and the difficulty of applying methods appropriate in the spheres of logic and mathematics to a sphere where they were scarcely applicable.

Looking back on the period when speculative metaphysics was in its heyday, it is impossible not to notice how much the programme of 'supplementing' the sciences by a different kind of knowledge was underpinned by theological assumptions. The difficulty of specifying what the object of supersensible knowledge was had indeed been met. The transcendent object which was the goal of speculative and, indeed, of ethical endeavour, was none other than God Himself. Now the seventeenth century was, in both science and philosophy, dominated by the figure of

Sir Isaac Newton, the advocate of experimental reasoning, the advocate of rejection of superfluous hypotheses and at the same time the firm believer in a universe which was the 'sensorium' of God. By the time Hume wrote his *Dialogues concerning Natural Religion* the strange amalgam of religious and scientific outlooks which had been epitomised in Newton had collapsed. It was the work of Hume which brought to the notice of philosophers how dubious was the theological foundation on which speculative metaphysical systems had been raised. The full weight of Hume's iconoclasm is seen, therefore, not in the *Treatise* so much as in the *Dialogues*, for the failure of the proofs of the existence of God is the crowning example of the impossibility of demonstrating matters of existence and it is, moreover, a failure which cuts the ground from beneath the edifice of traditional metaphysics. That 'experimental reasoning' is the only valid method which remains for the philosopher is the conclusion which inevitably follows.

The critical approach to philosophy belongs to modern times and is especially associated with the work of Locke, Hume and Kant (in ancient times Socrates was undoubtedly imbued with the critical spirit in its application to ethical problems). The critical approach consists in uncovering the basic concepts utilised by the sciences, or, as Collingwood has put it, uncovering the 'absolute presuppositions' of the sciences at particular stages in their history. Such an approach is avowedly historical. In our day, for example, concern with the concept of causality and substance has given way to concern with the theoretical implications of relativity and indeterminism. The critical approach does, in a sense, amount to one way of 'supplementing' the sciences, although it does at the same time amount to an attempt, as in the case of the work of Russell, to make philosophy itself scientific.

Existentialism and linguistic analysis respectively can to some extent be accommodated within the twofold classification of philosophies that has been under discussion. Existentialism belongs to the mainstream of metaphysical thought in so far as philosophers like Heidegger and Sartre are still preoccupied with the problem of Being, although, in so far as they refuse to regard man as a mere cogniser whose main aim it is to attach himself to the transcendent in a theoretical manner, existentialism constitutes a deliberate break with speculative metaphysics. Linguistic analysis falls within the critical movement, the difference being that, instead of advocating the analysis of experience or of knowledge or of science, its exponents advocate the analysis of language.

Although there is no single answer to the question as to what philosophy is, the reason being that philosophy itself has a history, (the historical character of philosophical problems has been stressed throughout the preceding chapters) we can perhaps speak of a common *activity of philoso phizing*, an activity without which there would not be any philosophy at all. To philosophize is to engage in a reflective activity analogous to questioning. But what exactly is the nature of those questions which may be described as typically philosophical? This is a matter which has especially exercised contemporary philosophers. Philosophers, perhaps because of their inevitable concern with definitions, have always shown a certain amount of interest in pinning down the difference between philosophy and the other disciplines. Whether or no there be certain 'eternal problems' in philosophy is something that can be debated. The speculative philosopher may maintain, in this connection, that questions like 'What is Being' or 'What is it to exist' are by no means residual but are foundational. To attempt to give answers to such questions is to practise metaphysics. The critical philosopher may, on the other hand, find an eternal problem in the task of making an inventory of the capacities of the human mind.

If the traditional question 'What is nature' has by now become the preserve of the sciences this should occasion no regret. An alternative task for philosophy, some may think, is set forth in the questions that dominated traditional metaphysics, questions as to what we are, whence we came and what we may hope for. These indicate with extraordinary pertinency the field in which philosophy may yet have its most significant contribution to make—the field of man himself. It by no means follows that, in accepting the centrality of these three questions, the three traditional concepts with which they were associated in dogmatic systems of metaphysics, that is to say, the concepts of God, freedom and the immortality of the soul, must be accepted too. On the other hand, it may be, of course, that these controversial concepts may take on a fresh significance, as happens, say, in the work of Gabriel Marcel.

In answering the question as to what we are there can be no doubt that if we neglect the fact that man is a language-using being we do so at our peril. The old definition of man as a rational animal was not as misguided as we sometimes take it to be. Man's rationality is, *inter alia*, exhibited in his use of language. The activities of man are diverse, comprising his cognitive, emotional and practical life. Now the status of language is peculiar in that not only must it be recognised as one among the many activities of man but it is tied up with all the other activities of man as well. If philosophizing is to concern man, therefore, we should expect that it should concern itself with language. But philosophical enquiries cannot be *restricted* to the investigation of language for language is a part of life, that is to say, there is more to life than can be found in language alone. It is for this reason that the philosopher must constantly return to the field from which his enquiries originally sprang, the field of human experience itself.

Selected Bibliography

PART I

GENERAL

Austin, J. L. *How to do things with words*, Cambridge, Mass., 1962.

Ayer, A. J. *Language, truth and logic*, London, 2nd ed., 1946.
Logical Positivism, New York, 1959.
Inaugural lecture, Oxford, 1960.

Barrett, W. *Irrational Man*, Garden City, New York, 1962.

Bergmann, G. *Metaphysics of Logical Positivism*, London, 1954.

Berkeley, George. *The Principles of Human Knowledge*, London, 1710.

Black, M. *Language and Philosophy, New* York, 1949.

Blackstone, William T. *The Problem of Religious Knowledge*, Englewdod Cliffs, N.J., 1963.

Buber, Martin. *I and Thou*. New York, 1958 (Eng. tr.).

Burtt, Edwin A. *Types of religious philosophy*, New York, 1951.
The Metaphysical foundations of modern science, London, 1932 (2nd. Ed.).

Carnap, R. *The logical syntax of language*, New York, 1937.
The philosophy of Rudolf Carnap (ed. by P.A. Schilpp), Chicago.

Chappell, V. C. *Ordinary language*, Englewood Cliffs, N.J., 1964.

Collingwood, R. G. *Metaphysics*, Oxford, 1940.
The Idea of Nature, Oxford, 1945.

Einstein, A. *Out of my later years* (Essay on 'Physics and Reality') New York, 1956.

Feigl, H. and Sellars, W. (eds.) *Readings in philosophical analysis* New York, 1949.

Flew, A. and Alasdair MacIntyre (eds.) *New Essays in Philosophical Theology*, New York, 1955.

Gellner, E. *Words and things*, Boston, 1960.

Gilson, E. *God and Philosophy*, New Haven, 1941.

Grene, Marjorie. *Introduction to existentialism, Chicago* 1948, London, 1959.

Harris, Errol E. *Nature, mind and modern science*, London, 1954.

Hegel, G. W. F. *Philosophy of religion* Eng. tr. 1895 by E. B. Speirs and J. B. Sanderson.

Heidegger, Martin. *Being and Time* (tr. by J. Macquarrie and E. S. Robinson), New York, 1962.

Heinemann, F. H. *Existentialism and the modern predicament*, New York, 1958, London, 1959.

Heisenberg, Werner. *Physics and Philosophy; the revolution in modern science*, New York, 1958.
Henle, Paul (ed.) *Language thought and culture*, Michigan, 1958.
Hick, John *Philosophy of Religion.*
Hoyle, Fred *Frontiers of Astronomy* chs 18-20, New York, 1955.
Hume, David *Enquiry concerning human understanding*, 1748.
Dialogues concerning natural religion, 1779.
Husserl, E. *Phenomenology*, Article in 14th Ed. of Encyclopedia Brittannica.
James, W. *Varieties of religious experience*, New York, 1902.
Kant, I. *Critique of Pure Reason*, 1781. Kemp Smith Edition, London, 1929.
Kierkegaard, S. *Either Or*, London 1944 (Eng. Ed.).
Concluding Unscientific Postscript, London, 1945 (Eng. Ed.).
Kraft, Victor *The Vienna Circle*, New York, 1953.
Lewis, H. D. (Ed.) *Clarity is not enough*, London, 1963.
Locke, John *An essay concerning human understanding* Pringle-Pattison Ed., Oxford, 1924.
Lunn, Arnold and Haldane, J. B. S. *Science and the supernatural*, London, 1935.
Macdonald, M. (ed.) *Philosophy and analysis*, Oxford, 1954.
Marcel, Gabriel *The Philosophy of Existence* (Eng. tr.), London, 1948.
Meyerson, E. *Identity and Reality*, London, 1930 (Eng. tr.).
Mitchell, Basil (ed.) *Faith and Logic*, London, 1957.
Newton, Sir Isaac *Philosophiae Naturalis Principia Mathematica*, 1687.
Ogden, C. K. and Richards, I. A. *The meaning of meaning*, London, 1923.
Popper, Karl *Conjectures and Refutations*, New York and London, 1963.
Quine, W. V. *From a logical point of view*, Cambridge, Mass., 1953.
Reichenbach, H. *The rise of scientific philosophy*, 1951.
Russell, B. *Our knowledge of the external world*, London, 1914.
Ryle, G. *Theory of Meaning* in "British Philosophy in Mid-Century" London, 1957.
Systematically misleading expressions in Proceedings of the Aristotelian Society, 1931.
Sartre, J. P. *Existentialism and Humanism*, London, 1948 (Eng. tr.).
Being and Nothingness (Eng. tr.) New York, 1956.
Critique de la raison dialectique, Paris, 1960.
Smart, Ninian *Reasons and Faiths*, London, 1958.
Stebbing, S. L. *Philosophy and the Physicists*, London, 1937.
Strawson, P. F. *Individuals*, London, 1959.
Urmson, J. O. *Philosophical Analysis*, Oxford, 1956.

Waismann, F. H. *Verifiability* in A. Flew (ed) Essays in Logic and Language, First Series, Oxford, 1951.
Language Strata in " " Second Series, Oxford, 1953.
White, A. D. *A History of the warfare of science with theology.* Dover publications, New York.
Whitehead, Alfred North *Science and the modern world,* 1938.
Wild, John *Challenge of existentialism* Bloomington : Indiana University Press, 1955.
Wisdom, John *Metaphysics and Verification,* Mind, 1938.
Wittgenstein, L. *Tractatus Logico-Philosophicus,* London, 1922.
Philosophical Investigations, Oxford, 1953.

PART II

THE NATURE OF KNOWLEDGE

Austin, J. L. *Sense and sensibilia,* Oxford, 1962.
Ayer, A. J. *Foundations of empirical knowledge,* London, 1940.
Philosophical Essays, London, 1954.
The Problem of Knowledge, London, 1956.
Banerjee, N. V. *Concerning human understanding,* London, 1958.
Berkeley, George *Theory of Vision,* 1709. *The principles of human knowledge,* London, 1710.
Blanshard, Brand *The nature of thought,* London, 1939.
Bradley, F. H. *Appearance and reality,* Oxford, 1893.
Collingwood, R. G. *Idea of nature,* Oxford, 1945.
Descartes, R. *Discourse on Method, Meditations, Principles of philosophy,* Eng. ed. by John Veitch, 1879.
Drake, Lovejoy, Pratt et alia *Essays in Critical Realism,* New York, 1920.
Ewing, A. C. *The idealist tradition from Berkeley to Blanshard,* Glencoe, Illinois, 1957.
Flew, A. (ed.) *Essays in logic and language,* First Series, Oxford, 1951.
Grice, H. P. and P. F. Strawson *In defence of a dogma,* Philosophical Review, 1956.
Hegel, *The phenomenology of mind,* Eng. tr. by J. B. Baillie, London, 1910.
James, W. *Pragmatism,* New York, 1907.
Joachim, H. *The nature of truth,* Oxford, 1939.
Kant, I. *Critique of Pure Reason,* 1781, Kemp Smith Edition, London, 1929. *Prologomena to any future metaphysic,* 1783.
Leibniz *New Essays,* 1702-3, Everyman Ed., 1934.
Lewis, C. I. *Mind and the world order,* New York, 1929.

Locke, John *An essay concerning human understanding,* Pringle-Pattison Ed., 1924.
Merleau-Ponty, M. *Phenomenology of Perception,* Eng. tr. London, 1962.
Moore, G. E. *Philosophical Studies,* London, 1922.
Perry, R. B. *The egocentric predicament,* Journal of Philosophy, Psychology and Scientific Methods, 1910.
Perry, Holt et alia *The New Realism,* New York, 1912.
Price, H. H. *Perception,* London, 1932.
Prichard, H. A. *Kant's theory of knowledge,* Oxford, 1909.
Quine, W. V. *Two dogmas of empiricism,* reprinted in 'From a logical point of view' Cambridge, Mass., 1953.
Russell, B. *Problems of Philosophy,* London, 1912.
Human Knowledge, its scope and limits, London, 1948.
Schilpp, P. (ed.) *The philosophy of Bertrand Russell,* Evanston and Chicago, 1944.
Stebbing, S. L. *Philosophy and the Physicists* (Part II), London, 1937.
Waismann, F. H. *Analytic-Synthetic* in "Analysis", 1949-52.
Walsh, W. H. *Reason and experience,* Oxford, 1947.
Whiteley, C. H. *An Introduction to metaphysics,* London, 1949.
Woozley, A. D. *Theory of knowledge,* London, 1949.
Wittgenstein, L. *Tractatus Logico-Philosophicus,* London, 1922.

PART III

MAN AND NATURE

Alexander, S. *Space, Time and Deity,* London, 1920.
Aristotle *Metaphysics,* and comm., W. D. Ross, 2 vols. Oxford, 1924.
Physics, text and comm., W. D. Ross, Oxford, 1936.
Ayer, A. J. *Language Truth and Logic,* London, 2nd ed., 1946.
Bergson, H. *Creative Evolution,* Eng. tr., 1911.
Berlin, I. *Historical Inevitability,* London, 1954.
Bernal, J. D. *Science in History,* London, 1954.
Bradley, F. H. *Appearance and Reality,* London, 1893.
Broad, C. D. *The mind and its place in nature,* London, 1931.
Campbell, C. A. *Scepticism and Construction,* London, 1931.
Cassirer, E. *Determinism and Indeterminism in modern physics,* New Haven, 1956.
Chardin, Pere Teilhard de *The Phenomenon of Man,* London, 1959.
Chatterjee, Margaret *Our knowledge of other selves,* Bombay, 1963.
Cohen, Chapman *Materialism restated,* London, 1927.
Cornforth, Maurice *Materialism and the dialectical method,* New York, 1953.
Darwin, Charles *On the origin of species by means of natural selection,* 1859.

Descartes, R. *Discourse on method, Meditations, Principles of Philosophy*, Eng. ed. by John Veitch, 1879.
Eliot, Hugh *Modern science and materialism*, London, 1919.
Ewing, A. C. *Kant's treatment of causality*, London, 1924.
Farrer, A. *The freedom of the will*, London, 1957.
Finite and infinite, London, 1960.
Gunn, T. A. *The problem of time*, London 1929.
Hampshire, S. *Thought and action*, London, 1959.
Hook, S. *From Hegel to Marx*, London, 1936.
Hoyle, F. *Man and materialism*, London, 1957.
Hume, David *Treatise of Human Nature*, 1739.
Jeans, J. *Physics and Philosophy*, Cambridge, 1943.
Kant, I. *Critique of Pure Reason*, 1781, Kemp Smith Edition, London, 1929.
Prologomana to any future metaphysic, 1784, Eng. tr. by Mahaffy and Bernard, London and N.Y., 1889.
Krikorian, Y. *Naturalism and the human spirit*, (ed.) New York, 1944.
Lange, F. A. *History of materialism*, London, 1925.
Laslett, Peter (ed.) *The physical basis of mind*, Oxford, 1951.
Leibniz *Correspondence with Clarke*, 1715.
Lenin, V. I. *Materialism and empirio-criticism*, Moscow, 1947.
Locke, *An essay concerning human understanding*, Pringle-Pattison Ed. Oxford, 1924.
Margenau, H. *The nature of physical reality*, New York, 1950.
Marx, Karl *Economic and Philosophic manuscripts* of 1844.
McTaggart, J. E. *The nature of existence*, Cambridge, 1921.
Nagel, Ernst *Are naturalists materialists?* reprinted in "Logic without Metaphysics," Ernst Nagel, Glencoe, Illinois, 1957.
Newton, Sir Isaac *Philosophiae Naturalis Principia Mathematica*, 1687.
Plato, *Timaeus*
Polanyi, Michael *The logic of liberty*, London, 1951.
Ramsey, Ian *Biology and Personality* (ed.), Oxford, 1966.
Russell *Our knowledge of the external world*, London, 1914.
Ryle, Gilbert *The concept of mind*, London, 1949.
Schroedinger, Erwin *What is life? Garden City*, 1956.
Simpson, G. G. *Meaning of Evolution*, London, 1950.
Spinoza, *Ethics*.
Stebbing, S. L. *Philosophy and the Physicists*, London, 1937.
Vesey, G. N. A. *Body and Mind* (ed.), London, 1964.
The embodied mind, London, 1965.
Whitehead, Alfred North *Adventures of Ideas* Harmondsworth, Penguin, 1942.
Whitrow, G. J. *The natural philosophy of time*, London and Edinburgh, 1961.
Wisdom, John *Problems of Mind and matter*, Cambridge, 1934.

PART IV

GOD, MAN AND VALUE

Anselm *Proslogion* chs 2-4
Aquinas *Summa Theologica*, Part I, Question 2, article 3.
Ayer, A. J. *Language, truth and logic*, London, 2nd Ed., 1946.
Barth, Karl *Anselm's Fides quaerens intellectum*, 1931, London, 1960.
Bosanquet, Bernard *The principle of individuality and value*, 1912.
Descartes, R. *Meditation V* (Veitch Ed.).
Farrer, A. *Finite and infinite*, London, 1960, (2nd Ed.).
Findlay, J. N. *Value and Intention*, London, 1961.
Flew, A. and Alasdair MacIntyre *New essays in philosophical theology*, New York, and London, 1955.
Hartmann, K. R. E. von *The philosophy of the unconscious*, Eng. tr. by Coupland, 1884.
Hume, David *Dialogues concerning natural religion* Parts V-VIII, 1779.
Joad, C. E. M. God *and evil*, London, 1942.
Kant, I. *Critique of Pure Reason*, Kemp Smith Ed., London, 1929. *Critique of Practical Reason* Book II, ch. II, Sections 4 & 5. *Critique of Judgement*
Laird, J. *A Study in realism*, Cambridge, 1920.
Leibniz,*Theodicy*.
Malcolm, Norman *Anselm's ontological arguments*, Philosophical Review, January 1960.
Mascall, E. L. *He who is*, London, 1943.
Mitchell, Basil (ed) *Faith and Logic*, London, 1957.
Moore, G. E. *Principia Ethica*, Cambridge, 1951.
Paley, W. *Evidences of the existence and attributes of the deity*, 1802.
Scheler, Max *The nature of sympathy*, Eng. tr., London, 1954.
Schopenhauer, A. *The world as will and idea*, 1819.
Shaffer, Jerome *Existence, predication and the ontological argument*, Mind, July 1962.
Spinoza *Ethics*
Temple *Nature, man and God*, London, 1934.
Tennant, F. R. *Philosophical Theology*, Cambridge, 1928-30.
Voltaire *Candide*, 1758.

Index

Abelard, 44
Absolute, The, 6, 10, 27, 41, 42, 158
    Hegelian Absolute, 87ff, 122ff, 237
    God and the Absolute, 90
    Pragmatist criticism of, 132
    Fichte, 89
    Schelling, 89
Acquaintance, theory of, 93ff., 117ff.
Alexander, S., 149, 152, 268
Anaxagoras, 48
Anaximander, 48
Anselm, 231ff.
A priori knowledge, 66, 77ff., ch. VI
Aquinas, St. Thomas, 42, 149, 172, 204, 217, Ch. XV passim.
Aristotle, 5, 10, 23, 39, 49, 65, 67, 79, 82, 85, 88, 135ff., 142, 145-6, 159, 162, 171-2, 185-6, 191ff., 198, 203
Arnauld, 92
Augustine, 38, 40, 46, 204, 217, 258
Austin, J.L., 35-6
Ayer, A.J., 34, 36, 99ff., 212-13, 226, 276ff.

Bacon, 1, 5, 142
Barth, Karl, 25, 257
Basic propositions, 58ff.
Behaviourism, 13, 178-9, 181-2
Being, 39, 47ff., 49, 50, 85, 185, 281, 282
Berdyaev, 38, 222
Bergson, H., 13, 20, 45, 63, 142. 155-6, 194ff., 222
Berkeley, 29-30, 33, 62, 70ff., 76 (Kant's criticism of), 81, 92, 97, 137ff., 153, 182, 206, 264, 280
Bernard, St., 44
Biran, Maine de, 43
Blanshard, Brand, 124
Blondel, 21
Boethius, 42
Bohr, N., 12
Boole, 111
Bosanquet, 140, 256, 272
Boyle 12, 138
Bradley, F.H., 60, 87, 89, 90, 140, 157, 164, 221, 256
Broad, C.D., 100, 152, 205
Buddhism, 16, 17, 256, 261
Burtt, E.A., 11
Butler, 91, 123

Caird, 26
Campbell, 222
Camus, A., 38
Carnap, R., 57ff.
Cassirer, E., 113
Causality, 52, Ch. X, Ch. XIII passim.
Chardin, Père Teilhard de, 188
Clarke, 151
Coherence, theory of, 121ff.
Collingwood, R.G., 9, 14, 128, 279, 281
Commonsense, 30ff.
Comte, A., 17, 61, 97, 142
Confucianism, 16, 17
Cook Wilson, 17
Copernicus, 1, 3, 10, 12, 96, 167
Correspondence, theory of, 115ff.
Cosmological proof, 237ff.
Criticism, critical movement, 51ff., 279ff.

Darrow, Clarence, 220, 246-7, 260
Darwin, C., 189ff., 215, 219, 247, 260
Deism, 11, 25, 243
Democritus, 133-4, 172, 191

Descartes, 2, 5, 10, 11, 50, 67ff., 103, 135ff., 148, 152, 172-5, 180ff. (Ryle's criticism of), 204ff., 218, 229, 234ff. (ontological argument)
Determinism, 219ff.
Dewey, J., 130ff., 274
Dilthey, W., 213, 223
Dostoievsky, F., 38
Driesch, 193

Einstein, A., 3, 15, 96, 151, 220
Emmet, D., 60
Empiricism, 10, 21, 24, 26, 31, 52ff., 78, 81-2, 119, 128, 137ff., 166, 207ff. (self)
Epicurus, 266
Essentialism, 5ff., 39ff.
Evil, problem of, 37, Ch. XVI
Evolution, Ch. XII
Ewing, A.C., 37
Existentialism, 8, 20, 21, 38ff., 60, 127, 213-14, 224, 227-8, 281
External relations, axiom of, 91ff.
Faith, 16ff., 43ff., 49-50, 55
Farrer, A., 206
Feuerbach, 140
Fichte, 82
Findlay, J.N., 37
Freedom, 23, 41ff., 50, 54, 213, Ch. XIV
Freud, S., 13

Galileo, 1, 11, 136, 137
Gaunilo, 233ff.
Gellner, E., 36
Gestalt psychology. 12
Geulincx, 175
God, 9, 10, 11-12, 37, 39-40, 43, 49, 50, 54, 55, 71ff., 135, 149, 150, 162, 191, 206, 216ff., Ch. XV, 274ff.
Grace, 19, 45. 49
Green, T. H., 89
Haeckel, 190
Hamann, 26, 252
Hampshire, S., 35, 36
Hare, R. M., 36, 60, 266, 269
Hartmann, K.R.E. von, 261
Hartmann, N., 266, 269, 273-4
Hegel, 5, 13, 23, 26, 40ff., 42, 44, 50, 84ff., 121ff., 224, 237, 256, 279
Heidegger, M., 41-2, 209-10, 281
Heisenberg, W., 12, 13, 96, 141 152
Heraclitus, 156, 197
History, study of, 86, 123ff.
Hobbes, T., 140, 152
Hoeffding, 26, 275
Holbach, 219
Howison, 91, 273
Hume, D., 5, 8, 11, 21, 25-6, 27, 30, 31, 33, 40, 45, 52ff., 56ff., 70, 78, 81
view of mathematics, 105ff., 148, 153
on causality, Ch. X passim, 202
self, Ch. XIII passim, 221, 224ff.
teleological proof, 244ff.
evil, 252ff., 276, 281

Idealism, 13, 43, 59, Ch. V passim
Immortality, 54
Induction, 61, 168ff.
Innate ideas, 102ff.
Internal relations, axiom of, 88
Intentionality, 183-4
Ionians, 38, 48ff., 133

James, W., 18, 26, 45, 89, 129ff., 145, 179, 208, 210, 221-2, 226, 272, 274
Jaspers, K., 42
Joachim, H., 123, 125
Joseph, H.W.B., 192
Jung, C. G., 13, 34

Kant, 5, 8, 9, 10, 12, 14, 15, 25, 26, 27, 29, 34, 42-3, 52ff., 57ff., 61, 70, 75ff., 82ff., 97, 127, 129, 132, 139, 141-2, 151ff., 157-8, 161, 182, 193, 194, 198, 206
space and time, 78-9, 151ff. and Hegel, 81ff.
a priori knowledge, 107ff.
truth, 120-21
criticism of Hume, 166ff., 211ff.

teleological proof, 245ff.
moral argument, 248ff.
value, 271ff., 275-6, 281
freedom, 224ff.
ontological proof, 234ff.
cosmological proof, 238ff.
Kepler, 1, 11, 136, 137
Kierkegaard, S. 18, 23, 41, 43ff., 250
'Knowing how' and 'Knowing that', 27
Knowledge, theories of, Ch. V

Lamarck, 189, 191
Language, copy theory of language, 33
emotive theory, 32
ordinary language, 3, 30-1
philosophy and language, 29ff., 36
scientific language, 3
Lashley, 177
Le Senne, Renè, 42
Leucippus, 133-4
Leibniz, II, 13, 25, 50, 59, 76, 82, 83, 85, 103-5, 136, 151ff., 175, 193, 204, 206-7, 243-4, 257, 260 236
Linguistic analysis, 13-14, 38, 63, 263, 276, 281ff.
Locke, 12, 22, 29, 31, 33, 51ff., 61, 68ff., 96, 104ff., 137ff., 152-3, 207ff., 237, 281
Logical atomism, 59
Logical positivism, 33, 56ff., 90, 276ff.
Lucretius, 172

Mach, E., 4, 62, 167
Macmurray, J., 36
McTaggart, J.E., 30, 91, 157-8
Marcel, G. 42ff., 228, 283
Marxism, Marx, 13, 20, 40, 41, 42, 56, 132, 140, 190, 220. 259
Materialism, 56, 140ff., 177ff., 196
Mathematics, 4, 7, 32, 54, 64, 132 102ff., 125
Matter, Ch. VIII
Meaning, The meaning of, 32
Mechanism, 141ff.
Meinong, 95, 267, 269
Memory, 127, 158, 201, 207
Meta-ethics, 37
Metaphysics, the possibility of, Ch. IV
Meyerson, E., 195
Mill, J.S., 22, 97, 100, 165, 219, 226, 246, 254
Mind and body, 163, Ch. XI
The Concept of Mind, 179ff.
Moore, G.E., 30ff., 56, 70, 74ff., 91, 92, 131, 222, 268ff., 276
Motion, 140, 145ff., 156-7, Ch. IX passim, Ch. X passim.

Naturalism, 36
Neurath, 57ff.
Newton, Sir I., 1, 3, 4, 11-15, 54 71, 76, 86, 139ff., 149ff., 159, 281
Nietzsche, F., 21, 188, 197
Nowell-Smith, 36

Objective idealism, 77, 81ff., 121ff.
Ontological proof, 52, 231ff.
Optimism, 260ff.
Otto, R., 18

Paley, W., 22, 244, 246
Pascal, 38, 40, 43
Pavlov, 56, 178
Pelagius, 217
Perception, Ch. V
Perry, R.B., 73ff., 91, 274
Person, Ch.III(b)passim, 184, Ch. XIII passim.
Pessimism, 260ff.
Phenomena and noumena 82, 97-8
Phenomenalism, 32, 96ff., 129
Berkeley, 98
Hume, 98-9
self, 207ff.
Phenomenology, phenomenological method, 43ff., 212
Plato, 20, 22, 29, 48, 49, 51, 54, 64-5, 87, 102-3, 145, 171, 203, 232, 244, 256, 265, 268, 270ff., 280

Plotinus, 172
Poincarè, H., 4, 62, 96, 150, 167
Popper, K., 2, 150, 165, 167
Positivism, 13, 28, 46, 56
Pragmatism, 21, 30, 128ff., 213, 274
Price, H.H., 21, 30, 37, 100
Protagoras, 64
Protocol propositions, 58ff.
Pythagoreanism, 65, 136, 265, 280

Qualities, primary and secondary, 3, 68, 71, 137ff.
Quine, 112-13

Rashdall, 273
Rationalism, 7, 33, 40, 50, 65, 103, 148ff. (time), 160ff. (causality), 203ff. (self)
Realism, 91ff
Reid, T., 74, 92, 164
Religion, Philosophy and, Ch. II
Representationism, 66ff., 92 (criticism of)
Ritschl, 26
Rousseau, J-J, 40, 45, 205
Royce, 89
Russell, B., 7, 10, 12, 13, 20, 31ff., 56ff., 90, 92ff., 99ff., 116, 150, 152, 156, 157-8, 166, 169, 179, 198-9, 246, 280-281
correspondence theory of truth 115ff.
Ryle, G., 34, 69, 164, 179ff., 201, 211, 224, 227, 236

Sartre, J.P., 41ff., 197, 281
Scheler, M., 266, 273-4
Schelling, F.W.J.von, 87
Schiller, 274
Schlick, 36, 38, 57ff., 226, 276
Schopenhauer, 197, 219, 261ff.
Science, Ch. I, 43, 46, 61, 63, 65, 66, 96, 125, Ch. X passim, 279ff.
Self, Ch. III (b) passim, 52, Ch. XIII, 223
Shaftesbury, 40, 245
Sidgwick, 221
Socrates, 10, 38, 102
Solipsism, 63
Soul, 55, *See also* Ch. XIII
Space, 52, 78ff., Ch. IX
Spencer, H., 25, 188ff., 259
Spinoza, 20, 49, 50, 54, 88, 136, 149, 175ff., 218, 236-7, 256, 280
Stevenson. C.L., 35, 36, 277
Stoics, 38, 103
Strawson, P.F., 6, 35, 36
Subjective idealism, 70ff.
Subjectivity, Ch. III (b) passim.
Synthetic *a priori* judgements, 53ff., 75ff., 107ff.

Tarski, 34
Tautologies, 110ff.
Teleology, 84, 141, 159, 191ff., 243ff.
Temple, W. 247, 257
Tertullian, 172
Thales, 48
Time, 52, 78ff., Ch. IX, Ch. X passim.
Transcendental philosophy, 55ff., 75ff., 93, 154
Truth, theories of, Ch. VII

Urmson, J.O., 269
Utilitarianism, 261, 276

Value, Ch. XVII
Verification principle, 57ff.
Vienna Circle, 57ff.
Voltaire, 260

Wach, J., 18
Waismann, F.H., 35, 161
Watson, J.B., 172
Westermarck, 266
Whitehead, A.N., 8, 13, 74, 111, 152, 164, 247
Whorf, 113
Wittgenstein, L., 5, 33ff., 59ff., 110, 179, 227, 276
Wolff, 243
Zeno, 156-8
Zoroastrianism, 255